INNOVATION AND THE SOCIAL ECONOMY

Innovation and the Social Economy

The Québec Experience

EDITED BY MARIE J. BOUCHARD

UNIVERSITY OF TORONTO PRESS
Toronto   Buffalo   London

© University of Toronto Press 2013
Toronto   Buffalo   London
www.utppublishing.com
Printed in Canada

ISBN 978-1-4426-4290-4

Printed on acid-free, 100% post-consumer recycled paper with vegetable-based inks

---

Library and Archives Canada Cataloguing in Publication

Innovation and the social economy : the Quebec experience / edited by Marie J. Bouchard.

Includes bibliographical references.
ISBN 978-1-4426-4290-4

1. Economics – Québec (Province) – Sociological aspects.   2. Social capital (Sociology) – Québec (Province).   3. Cooperative societies – Québec (Province).   4. Non-profit organizations – Québec (Province).   5. Voluntarism – Québec (Province).   6. Community development – Québec (Province).   7. Québec (Province) – Social policy.   I. Bouchard, Marie J.

HN110.Q8I55 2013   306.309714   C2012-908473-5

This book has been published with the help of a grant from the Canadian Federation for the Humanities and Social Sciences, through the Aid to Scholarly Publications Program, using funds provided by the Social Sciences and Humanities Research Council of Canada.

University of Toronto Press acknowledges the financial assistance to its publishing program of the Canada Council for the Arts and the Ontario Arts Council.

Canada Council   Conseil des Arts
for the Arts   du Canada

ONTARIO ARTS COUNCIL
CONSEIL DES ARTS DE L'ONTARIO
50 YEARS OF ONTARIO GOVERNMENT SUPPORT OF THE ARTS
50 ANS DE SOUTIEN DU GOUVERNEMENT DE L'ONTARIO AUX ARTS

University of Toronto Press acknowledges the financial support of the Government of Canada through the Canada Book Fund for its publishing activities.

Contents

Acknowledgments

This book represents the work of researchers involved in CRISES, the Centre de recherche sur les innovations sociales (Social Innovation Research Centre), and in ARUC-RQRP-ÉS, l'Alliance de recherche universités communautés, and le Réseau québécois de recherche partenariale en économie sociale (the Community University Research Alliance and the Québec Partnership Research Node on the Social Economy). I want to acknowledge the initiative of Juan-Luis Klein and Jean-Marc Fontan, who first had the idea for this book and invited me to lead the project. I also wish to acknowledge the participation of the authors who were involved in the planning of the book as well as the editing of its chapters.

The production of this book has been supported by the Canada Research Chair on the Social Economy, with funding from the Social Sciences and Humanities Research Council of Canada, and by CRISES, with funding from the Fonds de recherche du Québec Société et culture (Québec Society and Culture Research Fund).

I want particularly to thank Stéphane Guimont-Marceau and Monique K. De Sève for their help in coordinating this project, and to Hélène Gélinas, Florence Naud, and Caroline Dumulon-Morin for their assistance in producing the manuscript.

I am grateful to the peer reviewers and academic editors for their insightful and constructive comments. Finally, I wish to express my warm thanks to Jennifer DiDomenico for her invaluable editorial support in the preparation of this volume.

Contributors

Marie J. Bouchard is a professor at the Business School of l'Université du Québec à Montréal, director of the Canada Research Chair on the Social Economy, and a member of the Centre de recherche sur les innovations sociales (CRISES, the Social Innovation Research Centre). She was co-director of the Partnership Activities Workforce on Community Housing (Chantier d'application partenariale Habitat communautaire), Community University Research Alliance on the Social Economy (ARUC-ÉS). Marie is also a member of the Scientific Council of the International Center of Research and Information on Public, Social and Cooperative Economy (CIRIEC), and a board member of its Canadian section, CIRIEC-Canada.

Gilles L. Bourque holds a PhD in economic sociology from l'Université du Québec à Montréal. He is an economist at Fondaction (CSN) and general coordinator of the Éditions Vie Économique (EVE). Gilles is also the author of the book *Le modèle québécois de développement : de l'émergence au renouvellement*, published by Presses de l'Université du Québec in 2000.

Yvan Comeau is a professor at l'École de service social of Université Laval. He is director of the Chaire de recherche Marcelle-Mallet sur la culture philanthropique. His research and his teaching focus on community organizations. He participates in the CURA on Territorial Development and Cooperation (ARUC-DTC) and in the CURA on Social Innovation and Community Development (ARUC-ISDC).

Luc Dancause holds a PhD in urban studies from l'Université du Québec à Montréal. He is a research and planning agent at the Service des partenariats et du soutien à l'innovation of l'Université du Québec à Montréal, where he is in charge of developing a knowledge mobilization unit.

Jean-Marc Fontan is a professor of sociology at l'Université du Québec à Montréal. He was co-director of the CURA on the Social Economy (ARUC-ÉS) from 2003 to 2011. He coordinates the Innovation and Territory Axis at the Centre de recherche sur les innovations sociales (CRISES). He is also the director of l'Incubateur universitaire Parole d'excluEs (IUPE).

Corinne Gendron holds a PhD in sociology from l'Université du Québec à Montréal. She is a professor in the Department of Strategy, Social and Environmental Responsibility at the Business School of l'Université du Québec à Montréal. She is also director of the Chair in Social and Environmental Responsibility.

Louis Jolin holds a PhD in business law from l'Université de Lyon III. He is a professor in the Department of Urban and Tourism Studies at l'Université du Québec à Montréal. He is responsible for the scientific committee of the International Organization of Social Tourism (IOST) and was co-director of the CAP Loisir et tourisme social within the CURA on the social economy. He was also co-president of the CIRIEC-Canada Working Group on the Juridical Status of Associations.

Juan-Luis Klein is a professor of geography at l'Université du Québec à Montréal. He is director of the Centre de recherche sur les innovations sociales (CRISES). He was also the co-director of CAP Évaluation, CURA on the Social Economy (ARUC-ÉS).

Philippe Leclerc holds a master's degree in political science from l'Université du Québec à Montréal and is a doctoral student at Concordia University. His master's thesis was on the evolution of institutional arrangements and the relationship between the Québec state and the social economy within home care services, from 2003 to 2007.

Benoît Lévesque is an associate professor at l'École nationale d'administration publique and professor emeritus at l'Université du Québec à Montréal. He is the co-founder of the Centre de recherche sur les innovations sociales (CRISES) and of the Community University Research Alliance (CURA) on the Social Economy (ARUC-ÉS), organizations that he directed until 2003. He was also the president of the CIRIEC International Scientific Council from 2002 to 2010.

Marguerite Mendell is an economist, vice-principal and associate professor at the School of Community and Public Affairs. She is also the director of the Karl Polanyi Institue at Concordia University. She is a member of the board of directors, Chantier de l'économie sociale and ·of the Scientific Advisory Committee of the OECD-LEED Center on Local Development in Trento, Italy. She was co-director, CAP Finances, CURA on the Social Economy (ARUC-ÉS).

Richard Morin is a professor of urban studies at l'Université du Québec à Montréal. He is a member of the Inter-University Pole in Urban and Regional Studies, Villes, Régions, Monde (VMR) and a member of the Groupe de recherche sur l'action collective et les initiatives locales. He was also a member of the CAP Habitat communautaire, CURA, on the Social Economy (ARUC-ÉS).

Ralph Rouzier holds a PhD in economic sociology from l'Université du Québec à Montréal. His dissertation, *La caisse de dépôt et placement du Québec: portrait d'une institution d'intérêt général (1965-2000)*, was published by l'Harmattan in 2008.

Pierre-André Tremblay is a professor in the department of Human Sciences at l'Université du Québec à Chicoutimi. He is member of the Groupe de recherche et d'interventions régionales (GRIR) and of the Centre de recherche sur les innovations sociales (CRISES). He was a member of the CAP Développement regional, CURA, on the Social Economy (ARUC-ÉS).

Marie-France Turcotte holds a PhD in business administration from l'Université du Québec à Montréal. She is a professor in the Department of Strategy, Social and Environmental Responsibility at the Business School of Université du Québec à Montréal. She is also co-director of the Chair in Social and Environmental Responsibility.

Yves Vaillancourt is an associate professor in l'École de travail social at l'Université du Québec à Montréal. He is co-founder of the Laboratoire de recherche sur les pratiques et politiques sociale (LAREPPS). He is member of the Centre de recherche sur les innovations sociales (CRISES), and was co-director of the CAP Services aux personnes, CURA, on the Social Economy (ARUC-ÉS).

INNOVATION AND THE SOCIAL ECONOMY

Introduction: The Social Economy in Québec: A Laboratory of Social Innovation[1]

MARIE J. BOUCHARD

The social economy is not a new phenomenon. Over the past few decades, however, there has been renewed interest in it. Social, political and economic changes culminated in the 2008 crisis, raising important questions. The risks caused by the disconnection between the economy and society have been demonstrated in a number of painful ways, and the crisis now looks less like a conjunctural "shaking up" of the economy than a significant rupture of the model of development. It is within this context that interest in the social economy has increased. Another reason for this interest is that the social economy is perceived to be a laboratory of social innovation that may help, in conjunction with other social movements,[2] to create an economy that will not be disconnected from either the social or political arenas.

This book examines the social economy in Québec from the point of view of social innovation. The terms "social economy" and "social innovation" have recently become popular in Canadian scientific literature. Each expression has a different meaning, however, depending on the approach and objects discussed, and therefore we will define what is meant in this book by each of these terms.

What Is the Social Economy?

Although the definition tends to vary from one country to another, the social economy must be recognized and distinguished from other forms of economy (Defourny & Monzón Campos, 1992). Often called the "third sector," the social economy refers to organizations and enterprises that belong neither to the profit-seeking private sector nor to the public sector (state-owned corporations and public-administration organizations). It distinguishes itself from the capitalist economy and the public economy by combining modes of creation and administration that are private (e.g., autonomy and economic risk) with those that are collective (e.g., associations of persons), and because its aims are not centred on profit (mutual interests vs. private) (Defourny, 2005). Two conditions generally explain the creation and development of social economy organizations: the imperative to respond to an unfulfilled significant need, and the act of belonging to a social group that has a collective identity or common destiny (Defourny & Develtere, 1999).

Although different definitions have been given to the social economy,[3] all definitions can be grouped into two principal strains. The Anglo-Saxon approach to non-profit organizations (NPOs) emphasizes the non-distribution of benefits. The European and Québécois approaches to the social economy, however, place an emphasis on governance and the democratic functioning of a "family" of organizations, including cooperatives, mutual societies, and non-profit organizations that undertake an economic activity. The difference between these two strains is therefore not a profit-seeking versus non-profit orientation; rather, it is the difference between capitalist and "a-capitalist" organizations (Demoustier, 2001; Draperi, 2009), or "socio-economic" organizations (Evers & Laville, 2004), which emphasize generating an enhanced collective wealth, rather than a return on individual investment.

This book uses the Québécois definition of social economy, as defined in the general consensus adopted in Québec in 1996 (see Box 1.1). This definition blends the characteristics of legal and institutional forms of organizations – cooperatives, mutual societies, and non-profit organizations[4] (Desroche, 1983) – and the values, principles, and rules that these organizations all share: service to their members and to the community, democratization of the economy (Defourny & Monzón Campos, 1992; Vienney, 1980), and the hybridization of the economic principles identified by Polanyi (1944), which comprise market exchange, redistribution, and reciprocity (Eme & Laville, 1994). The social economy also refers to activities that seek to find new models of economic functioning and democratization, such as workers' funds, work insertion, micro-finance, and solidarity finance. Thus, the definition of social economy in Québec is based upon a social movement perspective, because it challenges social norms and proposes an alternative social order (Mendell & Neamtan, 2010).

BOX 1.1

DEFINITION OF THE SOCIAL ECONOMY IN QUÉBEC

The concept of "social economy" combines two often-opposing terms:

- "economy" refers to the concrete production of goods and services – the enterprise as an organizational structure – that contributes to a net increase in collective wealth

- "social" refers to the social (as opposed by and not just the economic) benefits of these activities. Social benefits are measured in terms of their contribution to democratic development, their support of an active citizenry, and their promotion of values and initiatives that further individual and collective empowerment. Social benefits therefore contribute to enhancing the quality of life and well-being of the population, particularly by providing a greater number of services. As with the traditional public and private sectors, social benefits can also be evaluated in terms of the number of jobs created. In its entirety, the social economy field covers all activities and organizations built on community-based entrepreneurship and operating on the following principles and rules:
  - the primary purpose is to serve its members or the community, rather than simply to make profits and focus on financial performance;
  - it is not government-controlled;
  - it incorporates in its bylaws and operating procedures a process of democratic decision-making that includes users and workers;
  - it places people and work above the pursuit of capital when distributing profits and revenues;
  - its activities are based on the principles of participation, empowerment, and the accountability of individuals and communities.

Source: *Excerpted from the report of the Task Force on the Social Economy,* Taking on the Challenge of Solidarity! *(TT), from the Summit Conference, October 1996.*

It is clear that the current understanding of social economy in Québec is quite different than the understanding of the term in other parts of North America. For example, in the rest of Canada, the social

Figure 1.1. Legal Status of Social Economy Organizations in Québec

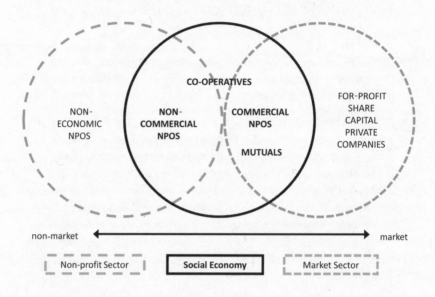

economy comprises not only market-based organizations but also all of organized civil society (such as volunteer and non-profit organizations, trade unions, social clubs, religious institutions, etc.), as well as public-sector non-profit organizations (such as hospitals, universities, and colleges) (Quarter, 1992; Quarter, Mook, & Armstrong, 2009). In addition, the definition of the volunteer/non-profit sector in the United States and English Canada is both more restrictive (because it takes into account only the legal status of a particular organization) and more extensive (because it includes all non-profit organizations, whether they have an economic vocation or not). In Québec, the social economy is understood to comprise both a wider scope of business organizations (because it includes cooperatives and mutual societies) and a narrower, civil-society scope (because it only includes organizations that produce goods or services with a social purpose).

Thus, a wide, inclusive definition of the social economy in Québec includes cooperatives, non-profit organizations that produce goods or services (market or non-market), and mutual societies. It does not include share-capital enterprises, whose goal is the individual distribution of profits, or non-profit organizations that do not engage in economic activities (Bouchard, Ferraton, & Michaud, 2006; Bouchard, Cruz Filho, & St-Denis, 2011).

The Social Economy: A Vector of Social Innovation[5]

The present work on Québec's social economy examines the phenomena that have appeared and become formalized over the past 30 years, at a time when important structural changes were reshaping the relationship between the economy and society. We believe that the present "crisis" is not only conjunctural, but is presenting itself, over time, as the height of a period of great change in the prevailing model of development, following many crises – of work and employment, the state, finance, global economics, and the environment. This period is marked by a growth in inequality, social exclusion, the "ungovernability" of states, the rise of individualism, and more. But it also accompanied by initiatives that seek to answer needs in such a way as to reinforce solidarity, rebalance power, redistribute wealth, etc.

The social economy, in this context, participates in seeking solutions to economic disparity and iniquity, as well as to inventing another model of development. At the local level, its initiatives multiply and are disseminated, bringing about structural impacts in living conditions, work, territory, and even the planning and implementation of public policy. The social economy is thus increasingly being perceived as part of the notion of social innovation.

Innovation is generally understood to be a new activity that takes shape and is disseminated within a given context. We can identify at least two major approaches to social innovation. The first approach is interested in solutions to major social problems, based on entrepreneurial initiatives that emphasize philanthropy, individual responsibility, and the market more than the state.[6] This approach is well represented by the Ashoka association, which values self-help and support to leading social entrepreneurs such as Muhammad Yunus (founder of the first microcredit institution in Bangladesh).

The second approach – which is given priority in this work – puts greater emphasis on the collective nature of the processes and products of social innovation. In this approach, although microsystems are often grounds for experimenting with new social regularities, innovation does not result solely from a voluntary and rational action. It also arises from the conjugation of structural impasses and the action of social movements (Comeau et al., 2007, pp. 370–1). In periods of crisis, macro-social rules (market, state, collective agreements) are shaken up, thus making more room for innovation and experimentation. New regulations originate from the relationships between leading social actors as well as from local experiments that extend to the whole of society. Innovations come about in clusters (Schumpeter, 1939; Porter, 1990) and work in systems that can characterize new development trajectories at the national level (Hollingsworth & Boyer, 1997; Strange, 1996; Crouch & Streeck, 1996). Innovation (economic and social) thus participates in the transition between one model of development and another (Lévesque, 2007).

Given this perspective, social innovation may be defined as "an intervention initiated by social actors to respond to an aspiration, to meet specific needs, to offer a solution or to take advantage of an opportunity for action in order to modify social relations, transform a framework for action, or propose new cultural orientations."[7] Social innovations are thus answers to specific necessities, but they are also proposals that aim towards social change to the extent that they imply "a new vision, a new way of seeing and defining problems, as well as solutions to these problems" (Lévesque, 2005, p. 13). This perspective has been adopted by researchers at CRISES (Centre de recherche sur les innovations sociales) and is used in this book. According to this approach, we can discern at least four types of social innovation (see Box 1.2, below), according to whether they involve relations of production (worker participation), relations of consumption (user participation), relationships between enterprises (cooperation and competition, non-market interdependencies or externalities), or the spatial configuration of social relationships (territorial governance).

BOX 1.2.
SOCIAL INNOVATION

Social innovation is "an intervention initiated by social actors, to respond to an aspiration, meet a specific need, offer a solution or take advantage of an opportunity for action in order to modify social relations, transform a framework for action or propose new cultural orientations."

There are four main types of social innovation:

- Relations of production: the involvement and participation of workers, new forms of work organization, the creation of self-managed businesses, workers' funds, and work insertion enterprises.
- Relations of consumption: involvement and participation of users, co-production of services to persons, co-construction of new programs and new rules, responsible consumption, responsible leisure time and tourism.
- Relationships between enterprises: cooperation and competition, non-market interdependencies (externalities), societal responsibility of enterprises.
- Spatial configuration of social relations: new forms of governance, community economic development.

Source: Centre de recherche sur les innovations sociales (CRISES)

The social economy is emerging to respond to collective aspirations and needs, often in new or underdeveloped sectors of activity, by proposing new ways of doing things that embrace the values of equity, equality, and social justice and are the result of a social and collective entrepreneurship driven by objectives other than personal monetary gain (Borzaga & Defourny, 2004; Nyssens, 2006). The social economy tends to address social demands and expectations that are unfulfilled either because the capitalist entrepreneur does not find a sufficient source of profit or because public powers are ineffective or delay their response (Vienney, 1980). It thus has the capacity to compensate for the market economy and make up for market failures (Hansmann, 1980), as well as to remedy public failures or even anticipate the insufficient production of public goods or trust goods (Weisbrod, 1977; Salamon & Anheier, 1997).

The social economy can also be an important vector for the different types of innovations developed by Schumpeter. We can illustrate these innovations using community housing (Bouchard & Hudon, 2008) and domestic help services (Vaillancourt & Jetté, 2009) as examples (see Table 1.1). The social economy widens the scope of products and services available to segments of the economy that are useful but not covered by the market or the state (new products or services). It also offers new opportunities for excluded or relatively dominated actors (new openings) and stimulates a new kind of social or collective entrepreneurship (new organizations). It contributes towards instituting new

Table 1.1. Examples of Social Economy Innovations

Innovation	Domestic help	Community housing
New products and services	Household cleaning services and domestic help offered to the entire population	Private rental housing at an affordable price
New openings	Creation of qualified jobs with good working conditions Poorly served clientele to date (e.g., the elderly, those with limited autonomy)	Collective overseeing of housing needs in decaying neighbourhoods Mixed or marginalized clientele (e.g., single-parent families)
New organizations	Creation of cooperatives and non-profit organizations with a board of directors composed of volunteers	Cooperatives that are the collective property of tenant-users Non-profit organizations that are administered by citizen members of the local community
New procedures	Partnership with the public health sector and social services via the CLSCs (Centres locaux de services communautaires); price setting according to household revenue; tax credits for the elderly	Joint construction of offer and demand by the users of housing and by professionals of the sector Co-construction of public policy with public authorities

norms and rules, notably on the level of intra- and inter-organizational practices of cooperation (new procedures).

As with any other organization, the social space that constitutes the social economy organization is created from the tensions between innovative and conservative behaviour (Bouchikhi, 1998). There are also different stages in the "life cycle" of social innovations (novelty, dissemination, maturity, decline), with institutionalization, trivialization, and even privatization marking the end of the movement. However, in the case of social innovation, institutionalization can also mean the pinnacle of success, to the extent that it allows for the dissemination of its contributions within the larger society (Bouchard, 2006; Bouchard, Lévesque, & St-Pierre, 2008). Thus, in a country where the welfare state is established and open to recognizing the social economy – as Québec has been, to a large extent, over the last 30 years – institutionaliza-tion can be seen as a desirable state, rather than regarded as a form of bureaucratization.

Social innovation in terms of the social economy thus enables the re-formulation and reframing of social questions with a global perspective in mind: It refutes the dichotomy between society and the economy, itself a source of many social problems. Practices are developed that question the separation between the private and public sectors as well as between economic development and social development. These practices also help create social and political coordination.

Two main factors help explain the innovative potential of the social economy. One of these factors is associated with the constraint of lim-ited or forbidden distribution of financial benefits and assets ("asset-lock"). This constraint makes social economy organizations particularly likely to develop products that have a strong public good component – i.e., whose market price is difficult to determine and for which con-sumers have a lack of information with regard to their quality, value, or utility (Hansmann, 1980, quoted in Ben Ner, 2001). Social economy organizations are even more capable than the state when it comes to fulfilling certain needs because, among other things, they can respond more rapidly to specific demands by mobilizing volunteer resources (volunteer work, donations, etc.) (Weisbrod, 1988). They are also more prompt in responding to needs, since they are oriented and governed by the principal stakeholders concerned with these needs (Ben Ner & Hoomissen, 1991). The constraint of non-distribution of surpluses ac-centuates the relationship of trust between consumer and producer. This factor is particularly developed by the Anglo-Saxon approach to non-profit organizations (NPOs) and remains focused on the non-market components of the social economy.

A second type of explanation applies to a wider notion of the social economy, including its predominantly market-based components (co-operatives and mutual societies). It takes into account other functions of the social economy, such as the creation of democratic spaces, the defence of social rights, and social integration (Enjolras, 2002). Thus, the social economy has a tendency to rethink institutions, in particular when those institutions are unable to respond to new social demands (Lévesque & Vaillancourt, 1998). A historical approach reveals that the process of innovation comes about in stages, often by contesting norms or rules, proposing alternatives, and then disseminating these alterna-tives within other organizations or sectors of activity.

This shows us that the social economy challenges institutions in terms of norms, rules, or society's values, but also that it tends to redefine the institutional dimensions of the model of development, such as the relationships between the market, state, networks, and communities (Lévesque, 2006). If innovations do not always have the effect of radically changing the way things are done, they do have, in certain cases, a widened or "generic" impact. For example, "the joint construction of offer and demand by professionals and users" (Eme & Laville, 1994; Bélanger & Lévesque, 1991) has been extended to numerous sectors (community housing, day-care centres, domestic help services, etc.). This co-construction presupposes the creation of public mini-spaces and is indicative of the political dimension of social innovation (Dacheux, 2003; Laville, 1994).

These two visions of factors favouring innovation in the social economy are complementary. The first sees the potential of the social economy to prevent or find solutions to social problems (Bouchard, 1999; Fraser, 2003). The second shows the finality of social innovation, which, contrary to technological innovation, is rarely promoted by the market but rather by change brought about in institutions. The criss-crossing of these two types of approaches and of the two major schools of the third sector – NPOs and the social economy - allows for the development of an original typology (see Table 1.2) of social economy initiatives that are founded, on the one hand, on the dynamics of an emerging organization (to respond to urgent needs or aspirations) and, on the other hand, on the type of activity in question (according to whether it is predominantly market or non-market based) (Lévesque, 2004).

How This Book Is Organized

This book presents recent research on contemporary issues vis-à-vis the social economy and shows how Québec's experience provides a rich source of information. Since the beginning of the 1980s, researchers have been interested in new practices and activities within Québec's social economy. Several of their studies have been initiated within CRISES, the Centre de recherche sur les innovations sociales (Social Innovation Research Centre), whose research program aims to explore how, in periods of crisis, a society can reconstruct itself. Without disregarding the negative effects of the global economic crisis, the hypothesis is that Québec society, like most societies, is experiencing a period of profound change: This is a very challenging period, but also one that is rich

Table 1.2. Typology of Social Economy Initiatives

Needs/Opportunities (Relationship to the Market)	Needs Linked to Aspirations	Needs Linked to Urgent Needs
Predominantly market-based (economic development)	Workers' cooperatives	Work insertion enterprises
Predominantly non market-based (social development)	Daycare centres	Collective kitchens

Source: Lévesque, 2004

in social innovation. This innovation relates to not only economic but also social development and, in particular, the link between the two, which the social economy attempts to create.

Since most social innovations are not recognized as such (at least a priori), one of the first functions of research is to identify and recognize them (i.e., to codify and formalize). Consequently, the methodology that underlies the basic research of this work has, to a large extent, counted on research partnerships with interested social actors, notably those associated with ARUC- ÉS and RQRP-ÉS, l'Alliance de recherche universités-communautés and le Réseau québécois de recherche partenariale en économie sociale (Community University Research Alliance on the Social Economy and the Québec Partnership Research Node on the Social Economy).

The goal of this work is to introduce the reader to some of the thematic elements that we believe are important from the perspective of the social economy's potential with regard to social innovation. The social economy is a complex reality that, by its very nature, calls upon a multi- or trans-disciplinary conceptualization. The chapters of the book have been written by researchers from the fields of sociology, business management, economics, political science, social work, the legal sciences, and geography. The authors were also involved in the planning of the book and the editing of its chapters.

The first four chapters lay out a general view of Québec's social economy vis-à-vis its institutional recognition, the close ties it nurtures with researchers, the partnership it bridges between the state and civil society, and the role its actors play in the conception and implementation of public policy. The next five chapters each address a particular topic: the legal status of non-profit organizations, financial instruments for the social economy, the links between sustainable development and the social economy, the role of the social economy in fostering local development, and working conditions in the social economy. The conclusion discusses the perspective taken in this book, and looks at some of the issues facing the social economy, as well as researchers working on it.

Institutionalization of the Social Economy in Québec

The social economy in Québec enjoys an institutional recognition that is unequalled elsewhere in Canada (Fairbairn, 2009; McMurtry, 2010; Quarter, Mook, & Armstrong 2009). The first chapter of this book traces the process that led to this recognition by underlining the characteristics of the Québec model of social economy. In Chapter 1, Benoît Lévesque first explores the conception of the type of social economy that prevails in Québec, whose form more closely resembles the European model (notably France and other Latin-European countries) than the model found in the rest of Canada or the United States. The chapter presents the recent history of Québec's social economy, offers a panorama of what it is today, and shows the trajectory of its institutional recognition. This recognition has not been smooth: It has been marked by, among other things, tension among social economy families. The social economy has gone through different successive configurations that, like the present configuration, were challenged by actors in the sector themselves. This historical review allows us to take a fresh look at the tensions and compromises that imbue the present configuration of the social economy.

A New Research Practice

One of the unique characteristics of Québec's model of social economy is the role played by universities in both promoting and conceptualizing the field, even to the extent of having an influence on the co-creation of knowledge, achieved through research produced in collaboration with actors in the social economy community. In Chapter 2, Jean-Marc Fontan explores this new type of research. Partnership research is a non-traditional way of producing knowledge by bringing together practitioners – who sometimes, but not necessarily, have the status of institutional researchers – and university researchers. Both are involved in all stages of a research project, from conception to realization, including the dissemination and transfer of information, and the training of students. Mixing formal and tacit knowledge, as well as having privileged access to data, leads to the development of objectives and work methods that are appreciably different from those reached by more traditional approaches. The challenge for researchers is to no longer regard the practioners' communities solely as objects or subjects of study, but rather to see them as active research participants. It also challenges researchers in terms of maintaining a critical distance in order not to simply serve as instruments for practitioners. This is a new research culture that requires learning on both parts.

Governance

Partnership also characterizes the new relationships between the state and the social economy. In Chapter 3, Luc Dancause and Richard Morin explore the transformation of the state and its modes of intervention, notably territorial decentralization and the appeal to non-profit organizations for the delivery of services. The authors show different trajectories, beginning with examples taken from Québec and elsewhere (English Canada, the United States, France, and the United Kingdom). While partnership represents an opportunity for recognition and financing for the social economy, it also involves risks, and the authors identify three of these: instrumentalization, marketization, and democratic deficit. Partnership cannot be solely a strategy for entrusting the dispensation of public services or the management of social problems, through subcontracting to non-profit organizations. If it is, it becomes a tool for controlling community organizations and sectors, which reduces their autonomy and tends to standardize their practices. It can also be seen as a weakened form of democracy, where professionals replace true social representation. On the other hand, partnership can favour the participation of workers, members, and users in the strategic decision-making of organizations and even encourage representation of the social economy in local consultation bodies. Thus, the principal challenge that social economy organizations must meet in order to overcome the above-mentioned risks is to have an influence on the definition of public policies and their resulting programs.

The Construction and Orientation of Public Policies

Chapter 4, by Yves Vaillancourt and Philippe Leclerc, explains the influence of social economy actors on the definition of public policies
and their resulting programs. They analyse the partnership nature of
the formulation and implementation of social policies over the past 20
years in Québec. They show the role played by non-state actors in the
creation and orientation of policies (which they call "co-construction").
They formulate four models: mono-construction, where this type of
contribution does not exist; neo-liberal co-construction, which involves
the business world; corporatist co-construction, which favours cooperation with employer or union bodies; and democratic, solidarity-based
co-construction, which contributes to a participative reform of the state
by mobilizing diverse groups within society that have collective interest objectives.

Four factors characterize the democratic, solidarity-based model.
The first is the relationship between the "co-architects" of public policy, which remains unequal, since it is the state that, in the end, arbi-
trates and adjudicates. The second is the plurality of involved actors,
who come from both the market and the civil society. The third is the
existence of governance spaces and mechanisms that are open to debate, thus promoting "the best of representative and deliberative democracy." The fourth is a recognition of the participation of actors from
the social economy in a partnership relationship that does not instrumentalize the social economy and that recognizes its autonomy vis-à-
vis the state. The authors illustrate their thesis by describing the recent
evolution of community (cooperative and non-profit) social housing
programs and institutions in Québec.

Associative Law

How does the law reconcile the fact that social economy associations –
non-profit organizations – are also businesses? Expectations have been
drawn up to reform the legal status of associations in Québec, but points
of view on the subject are divergent. The debate, which Louis Jolin discusses in Chapter 5, deals with, among other things, the conception of
the association as a contract or institution. If considered as a contract
between persons, the association would be controlled by civil law and
the state would have to limit rules that interfere with contractual freedom, a guarantor of the freedom of association. The only acceptable

imperative rules would be those that aim to protect third parties and public order. In the second case, the association is perceived as an organization that enjoys certain privileges (notably fiscal), not only because it is a not-for-profit institution but also because it contributes towards democracy by facilitating the expression and action of its citizens. Consequently, the association requires imperative rules in order that the rights of third parties and the public order are respected, and that the associative "foundation" – democratic governance – is secure.

Another controversy concerns the ability – or lack thereof – to issue associative capital. If an association is governed by civil law and is authorized to pursue "any goal provided that its sole purpose is not the sharing of profits among members," why not allow it to issue shares, as cooperatives do, ensuring limited remuneration and decision-making power over the future of the association, this power remaining in the hands of its members? For the advocates of an institutional and democratic approach, to authorize the issuance of an associative capital would likely cause the real risk of lessening public confidence in associations and a reduction in public financing. The debate reflects back to the meaning itself of an association and its role within the third sector and in society in general.

Financing

How can the social economy be financed while still respecting its unique characteristics and purpose? Social economy organizations develop economic activities that have a social end. They generally mobilize a mixture of resources from sales, subsidies, donations, and volunteer work. These resources are not always sufficient to insure growth, however, and access to capital becomes an important factor. In Chapter 6, Gilles L. Bourque, Margie Mendell, and Ralph Rouzier outline the instruments of financing available to social economy enterprises through solidarity financing, instruments that are considered to be one of the most significant initiatives of Québec's social economy. Loan capital (debt instruments) and development capital (long-term investment) instruments have been developed to facilitate the financial setup of social economy projects. These range from micro-credit to financial institutions. The actors differ according to their socio-economic objectives and a logic that includes non-financial dimensions in the analysis of projects (job development, territory consolidation, etc.). The role of the state as facilitator and partner in solidarity-based financing is crucial, but the governance of these institutions remains plural and autonomous. The 2008 financial crisis accentuated the need for such tools in a responsible economy that is anchored in concrete values, and the authors believe that future developments will increase and disseminate the impact of these social innovations.

Sustainable Development

Is the social economy better able to meet society's expectations in terms of the social and environmental responsibilities of economic actors in relation to sustainable development? In Chapter 7, Corinne Gendron and Marie-France Turcotte ask this question as they explore how the concepts of social economy and sustainable development work together. Until now, the environmental angle of sustainable development has attracted researchers, with the social angle coming in a poor second. At the same time, sustainable development issues are part of the fundamental questioning raised by the social economy movement. The social economy therefore appears to be fertile ground for better understanding sustainable development, not only empirically but theoretically as well. These two arenas – the social economy and sustainable development – can thus work together in several ways: (1) They can be based on similar principles, such as autonomy and development that is centred on the satisfaction of human needs and on democracy; (2) they can suggest alternative ways to satisfy social needs; and (3) they can be used to thoroughly explore the definition of the common good, collective social welfare, and, to a larger extent, the question of general interest.

Of course, sustainable development has dimensions that are not necessarily integrated into the social economy, and the social economy does not necessarily bring about sustainable development. On the other hand, social economy enterprises are already accustomed to operating and being evaluated within a context of multiple bottom-line objectives according to a hierarchy that is supposed to favour the common interest (or at least the collective interest of its members). This in itself constitutes an essential ingredient of sustainable development.

Local Development

As a result of globalization, new forms of social inequality have emerged on both national and local levels. In Chapter 8, Juan-Luis Klein and

Pierre-André Tremblay explore the capacity of social economy organizations to support local actors in their efforts to deflect this inequality and even to generate a specific project for local development. Since social economy organizations are rooted in communities, they act as a support for local territories. The effects they have can be considered beneficial when they contribute to the reinforcement of local markets, the construction of local skills, the implementation of local governance bodies, and new ways of responding to social problems. The role of the social economy can prove to be negative, however, when it becomes immersed in a political context that dualizes society and contributes to the institution of an economy of poverty. To avoid this trap, organizations must go beyond local resources and networks and must collaborate, first with each other, on various levels, and then with public and private actors. Klein and Tremblay present Québec examples of local initiatives in both urban and rural communities that illustrate the conditions allowing the social economy to act as a real support for a more sustainable and solidarity-based local development. There are still challenges, of course, notably the search for financial aid that is not solely oriented towards profit-making, the overlapping of local and national governances to lessen inter-territorial competition, and the embeddedness within emerging social practices that serves to preserve and reproduce the capacity of local communities to diagnose and identify solutions.

Work

Does the social economy encourage poor working conditions? Or is it a space in which a workers' democracy can be created? In Chapter 9, Yvan Comeau, who has carried out several empirical studies, offers subtle answers to these questions. His analysis, which goes beyond a strict examination of working conditions (direct and indirect wages, benefits, etc.), examines wage relationships, taking into account the degree of worker inclusion in the enterprise's power structure. The studies quoted show that, in terms of determining working conditions, there exist common phenomena with other types of organizations. Thus, when social economy organizations are located in outlying and underprivileged areas, when they invest in fields of activity that are not very lucrative, and when they are small, there is a good chance that working conditions will be poor. In addition, working conditions are also influenced by the "rules of the game" and the strategies of the groups that produce, in some social economy cases, an original wage relationship. This is particularly true for worker cooperatives, worker shareholder cooperatives, and solidarity cooperatives. The social economy offers no guarantees, however. The author therefore calls upon strategies to enhance the reflective capacities of social economy actors in order to better include workers in the management process. This would result in encouraging a better recognition of social economy workers by governments (similar to what is already happening in the construction and health sectors). It would also help workers gain access to mutual help initiatives, such as insurance and retirement plans, and unions develop new protocols to achieve compromise with state partners.

* * *

In this point in time, when the system seems to be exhausted from facing social and economic challenges, social innovations are clearly needed boosts. While not a panacea, the social economy has proven to offer durable alternative solutions to the dual – and not always viable – options of either asking for more public services or letting the market solve everything. The Québec social economy experience demonstrates how social innovations can affect society as a whole. It enabled the reformulation and reframing of social questions while refuting the dichotomy between society and the economy, in itself a source of many social problems. This book should therefore be of interest not only to scholars but also to practioners and policy makers, as we believe it offers grounds for a larger policy debate beyond what has begun in Québec.

NOTES

1   I wish to thank Karen Simon for the translation of this introduction.
2   Such as the workers' movement, the women's movement, the environmental movement, and the alternative-globalization movement.
3   The social economy is defined either by its definite or indefinite components (Desroche, 1983), its rules of functioning (Vienney, 1980), its dynamic of reciprocity and solidarity (Eme & Laville, 1994), its logic of action (Enjolras, 1994), its place within a plural economy (Evers & Laville, 2004), its non-profit character (Ben-Ner & Van Hoomissen, 1991; Anheir & Ben-Ner, 2003; Salamon & Anheier, 1997), its entrepreneurial character (Dees, 1998; Borzaga & Defourny, 2004; Nyssens, 2006), etc.

4 In some countries like France, foundations are increasingly being included as well.

5 These ideas are developed in a chapter of a work on social innovation that appeared in the Presses de l'Université du Québec under the direction of D. Harrisson and J.-L. Klein following a colloquium of CRISES (see Bouchard, 2007) and in a paper presented to the Réseau interuniversitaire de l'économie sociale et solidaire in Luxemburg, in June 2010 (see Bouchard & Lévesque, 2010).

6 "A new name for brains and money" is how an article in *The Economist* put it on 12 August 2010.

7 Definition of the Centre de recherche sur les innovations sociales (CRISES).

REFERENCES

Bélanger, P.R., & Lévesque, B. (1991). La "théorie" de la régulation, du rapport salarial au rapport de consommation. Un point de vue sociologique. *Cahiers de Recherche Sociologique, 17*, 17–52.

Ben-Ner, A. (2002). The shifting boundaries of the mixed economy and the future of the nonprofit sector. *Annals of Public and Cooperative Economics, 73*(1), 5–40. http://dx.doi.org/10.1111/1467-8292.00184

Ben-Ner, A., & Van Hoomissen, T. (1991). Nonprofit organizations in the mixed economy: A demand and supply analysis. *Annals of Public and Cooperative Economics, 62*(4), 519–50. http://dx.doi.org/10.1111/j.1467-8292.1991.tb01366.x

Borzaga, C., & Defourny, J. (Eds.). (2004). *The emergence of social enterprise.* London: Routledge.

Bouchard, C. (1999). *Contribution à une politique de l'immatérie: Recherche en sciences humaines et sociales et innovations sociales.* Québec: Conseil québécois de la recherche sociale, Groupe de travail sur l'innovation sociale.

Bouchard, M.J. (2006). De l'expérimentation à l'institutionnalisation positive, l'innovation sociale dans le logement communautaire au Québec. *Annales de l'économie publique, sociale et coopérative, 77*(2), 139–66. http://dx.doi.org/10.1111/j.1370-4788.2006.00301.x

Bouchard, M.J. (2007). Les défis de l'innovation sociale en économie sociale. In J.-L. Klein & D. Harrisson (eds.), *Innovations sociales et transformations sociales* (pp. 121–38). Québec: Presses de l'Université du Québec.

Bouchard, M.J., et al. (2008). *Portrait statistique de l'économie sociale de la région de Montréal.* Montréal: Conférence régionale des élus de Montréal et UQAM, Chaire de recherche du Canada en économie sociale.

Bouchard, M.J., Cruz Filho, P., & St-Denis, M. (2011). *Cadre conceptuel pour définir la population statistique de l'économie sociale au Québec.* Report for the Québec Institute of Statistics (Institut de la statistique du Québec). Montréal: UQAM, Chaire de recherche du Canada en économie sociale, R-2011–02.

Bouchard, M.J., Ferraton, C., & Michaud, V. (2008). First steps of an information system on the social economy: Qualifying the organizations. *Estudios de Economía Aplicada, 26*(1), 7–24.

Bouchard, M.J., & Hudon, M. (Eds.). (2008). *Se loger autrement au Québec. Le mouvement de l'habitat communautaire, un acteur du développement social et économique.* Montréal: Éditions Albert St-Martin.

Bouchard, M.J., & Lévesque, B. (2010). *L'approche de la régulation au cœur de la construction québécoise de l'économie sociale.* Montréal: CRISES and Chaire de recherche du Canada en économie sociale, no. ET1103 and R-2010–04.

Bouchard, M.J., Lévesque, B., & St-Pierre, J. (2008). Modèle québécois de développement et gouvernance: Entre le partenariat et le néolibéralisme. In B. Enjolras (Ed.), *Régimes de gouvernance et services d'intérêt général, une perspective internationale* (pp. 39–65). New York, Bern, Berlin, Brussels, Frankfurt am Main, Oxford, Vienna: PIE Peter Lang Publishers.

Bouchikhi, H. (1998). Living with and building on complexity: A constructivist perspective on organizations. *Organization, 5*(2), 217–32. http://dx.doi.org/10.1177/135050849852004

Comeau, Y., et al. (2007). Axe 2 – Conditions de vie. In J.-L. Klein & D. Harrisson (Eds.), *L'innovation sociale: Émergence et effets sur la transformation des sociétés* (pp. 361–76). Québec: Presses de l'Université du Québec.

Crouch, C., & Streeck, W. (Eds.). (1996). *Les capitalismes en Europe.* Paris: La Découverte.

Dacheux, É. (2003). Un nouveau regard sur l'espace public et la crise démocratique. *Hermes, 36*(36), 195–204. http://dx.doi.org/10.4267/2042/9376

Dees, J.G. (1998, Jan–Feb). Enterprising nonprofits. *Harvard Business Review, 76*(1), 54–67. Medline:10176919

Defourny, J. (2005). L'économie sociale. In J.-L. Laville & A.D. Cattani (Eds.), *Dictionnaire de l'autre économie* (pp. 233–42). Paris: Desclée de Brouwer.

Defourny, J., & Develtere, P. (1999). Origines et contours de l'économie sociale au Nord et au Sud. In J. Defourny, P. Develtere, & B. Fonteneau (Eds.), *L'économie sociale au Nord et au Sud* (pp. 25–56). Paris, Brussels: DeBoeck & Larcier.

Defourny, J., & Monzón Campos, J.L. (Eds.). (1992). *Économie sociale: Entre économie capitaliste et économie publique/The Third Sector: Cooperative, mutual and nonprofit organizations.* Brussels: CIRIEC and De Boeck-Wesmael.

Demoustier, D. (2001). *L'économie sociale et solidaire: S'associer pour entreprendre autrement*. Paris: Syros.

Desroche, H. (1983). *Pour un traité d'économie sociale*. Paris: CIEM

Draperi, J.-F. (2009). L'entrepreneuriat social, un mouvement de pensée inscrit dans le capitalisme. *RECMA Revue internationale de l'économie sociale*. Accessed 11 Jánuary 2011. http://www.recma.org/node/974.

Eme, B., & Laville, J.-L. (Eds.). (1994). *Cohésion sociale et emploi*. Paris: Desclée de Brouwer.

Enjolras, B. (2002). *L'économie solidaire et le marché*. Paris: L'Harmattan.

Evers, A., & Laville, J.-L. (2004). *The third sector in Europe*. Cheltenham: Elgar.

Fairbairn, B. (2009). Imagination and identity: The social economy and the state in Canada. In J. Defourny et al. (Eds.), *The worldwide making of the social economy: Innovations and change* (pp. 129–48). Leuven/ The Hague: Acco.

Fraser, M. (2003). *Les organisations oeuvrant dans le domaine de l'innovation sociale: Résultats d'une recherche dans Internet*. Québec: Conseil de la science et de la technologie.

Groupe de travail sur l'économie sociale. (1996). *Définition de l'économie sociale*. Québec: GTES.

Hansmann, H. (1980). The role of non-profit enterprise. *Yale Law Journal, 89*(5), 835–901. http://dx.doi.org/10.2307/796089

Hollingsworth, R.J. (2000). Doing institutional analysis: Implications for the study of innovations. *Review of International Political Economy, 7*(4), 595–644. http://dx.doi.org/10.1080/096922900750034563

Laville, J.-L. (Ed.). (1994). *L'économie solidaire: Une perspective internationale*. Paris: Desclée de Brouwer.

Lévesque, B. (2004). Les entreprises d'économie sociale, plus porteuses d'innovations sociales que les autres? In *Le développement social au rythme de l'innovation*. Québec: Presses de l'Université du Québec and Fonds de recherche sur la société et la culture, 51–72.

Lévesque, B. (2006). Le potentiel d'innovation et de transformation de l'économie sociale: Quelques éléments de problématique. *Economie et Solidarités, 37*(2), 13–48.

Lévesque, B. (2007). L'innovation dans le développement économique et le développement social. In J.-L. Klein & D. Harrisson (Eds.), *L'innovation sociale: Émergence et effets sur la transformation des sociétés* (pp. 43–70). Québec: Presses de l'Université du Québec.

Lévesque, B., & Vaillancourt, Y. (1998). *Les services de proximité au Québec: De l'expérimentation à l'institutionnalisation*. Montréal: Université du Québec à Montréal, Centre de recherche sur les innovations sociales, collection Recherche, no. 9812.

McMurtry, J.J. (Ed.). (2010). *Living economics: Canadian perspectives on the social economy, cooperatives, and community economic development.* Toronto: Emond Montgomery Publications Limited.

Mendell, M., & Neamtan, N. (2010). The social economy in Québec: Towards a new political economy. In L. Mook, J. Quarter, & S. Ryan (Eds.), *Researching the social economy* (pp. 63–83). Toronto: University of Toronto Press.

Nyssens, M. (Ed.). (2006). *Social enterprise.* London: Routledge.

Polanyi, K. (1944). *The great transformation.* New York: Rinehart.

Porter, M.E. (1990). *The competitive advantage of nations.* New York: The Free Press.

Quarter, J. (1992). *Canada's social economy: Cooperatives, non-profits and other community enterprises.* Toronto: James Lorimer & Company Publishers.

Quarter, J., Mook, L., & Armstrong, A. (2009). *Understanding the social economy: A Canadian perspective.* Toronto: University of Toronto Press.

Salamon, L.M., & Anheier, H.K. (1997). *Defining the nonprofit sector: A cross-national analysis.* Manchester and New York: Manchester University Press, Johns Hopkins Nonprofit Sector Series 4.

Schumpeter, J.A. (1939). *Business cycles: A theoretical, historical and statistical analysis of capitalist process* (2 vols.) New York, London: McGraw-Hill.

Strange, S. (1996). L'avenir du capitalisme mondial: La diversité peut-elle per-sister indéfiniment? In C. Crouch. and W. Streeck (Eds.), *Les capitalismes en Europe* (pp. 246–71). Paris: La Découverte.

Vaillancourt, Y., and Jetté, C. (with P. Leclerc). (2009). *Les arrangements institu-tionnels entre l'État québécois et les entreprises d'économie sociale en aide domes-tique: Une analyse sociopolitique de l'économie sociale dans les services de soutien à domicile.* Montréal: Les Éditions Vie Économique.

Vienney, C. (1980). *Socio-économie des organisations coopératives.* Paris: C.I.E.M.

Weisbrod, B.A. (1977). *The voluntary nonprofit sector.* Lexington, MA: Lexington Books.

1 How the Social Economy Won Recognition in Québec at the End of the Twentieth Century[1]

BENOÎT LÉVESQUE

Introduction

When the social economy finally won recognition in Québec in the mid-1990s, it did so following a long process initiated in the late 1960s. Thus, 1996 did not mark the beginning of the social economy, although it was in fact the starting point for a new social dynamic (economic and political) that would affect all of its sectors. From this point forward, these sectors would interact more frequently and share the tools of their trade. Of course, 1996 also represented a watershed; the social economy received institutional recognition per se (Lévesque, 2007).

Keeping this in mind, it is important to understand that, several decades earlier, the cooperative movement was torn between two divergent outlooks. One saw the movement as a means to achieve a social vision; the other saw it as an end in itself (which made it more difficult to include categories of associations that were not explicitly cooperative in their orientation).[2] The Quiet Revolution would pave the way for a compromise between these two views, while the social movements and the economic crisis of the early 1980s would favour the rise of a new generation of cooperatives. Some of these organizations would have close contact with projects initiated by civil society associations, especially those involved in local, community-based services, job creation, and local development. By understanding this earlier history, which was still far removed from the recognition that would be accorded the social economy in later years, we can construct a somewhat different interpretation of the more recent context – of the initial compromise of 1996 – and make a better assessment of the major issues that would affect the future of the social economy in Québec. Before going any further, however, a brief discussion of what we mean by the social economy and its institutional recognition is in order.

Broaching the question analytically, we can identify two major approaches to the social economy[3] (or what some call the third sector): (a) one generally identified as the American approach, which includes non-profit organizations (NPOs) and whose leading light is Lester M. Salamon (1987 et al., 1996, 1999); and (b) one identified as the European approach, which is propagated, by, among others, CIRIEC (Centre International de Recherches et d'Informationsur l'Economie Publique, Sociale et Coopérative) and a new generation of researchers following the original work of Henri Desroche (1983, 1987) and Claude Vienney (1994) (Evers & Laville, 2004; CIRIEC, 2000; Defourny & Monzon Campos, 1992; Fecher & Lévesque, 2008). These two major theoretical approaches, which exist side by side in Canada (Vaillancourt, 2006), reveal that the organizations in question (cooperatives, mutual societies, associations, and foundations)[4] have at least four characteristics in common: democratic governance, the non-profit-making character of their activity (the goal of the service), voluntary membership, and independence vis-à-vis the state.

There are also fundamental differences between the two approaches, however. Salamon, for example, places NPOs at the centre of a triangle, each angle of which represents cooperatives, mutual societies, or foundations. In the European approach, cooperatives are located at the centre of the triangle, with the other components located on each side. In the American approach, the non-profit-making character of the activity and the fact that it is provided free of charge (on a voluntary basis) is considered the quintessential way of serving the public interest; in the European approach, democracy allows market activities to be included so as to make them compatible with the collective interest. Because of this major difference, Salamon selects only cooperatives that work with the poor, whereas the approach we favour includes large cooperatives as well as solidarity-based cooperatives. Lastly, the American approach does not exclude associations that provide collective services (such as hospitals or universities), something the European (and Québec) approach rejects, on the grounds that education and health services are public services and thus the concern of the state, notwithstanding the fact that some of the institutions delivering these services have NPO legal status.

The social economy has its origins in the second half of the nineteenth century, when mutual benefit societies emerged (Petitclerc,

2005; Gueslin, 1998). This should not lead us to conclude, however, that since that time the various sectors of the social economy have rallied round the concept per se (Lévesque, 2007; Deschênes, 1976, 1981, 1982; Felteau, 1989, 1992; Lévesque & Malo, 1992). Institutional recognition of the social economy assumes at a minimum that the social forces directly involved interact and view themselves as part of the same grouping. It also assumes that governments acknowledge this, employing guidelines that help to define the social economy and the support systems that are consistent with its undertakings. While researchers' definitions of the social economy vary according to the theoretical currents to which they subscribe, for any given society there can only be one institutional definition, which may even be specific to that society (although this does not rule out ambivalent definitions, of course). In reality, cooperatives, mutual societies, and associations will tend to group together spontaneously, according to their legal status or sector. The understanding of the cooperative movement as a means to implement a particular social blueprint or vision[5] would make it easier to unite its various sectors under a single banner, without requiring that these sectors give up their individual identity, which is what makes them unique.

A New Generation of Cooperatives and Socio-economic Initiatives Questions the Established Cooperative Movement

In Québec, a "golden age" of cooperation followed the Great Depression, forming part of a social reform project (Martel, 1986, 1987, 1988). In its most extreme form, the reform project sought to create a Christian social order (Cloutier, 1932). The corporatist approach to cooperation also found expression in mobilizing the cooperative movement to ensure the success and interests of a particular social category, such as farmers or even the working class. This view of the cooperative movement as a vehicle for a broader project (in Québec at that time, the project had a conservative and anti-state orientation) was very different from the view of the movement as an end in itself, the notion advanced by Father Georges-Henri Lévesque in 1940. To ensure the unity of the cooperative movement, he affirmed its apolitical, non-ethnic, and non-denominational character, even if this ran counter to the convictions of the "social and religious authorities" and the majority of cooperatives of the time.[6]

The liberal approach of Father Lévesque emerged only gradually, however, so the first concern of the Conseil supérieur de la coopération

(CSC, the "supreme council" of the cooperative movement) was to pre-serve the authenticity of cooperatives and promote cooperation as an end in itself. Accordingly, mutual benefit societies, which had been the principal component of the cooperative movement from 1840 to 1880, would not be invited to join the CSC. The latter would even be reluc-tant to recognize mutual societies, since it believed that their business practices differed only very slightly from those of insurance compa-nies (Deschênes, 1976, p. 548; Lamarre, 1991, p. 56). Thus, "it took until 1944, following an exhaustive study of the by-laws of five societies by legal advisors for the Conseil supérieur de la coopération, that mu-tual aid societies were recognized as cooperatives" (Deschênes, 1976, p. 548; 1982, pp. 20–1). The CSC concluded that, "the Société des artisans was of the cooperative type, notwithstanding its ethnic and denomina-tional orientation" (ibid.). In short, the CSC recognized the mutual so-ciety form by placing the accent on its cooperative principles. While the issue was ostensibly settled once and for all in 1957 by revising coopera-tives' criteria, by 1962 these criteria had expanded to include the follow-ing: democratic control (direct or indirect), a positive attitude towards the cooperative movement, and avoidance of profit (Lamarre, 1991, p. 49). These criteria could have led to a broader coalition while still al-lowing cooperatives to maintain their position of leadership,[7] especially since the CSC had from the very start accepted "para-cooperatives" (or quasi-cooperatives) as charter members.

The 1950s were a period of crisis for the cooperative movement. Dur-ing this time, most cooperative sectors, with the exception of the caisses populaires (a type of credit union), stagnated and some even waned (Deschênes, 1982, p. 6). On a deeper level, the ideas of social corpo-ratism, agriculturalism, anti-statism, and a conservation-centred view of development, all of which sustained the social restoration program, were practically worn out. The momentum was elsewhere, as revealed by the advent of the Quiet Revolution, of which Father Lévesque was considered a leading figure (Rocher, 1984a, 1984b). Still, Québec would have to wait until 1965 for cooperatives to fully endorse the trend to-wards economic modernization and join in a dialogue with the private sector and other intermediary bodies, as proposed by the state (La-marre, 1991, pp. 73–4). Consequently, a compromise between the two conceptions of cooperatives was required: On the one hand, the cor-poratist view (conservative and nationalistic) accepted the objective of modernizing Québec; on the other, the ideological view (liberal) now supported economic nationalism and francophone control over the economy ("to be masters of one's own house"). In the same period, several economically active Catholic unions and associations, especially in the area of services, decided to become non-denominational, in order to participate in the modernization of Québec under the aegis of the state. While centripetal forces in the field of cooperatives and associations dominated for a few years, this period would also witness the rise of a new generation of cooperatives and associations that were independent (vis-à-vis the church and the state), such as the first citizen committees (Bélanger & Lévesque, 1992). It is this period to which we need to refer if we want to identify the long process that eventually led to the founding compromise of 1996 and to the recognition that community-based movements were stakeholders in economic development.

A New Generation of Cooperatives and Civil Society Initiatives

While citizen committees in the second half of the 1960s started off by demanding better services from the authorities, by the early 1970s they had become involved in socio-economic experiments that helped them realize their aspirations for autonomy, self-management, and "living and working differently." Thus, a significant proportion of educated intellectual workers and a greater-than-ever number of women, youth, and "city folk" chose the cooperative formula, usually the NPO formula, since cooperative accreditation was more difficult to obtain. Thus, there was a remarkable upsurge in associations, whose number increased from 5,302 in 1956 to 23,330 in 1976 (Levasseur, 1990, p. 156). In Europe, some of these socio-economic initiatives were characterized as "new frontier cooperatives," "quasi-enterprises of socio-cultural consumption" (Laliberté, 1973, p. 49, n. 30), or "new-wave cooperatives" (Rioux, 1989, p. 177), and, even more often, as "new cooperatives" (Defourny, Simon, & Adam, 2002). These "social enterprises" developed primarily in sectors linked to the environment and to culture: natural food, health clinics, food banks, day-care centres, housing, community-based media, theatre, etc. They viewed their form of participatory democracy as an essential complement to representative democracy.

As well, an employment crisis followed this work crisis, while the inability of the welfare state to assume responsibility for new social needs prompted people to increasingly challenge its bureaucratic model and weak form of democracy. Meanwhile, there was a meeting of minds between associations initiating projects inspired by research on alternatives and those driven by the new social needs and other pressing concerns.

For the movement as a whole, the rise to power in 1976 of the Parti Québécois raised hopes, especially since this party was favourably disposed towards cooperatives (Landry, 1980, p. 411). Thus, in 1977, a Société de développement coopératif (SDC) was created as a mixed enterprise.[8] The most eagerly awaited event, however, was the 1980 "Conférence socio-économique sur la coopération,"[9] the theme of which was "The Role of the Cooperative in Economic Development." Still, in the short term, the direct spin-offs from this major meeting were minor. According to a former deputy minister for cooperation, it revealed "the wide gap that separated the organized cooperative movement, represented by the Conseil de la coopération du Québec, from the non-organized cooperatives, especially those that worked in new sectors and regarded themselves as innovative in terms of cooperative ideology" (Rioux, 1989, p. 177). It also brought to light the inadequate representativeness of the CCQ in this period, since "75 per cent of the members of the board of directors came from the insurance and loan and credit sectors," whereas "90 per cent of non-financial cooperatives were not represented on the board" (Lamarre, 1991, p. 118; Joron, 1980, p. 163). In defence of the CCQ, most "new cooperatives" either had no sector federation or did not wish to join such a federation even when one existed.[10] Thus, it was necessary to reform CCQ structures in order to endow them with the representativeness implied by its mission, as well as government assistance to promote the grouping together of new cooperatives into federations.

The economic crisis of the early 1980s would give rise to two paradoxical phenomena: namely, the disappearance of certain mature cooperative sectors and the emergence of new cooperatives (which were often similar to socio-economic projects found in civil society). The two phenomena caused new tensions within the cooperative movement. The collapse of certain mature cooperatives raised questions about the solidarity among federations in the CCQ, since it was clear that intercooperation had proved of no benefit to cooperatives that found themselves in difficulty. Following the "series of liquidations, mergers and transformations" (Lamarre, 1991, p. 116), it seemed as if inter-cooperation and government support for cooperatives no longer constituted assets. In addition, in certain sectors, such as agri-food cooperatives and savings and credit institutions, competition had a profound effect on the relations among cooperatives. As well, the disappearance of the cooperative newspaper *Ensemble!* reflected a decline in solidarity. The "institutions that were members of the Conseil" demonstrated "a sort of egoism and disengagement. Of course, sometimes this was unavoidable, but at other times it was unwarranted" (Lamarre, 1991, p. 116). In sum, "several signs" led to a belief that there had been a "dismantling of, divisions among and possibly an atomization of organizations and cooperative initiatives; this contrasted with the image attributed to it in previous years" (Martel, 1988, p. 48).

Thus, the cooperative movement was divided into two cooperative missions (Baribeau, 1981; Lévesque, 1981). The first, supported mainly by previous generations of federations and cooperatives, continued to be characterized by government-supported economic nationalism, regardless of the party in power. The second, promoted through civil society projects in the areas of living conditions and job creation, questioned economic nationalism while supporting an alternative vision of society, admittedly one drawing on several sources (although this is typical of new social movements) (Bélanger & Lévesque, 1992). Within this framework, "the most radical wing" of the "new cooperatives" challenged the development strategy of the "structured cooperatives," which, following the line of economic nationalism cum private sector development, were accused of sleeping with the enemy while paying too little attention to the development of cooperatives[11] (Larivière 1980, p. 54; Laliberté, 1973, p. 325). The Associations coopératives d'économie familiale (ACEF) strongly supported this radical position. The ACEFs, which were created in 1965, were "cooperatives with a social purpose."[12] They were an initiative of the CSN (Confédération des syndicats nationaux, a trade union), and created in collaboration with caisses populaires and credit unions, to combat the abuse of consumer credit. Admitted in 1970 as a federation within the CCQ, the ACEFs considered themselves closer to NPOs than to cooperatives. Thus, "the CCQ which was trying to deal with requests from groups of this type to help them form cooperatives, advised the government to pass a special law to make a distinction between cooperative groups and community groups" (Angers, 1974, p. 174). With the introduction of this law, the integration of para-cooperatives and pre-cooperatives (or quasi-cooperatives) into the cooperative movement would now become even more difficult.

The unionization of the largest cooperatives was a further source of conflict. The central labour bodies were very critical of the mature cooperatives, which they considered worse than capitalist corporations, at least when it came to collective bargaining (Lévesque, 1991). While some unions supported consumer and worker cooperatives, which they saw as liberating workers, others challenged cooperatives' support for economic nationalism, since the latter tended to subordinate worker control to control by the French-speaking bourgeoisie (Centre coopératif de recherche en politique sociale, 1975, p. 3). As well, the difficulties experienced in incorporating new cooperatives into the cooperative movement were not limited to the most radical cooperatives or to para-cooperatives. For example, some housing cooperatives believed that the CCQ obstructed the issuing of favourable opinion that would have facilitated their obtaining cooperative status, because, amongst other reasons, these cooperatives did not have a "policy regarding rentals at market prices" (Larivière, 1980, p. 53). Similarly, in the case of worker cooperatives, the CCQ hesitated to give a favourable opinion on this type of cooperative, Tricofil being a case in point.[13] Not until the mid-1980s, with the adoption of changes to the Cooperatives Act, would new cooperatives be as easy to develop as other cooperative sectors (Lévesque et al., 1985).

Because of the setbacks experienced by certain mature enterprises and the challenges raised by the new cooperatives, the first half of the 1980s was "the gloomiest and most trying period, but also the most unpredictable in the existence of the Conseil" (Lamarre, 1991, p. 115). At a 1987 conference of the CCQ, Claude Béland, chairman of the Mouvement Desjardins, suggested holding an estates-general on the cooperative movement, and immediately recognize that cooperative enterprises had reached "a point where it was necessary to ascertain the depth of their cooperative project" (Béland, 1987, p. 20). Four years later, as chairman of the CCQ, he confessed that "the Conseil had gone through a rough time. The fact that the Conseil had put so much on the back burner for several years was due to internal struggles" (Béland, 1991, p. 148). Thus, the cooperative movement, especially the structured cooperatives, seemed to lack a broader social vision (or at the very least was a victim of the crisis that befell the economic nationalism project). By contrast, some new cooperatives, like a large part of the community-based movement, advanced a plan for self-managed socialism that was unable to make an impact on society as a whole. In reality, even if we exclude social cooperatives such as the ACEF, the cooperative project still had two sides. One was highly integrated into the dynamics of Fordist economic development, and the other was oriented towards an alternative form of development, which was associated with an end to the crisis (Bélanger, Boucher, & Lévesque, 2007). The long-lasting economic crisis would give these two sides ample opportunity, however, to coexist while using a development model that was open to a plural economy and to a civil society supportive of improved governance.

The Repositioning of Social Forces in the Search for a New Convergence

The economic crisis and the crisis in the welfare state prompted civil society to find solutions to the very real problems of chronic unemployment, social exclusion, unfulfilled social needs, and other issues of social urgency. Given the circumstances, the government could not hold back support for civil society projects. Consequently, the search for new solutions no longer concerned only those who challenged the dominant model, but all dynamic forces in society, even if their visions covered a wide range of possibilities. The government's explicit recognition of the social economy was preceded by de facto recognition of its various components or sectors. This was marked by stormy debate, as noted above, but also increasingly through deliberation and dialogue to find new solutions.

Of the public forums that favoured convergence between community groups and the cooperative movement, the most innovative was, without question, the Forum pour l'emploi (a forum on employment),[14] a non-governmental initiative created in 1987 that continued until the early 1990s. By bringing together trade unions and all sectors of the social economy, and by entrusting the chairpersonship to Claude Béland, president of the Mouvement Desjardins, the Forum created a pivotal experiment in joint action on employment, promoting regional and local initiatives. In addition, community groups themselves worked together to generate joint action on economic development. The first symposium, held in 1986, was an initiative of Victoriaville's Corporation de développement communautaire (CDC), and played a decisive role in clarifying the concept of community, and identifying the scope of the movement and forging its identity (CDC des Bois-Francs, 1987, pp. 17–18). It proposed the term "community enterprise"[15] to refer to the entire range of community groups, including grassroots community groups, as well as service groups and cooperatives, although a number of advocacy and adult education groups had reservations about this proposal (ibid., p. 221). This initial major meeting was followed by two international symposia,[16] Le local en action (action at the local level) in 1989 and Stratégie locale pour l'emploi et l'économie sociale (local strategies for employment and the social economy) in 1997. Another joint action initiative was Urgence rurale, which became Solidarité rurale following the États généraux du monde rural held in February 1991 (Larocque, 1991). Thus, all dynamic forces in rural Québec were brought together to promote a new view of rural development (Vachon, 1993, p. 55). Solidarité rurale is still in operation. Lastly, when unions launched their worker funds – the QFL (Quebec Federation of Labour) in 1983 and the CSN in 1996[17] – they took the opportunity to hold debates on the cooperative movement and the social economy.

During the same period, cooperators analysed[18] the relevance of the cooperative movement and the need to revive the CCQ, even though this implied including a broader range of partnerships. Under the leadership of Claude Béland, the CCQ organized a symposium in 1990 to launch the Estates-General on Cooperation. In the spring of 1992, following the symposium, 30 Québec towns held meetings that ended with the holding of "national" conferences. The latter allowed "cooperators and their partners to coalesce around numerous projects calling for joint action, networking and solidarity" (Béland, 1992, p. 3). On this occasion, participants adopted a new Cooperation Manifesto, the demand for which had been made for several decades (CCQ, 1992, p. 1). The CCQ then became involved in follow-up activities relying on, among other things, creating a cooperative education fund, organizing a summit on cooperative education, giving a new boost to Cooperation Week (especially to its up-and-coming personnel), opening up regional funds to cooperatives, launching a people's college cooperative, and creating a cooperative enterprise network (CCQ, 1992). The relevance of cooperatives was reaffirmed for both old and new sectors, including those involved in regional development, health, and personal services (Lévesque, Malo, & Girard, 1999).

In the end, research took the debate to a new level, notably by proposing that the social economy serve as a rallying or unifying concept. Thus, the initial research designed to delimit the social economy in Québec was carried out in 1990, within the framework of a CIRIEC International research group. It bore the evocative title *The Social Economy in Québec: A Misunderstood Concept, but a Significant Economic Fact* (Lévesque & Malo, 1992). CIRIEC Canada, which brings together academic researchers and social economy and public enterprise directors, quietly helped to disseminate the idea that converging practices were initiated during this period by the cooperative movement, the union movement, community groups, and women's groups (Lévesque, 2009).

It was assisted in this task by its journal, *Coopératives et Développement* (now known as *Économie et Solidarités*), in collaboration with the various research centres and chairs with which it was associated. This academic network was favourably disposed towards European research, and during their visits disseminated works by Henri Desroche and, more recently, those of Jean-Louis Laville, who has promoted the concept of the solidarity-based economy (Laville, 1994; Palard, 2005; Aubry & Charest, 2005).

From Institutional Recognition of the Social Economy to the Current Situation

The more recent context in which institutional recognition of the social economy has taken place is better known than its older, more distant counterpart, already discussed in this paper (Lévesque, 2007; D'Amours, 2006; Lévesque & Mendell, 2004; Favreau & Lévesque, 1996). One of its landmarks was a concern revealed through the June 1995 Women's March Against Poverty, For Bread and Roses, when various women's groups demanded that the Québec government invest in social infrastructure in order to to improve living conditions, an area in which women currently play a huge role. Also noteworthy was the autumn 1996 "Summit on the Economy and Employment," which helped define the broad lines of a new social covenant, one of the basic elements of which was a policy of a zero government budget. The 1995 march generated discussion on and gave rise to regional committees on the social economy. The "Summit on the Economy and Employment" created the Groupe de travail sur l'économie sociale (GTES, working group on the social economy), chaired by Nancy Neamtan and made up of representatives from cooperative groups, unions, the private sector, and community and women's groups. It came up with a founding compromise in accordance with the mandated entrusted to it.[19]

Definition of the Social Economy and the Founding Compromise

The definition of the social economy proposed by the GTES (Chantier de l'économie sociale, 1996), and accepted at that time, was considered broad, inclusive, and even unifying. It had three major dimensions. The first involved the meaning of "economy" (its substance), namely "the concrete production of goods and services"; and "social," defined both as the "the improvement of the population's quality of life and welfare" and "democratic development," which included taking an active part in citizenship. The second consisted of ethical principles, which closely resembled cooperative principles. The third was the legal status of the various types of social economy enterprises and organizations, namely cooperatives, mutual societies, and associations. The process for defining the social economy formed part of a strategy for recognizing it as a full partner in economic and social development, following the example set by the cooperative movement. The requirement that all of the social partners take a position would have been more difficult to implement had there been no "national" joint action on the economy and employment, which provided a suitable framework. On the other hand, this type of framework raised fears that the social economy could be downgraded to projects involving socio-economic insertion and the war on poverty, as legitimate as these objectives might be.

The definition and the development plan put forward at that time meant that stakeholders would have to make compromises (GTES, 1996). The Government of Québec hoped that the social economy might meet new needs (such as home care) at a lower cost, while giving a boost to job creation. Cooperatives and associations saw an opening for strengthening and broadening their spheres of activity, and were convinced that they could do a better job than the public or private sectors. The unions that were supportive in principle would nonetheless demand that the social economy jobs be long term, skilled, pay more than the minimum wage, and, above all, not replace those in the public sector (or those in the private sector, employers would add); in this way, it would channel the social economy towards emerging sectors. These conditions resembled those demanded by women's groups, which also wanted the social economy to include advocacy associations and the hidden, unpaid work performed by women. On the other hand, independent community activists and social advocacy groups refused to take part, maintaining that they deserved to be subsidized for their work, much of which involved policy formulation and demands (D'Amours, 2002). Lastly, the caisses populaires Desjardins, which were firmly rooted in local communities, would go as far as to provide the GTES with personnel, as well as premises. The founding compromise, as well as the definition to which it gave rise, were not immutable, although they henceforth constituted an indispensable point of reference in evaluating progress or decline.

The development plan proposed at that time by the GTES involved two main approaches. In the first approach, proposed projects would be primarily of the pilot-project type or those that reproduced success-ful experiments (e.g., home care services). Such projects had the advan-tage of avoiding both job substitution and the over-identification of the social economy with social insertion, while bolstering the social econ-omy's potential for full participation in Québec's socio-economic de-velopment. These projects mainly involved the personal services sector and sectors with an impact on local development, the revitalization of neglected rural environments, and sustainable development. To create 300 enterprises and 20,000 jobs,[20] they relied not only on NPOs but also on cooperatives, especially housing cooperatives, home care service co-operatives, consumer cooperatives, youth services cooperatives, funeral cooperatives, and multiservice solidarity cooperatives. The second ap-proach had a prerequisite: recognition by the state and government in-stitutions that the social economy was a social and economic partner. Of the tools it identified, funding was the most important. Funding in-cluded "grants" for community action[21] and tools appropriate to the social economy, namely regional and local funds and NPO access to In-vestissement Québec. In addition, it suggested giving priority to three types of action: strengthening agencies that support the social economy (GRT and CDR),[22] encouraging networking among enterprises, and de-veloping new forms of partnership with the private sector (patronage and sponsorship). In the area of training, the plan recommended creat-ing a comité sectoriel de formation de la main-d'œuvre (sector-based labour-force training committee). It also proposed updating legislation concerning NPOs and cooperatives, especially vis-à-vis the creation of solidarity cooperatives. Lastly, the GTES recommended establishing a monitoring structure representing the social economy. It would oper-ate for two years and come under the direct authority of the Conseil exécutif du Gouvernement du Québec (cabinet of the Government of Québec).

Current Composition of the Social Economy

The social economy currently has at least four major sectors: coop-eratives, mutual societies, associations with economic activities, and worker funds (and other union enterprises). We could also include other elements, including foundations,[23] especially Centraide du grand Montréal, which supports numerous community organizations; and private foundations, which have relatively independent boards of di-rectors and perform an important task.

COOPERATIVES AND MUTUAL SOCIETIES

A new paradigm for cooperatives has been taking shape since the mid-1990s (Côté, 2000), and the number of cooperatives is increasing once again, especially in the new sectors. By the end of 2004, there were 2,834 cooperatives and 39 mutual societies, accounting for 77,025 jobs, a turnover in the economy of nearly $19.3 billion, and more than $111 billion in assets (Ministère du Développement économique, de l'Innovation et de l'Exportation [MDEIE], 2007). Québec has more cooperatives than any other province in Canada: it accounts for 25 per cent of the country's population, 39 per cent of its cooperatives, 42 per cent of cooperative memberships, and 45 per cent of the jobs in the area of cooperatives. As well, while there are more cooperatives and mutual societies in Québec than anywhere else in Canada, non-financial cooperatives account for only 3.2 per cent of Québec's gross domestic product. Nonetheless, its strong concentration in a few sectors, such as agri-food and financial services, allows it to play a strategic role in economic development (Lévesque, 1989). Similarly, the comparatively important role that cooperatives play in certain regions means that they have an important influence on regional development.

There are cooperatives in about 40 "major sectors."[24] The financial sector and the agri-food sector, which date back to the early twentieth century, carry the most economic weight, given that they account for 98.2 per cent of the assets, 88 per cent of the membership, and 74 per cent of the jobs in the cooperative and mutual society movement as a whole. In 2009, the Mouvement Desjardins, Québec's leading financial institution and Canada's leading financial cooperative, had over 5.8 million members, $157 billion in assets, and 42,273 employees (Desjardins, 2009), while Québec's mutual societies (the largest being SSQ Groupe financier, with $2 billion in assets, and La Capitale, with $1.7 billion in assets) had 1.4 million members, $5.9 billion in assets, and 4,613 people providing them with services (Ministère du Développement économique, de l'Innovation et de l'Exportation, 2007). The agri-food sector had 35,919 members and $2.3 billion in assets, and accounted for 17,266 jobs. The largest cooperatives in the sector were Coopérative fédérée, which had 12,287 employees, economic turnover of $2.7 billion, and $754 million in assets (taking into account its 97 affiliated cooperatives), and Agropur, which had 4,200 members (50 per cent of all Québec milk producers, 3,000 employees, and economic turnover of $1.9 billion). Other sectors, too, made their presence felt: The housing sector had 1,040 cooperatives (accounting for 47.2 per cent of all non-financial cooperatives) and 26,114 members (high-use intensity), while the forestry cooperatives had an economic turnover of $332 million and 5,058 employees, mainly in local communities of resource regions.

In sum, the cooperatives that have emerged over the last three decades account for over 60 per cent of all non-financial cooperatives. The total number of non-financial cooperatives in 2005 was 2,589; 1,571 cooperatives were formed over the last 10 years, primarily solidarity cooperatives (31 per cent), work cooperatives (24 per cent), producers' cooperatives (18 per cent), worker-shareholder cooperatives (11 per cent), and housing cooperatives (10 per cent) (MDEIE, 2007, pp. 16, 18). The survival rate of cooperatives after five years and 10 years is much higher among private enterprises, but varied greatly among the cooperative sectors[25] (Bond, Clément, Cournoyer, & Dupont, 1999, pp. 15–16). Cooperatives have entered a new era of growth, as clearly demonstrated by both the number of cooperatives created and the success of the older cooperatives in raising their status. Also noteworthy in this regard is the establishment in 2001 by the Mouvement Desjardins of an investment fund, Capital régional et coopératif Desjardins, whose assets at year-end 2006 were $650 million, part of which will be used to capitalize cooperatives.[26] Lastly, the Conseil québécois de la coopération et de la mutualité is itself a stakeholder in this new dynamic situation, as indicated by its name change and incorporation as a cooperative (Conseil québécois de la coopération et de la mutualité [CQCM], 2007).

WORKERS' FUNDS: SOCIAL ECONOMY ENTERPRISES

The 1982 socio-economic summit occurred amidst a growing crisis in employment. In response, the Fédération des travailleurs et travailleuses du Québec (FTQ) proposed creating a development fund designed to preserve and create jobs through investments in SMEs (small and medium-sized enterprises) (Lévesque, Bélanger, Bouchard, et al., 2000). Worker funds created in this way constituted a major innovation: Unions were now key players not only in negotiating working conditions but also in developing the economy. As the first worker fund in Canada, the Fonds de solidarité (FTQ) played a pioneering role.[27] It innovated in more than one way, particularly by (a) creating local representatives (LRs, or "worker brokers"), (b) supplementing the financial analysis with a social responsibility report, and (c) setting up an economic education program for workers. The Fonds de solidarité is the largest venture capital fund in Canada: at year-end 2010, it had 577,511 shareholders and assets of $7.2 billion, of which $4.7 billion were invested in 2,052 Québec enterprises. Since its inception, it has helped to create and preserve about 116,644 jobs (Fonds de solidarité, 2007). With over 100 affiliates, it plays a role in local and regional development, as well as in the new economy, and occasionally has a hand in giving a boost to enterprises threatened with closure. The very close links between the *Fonds* and the QFL plays an important role when it comes to governance. Thus, the presidents of the various unions (in sectors such as metallurgy and automobiles), and a few representatives of socio-economic organizations have seats on the board of directors. There are also union representatives on the boards of regional and local funds. Overall, this Fund has strengthened union activity in Québec, while making a significant contribution to the development of Québec.

The Fondation pour la coopération et l'emploi (CSN), which was created in 1996, drew its inspiration from the Fonds de solidarité des travailleurs (Solidarity Fund, FTQ) but has also been differentiated from it in accordance with a long tradition of CSN involvement in the cooperative movement and the social economy.[28] Thus, in its method of governance it has considered itself more or less independent of the central labour body, while maintaining strong ties with the "collective tools" to which it has had access. In addition, it took on the mission of increasing its investment in social economy and sustainable development enterprises, even though these did not play a dominant role in its investments as a whole. At the end of fiscal year 2010, the fund had more than 99,000 shareholders and assets of $699 million. Amongst other things, this allowed it to play a role in local development through its subsidiary, Filaction; in sustainable development, with the Fonds d'investissement en développement durable; in cooperatives, with the Fonds de financement coopératif (managed by Filaction); and in microlending, through the Fonds d'emprunt économique communautaire de Québec and other institutions (Fondaction, 2006). This gave a tremendous boost to its membership in the cooperative, ethical investment (Global Reporting Initiative) and social economy communities, as demonstrated over the last few years by its extensive involvement with CIRIEC-Canada, its participation in the CQCM and its partnership with RISQ, to cite but a few examples. In sum, the Fondaction (CSN) has in numerous ways endorsed and expressed its commitment to the social economy.

These two workers' funds met practically all of the criteria contained in the definition of social economy adopted in 1996. Their boards of directors consisted primarily of representatives of the central labour bodies involved. The socio-economic objective of the first fund was creating jobs, developing Québec as a whole (as well as individual regions), and educating workers about the economy, while that of the second fund was creating jobs and promoting sustainable development and cooperation. They helped shift the emphasis of financialization by directing employee investment funds towards sectors and territories neglected by big business. In addition to democratizing the economy and encouraging the participation and education of workers, they assisted in the plan to promote francophone control of the economy – a project considered to be in the public interest (Lévesque et al., 2001). Related to their mission was their support of numerous community development initiatives, including the Fonds de développement Emploi-Montréal (FDEM) (for the Fonds de solidarité) and the Société de développement Angus (for Fondaction). More recently, they contributed to the new Fiducie[29] du Chantier de l'économie sociale, whose total capitalization reached $52.8 million. Since 2000, the two funds have also been partners in the Alliance de recherche Universités Communautés en économie sociale (ARUC-ÉS). On an even broader level, they have had financial involvements with several institutions associated with the social economy, such as credit unions and the SSQ mutual society. This indicates the prospect of a sort of union-oriented financial network that might complement that of the Mouvement Desjardins.

ASSOCIATIONS WITH ECONOMIC ACTIVITIES

The flexibility of the NPO legal status partially explains its popularity, although it produces certain reservations on the part of organizations that have a different status. One thing is certain, however: Associations are more difficult to define than other organizational forms, and even more so when considered from the standpoint of the social economy. How does one differentiate an association with economic activities (producing goods or services) from one that does not? To be sure, salaried personnel and diversified sources of income indicate the presence of economic activity. However, if one wishes to employ this criterion to explain the difference between the two types, certain important distinctions must be kept in mind. Traditionally, there was a clear distinction between associations and cooperatives: The former had non-market activities and provided services to non-members (administrators did not benefit from the activities), while the latter had market activities and provided services to its members, based on the principle that members could also be users (Gui, 1991). More than a decade has now passed, and the situation is less clear. For example, some cooperatives, such as solidarity cooperatives, have various types of stakeholders (including stakeholders for whom the user role is weak or even non-existent), and many associations have market activities (which, incidentally, gives rise to the term "social enterprise") and often lump together users of their activities with other stakeholders. Several analysts of cooperatives now refer to a "hybridization of cooperatives and associations," especially in the field of local community-based services, and health and social services (Munkner, 2004; Draperi, 2000; Girard, 2004; MacPherson, 2004).

In most developed countries, the number of associations has increased. Associations account for a growing number of jobs: 14.4 per cent of the active labour force in the Netherlands, 11.1 per cent in Canada, 10.9 per cent in Belgium, and 9.8 per cent in the United States (Hall et al., 2004, p. 11). Before the advent of the welfare state, a large proportion of associations – which in Québec provided services in the fields of education, health, and social services – was controlled by the Church. Three socio-political forces reshaped associations (excluding certain charitable associations, such as Saint-Vincent de Paul, which continued to have ties to the Church): direct state control of associations (still in progress) providing services (e.g., CLSCs);[30] empowerment (through decentralization) of philanthropic associations such as Centraide[31] (United Way); and, lastly, empowerment (through decentralization) of associations with economic activities in the fields of recreation and social tourism. The latter were similar to associations, such as the CAA, that were even older and had diversified their economic activities (e.g., insurance and travel agencies). However, what was new in the 1970s and 1980s were civil society projects creating associations for the defence of people's rights and, later, groups providing services, such as local community-based services (in Europe, sometimes referred to as proximity services), local development services, and employment services (see "A New Generation of Cooperatives and Civil Society Initiatives, above). A significant proportion of these civil society initiatives, especially those producing goods and services, were recognized by the social economy.

Canada (according to a 2005 study) had 161,000 non-profit organizations (NPOs) with a combined economic turnover of $36.9 billion (of which 39 per cent came from the government). These NPOs had 1,016,856 full-time equivalent, paid employees, not including hospitals, colleges, and universities with NPO status (Hall et al., 2004, pp. iv, 9; Imagine Canada, 2005). The level of service delivery and government assistance in this sector invites comparisons with countries such as the Netherlands, Belgium, France, Germany, and Ireland. From the standpoint of voluntary work and civil society, however, Canada combines the social assistance partnership model with the Anglo-Saxon model. With 46,000 non-profit organizations,[32] Québec accounted for 29 per cent of Canada's associations, which is a higher proportion than its share of the country's population. The revenue of these associations, not including hospitals, colleges, and universities with NPO status, was $17 billion, while the dependent labour force consisted of 324,000 persons (Imagine Canada, 2005). In terms of groupings or coalitions, these associations were fragmented, with almost 250 national, sector-based, and regional coalitions in the community sector alone (Secré-tariat à l'action communautaire autonome [SACA], 2005). Taking into account associations with employees producing goods and services – but that were neither quasi-governmental, religious, rights advocacy, nor professional organizations – we estimate that about 10,000 of these could fall within the social economy sphere (Hall et al., 2004). The 3,941 NPOs identified by the Bureau de l'économie sociale and the Chantier de l'économie sociale are found primarily in culture (37.9 per cent), recreation and tourism (24.3 per cent), day-care centres (22.8 per cent), housing (6.1 per cent), community-based media and information and communication techniques (3.8 per cent), social enterprises for work integration and adaptive aid (2.8 per cent), home care services (1.6 per cent), recycling (0.7 per cent), and perinatality (0.2 per cent). As is evident, the numerous associations emerging in the areas of social services and health are not well represented in this inventory; this is due to the founding compromise.[33]

Coalitions and Their Relationship to the State

For the purposes of incorporation, almost all cooperatives, mutual societies, and associations come under the authority of the Québec government. For the purposes of policy and development strategy, however, each of the social economy's principal sectors is controlled by different departments or government branches. For example, until recently, while the sectors had, in principle, been under the authority of the same ministry, the Ministère du développement économique, de l'innovation et de l'exportation (MDEIE), they were in reality controlled by two different branches, the Direction des coopératives[34] and the Bureau de l'économie sociale, whose area of competence is, theoretically, not limited to NPOs alone (this office now comes under MAMROT, the ministère des Affaires municipales, des Régions et de l'Occupation du territoire). Two coalitions have the primary responsibility for delineating strategic directions for the development of the social economy: the CQCM, in the case of cooperatives and mutual societies, and the Chantier de l'économie sociale, in the case of the social economy.

THE CQCM AND GOVERNMENT SUPPORT

The Conseil québécois de la coopération et de la mutualité (CQCM), which is now incorporated as a cooperative, "coordinates dialogue and joint action among the cooperative and mutualist sectors and their partners; represents and defends the interests of the entire Québec cooperative and mutualist movement; and fosters the development of cooperatives and mutual societies to increase the benefits of cooperation for its members and the population" (CQCM, 2007, p. 2). It has seven associate members, in addition to its 35 members. The members comprise three mutual societies (SSQ Groupe financier, la Capitale, and Promutuel, the latter serving to unite 39 other mutual societies), a number of cooperative federations (11 regional development cooperatives and their federation, eight federations of housing cooperatives and their confederation, and 11 sectoral federations: Caisses Desjardins, Coop fédérée, the food sector, cable television, home care services, worker–shareholders, paramedics, New Québec, funeral homes, and the education and forestry sectors) and Agropur, the largest agricultural cooperative in milk processing. Unlike similar organizations in previous periods, the CQCM represents the entire cooperative and mutualist movement.

For over a decade, the CQCM has been responsible for defining the strategic orientation and development strategies of cooperatives. Thus, when ministers formulate policies for cooperatives, negotiation and cooperation figure prominently. Over the last 10 years, the Conseil has introduced two strategic plans. The first (2000–2003) aimed to cast the cooperative movement in a new light and come up with a development strategy that responds to new social needs and aspirations. Using a "targeted networking strategy," the cooperative movement sought "to become a democratic alternative to the concentration of economic power stemming from globalization, and a driving force behind enterprises and jobs meeting the current needs of the population in a relevant way" (CCQ, 2000, p. 4). The second plan was the Plan d'ensemble 2004–2007 du développement coopératif québécois, La formule coopérative, solution durable (CCQ, 2005). Some of the issues identified – including capitalization, new measures to support cooperatives, and the development of new sectors (such as health) – were, in fact, not new. On the other hand, revitalizing governance was, in fact, a new issue on the agenda, especially the desire to have the Coopératives de développement régional (CDR, or regional development coooperatives) serve as hubs or focal points of governance, similar to the role played by sectoral groupings. While this may be a historical turning point, we need to realize that any new sectoral or territorial structuring raises issues that could remain on the agenda for several years. The term "social economy," which over the last few years had always been mentioned several times in its annual reports, is not mentioned at all in this plan.

The Government of Québec's policy on the cooperative movement was first formulated in 2001 in the *Avant-project de Politique de développement des coopératives* ("Draft Proposal for a Policy on the development of Cooperatives," Ministère de l'Industrie et du Commerce, 2001), which accompanied the proposed revision of the Cooperatives Act. The change of government in April 2003 delayed the revision by several months and cast uncertainty over certain proposals in the draft version of the *Politique de développement coopératif.* For example, the changes made to the Act in 2006 concerned the minimum number of administrators (which had been reduced to three); the requirement that at least 50 per cent of a cooperative's operations involve participation by members themselves; and the power of the assembly, which may not submit to its authority the exercise of powers vested expressly in the board of directors by the Act. In January 2005 (after the policy had been adopted), the Ministre du développement économique et régional et de la recherche (MDERR) and the CCQ signed an initial partnership agreement for a period of three years: $13.5 million were awarded to the CCQ for the period covering 2004–7 to support, amongst others, the CDR and the sector federations in starting up and coaching cooperatives (MDERR and CCQ, 2005, p. 4). The CCQ and its members agreed to provide $500,000 each year over the same period. With regard to issues of succession and the younger generation, the Ministère Développement économique, innovation et exportation (MDEIE) subsidized the creation of "11 positions of promotional officer in the area of collective youth entrepreneurship in 10 regional development cooperatives and at the Fédération des coopératives québécoises en milieu scolaire" (MDEIE, 2005b, p. 27). To assist in the financing and capitalization of cooperatives, the moratorium on the RIC (Régime d'investissement coopératif) was lifted and the upper limits for Fondaction and the CDRC (Desjardins) were raised. As well, the Programme favorisant le financement de l'entreprenariat collectif and the Programme favorisant la capitalisation des entreprises de l'économie sociale would allow Investissement Québec to invest $21.1 million in cooperative projects, for a total value of $43.2 million (Investissement Québec, 2005, p. 25).

In 2006, the previous partnership agreement was renewed for the period 2007–10 (MDEIE and CQCM, 2006). It had four objectives: (1) promoting the cooperative formula and joint initiatives among cooperatives around the province, in cases where the principal organizations eligible for funding were CDRs; (2) delivering technical services to promoters of new cooperatives in cases where the organizations eligible for funding were CDRs and sector federations; (3) delivering specialized follow-up services and coaching to existing cooperatives in cases where principal eligible organizations were provincial sector federations that were also members of the CQCM; and (4) carrying out formative activities in cases where the principal eligible organizations were provincial federations. (For the fourth objective, the projects presented by the federations received authorization in writing from the CQCM, but those carried out by the Conseil itself had to obtain written authorization from the minister). In case of disagreement between a federation and a CDR (a situation that could arise from the sharing of responsibilities), especially concerning services provided to existing cooperatives (objectives 2 and 3), the CQCM could either take a decision or resort to an adjudicative process. The organizations agreed to maintain a self-financing rate of at least 60 per cent. In cases of disagreement or misunderstanding between representatives of the minister and the CQCM, the minister would resolve issues by making a final decision that applied to both parties. The CQCM was in charge of managing the agreement, whose performance criteria were defined beforehand. The amounts paid by the MDEIE were slightly less than those of the previous agreement: $12.9 million over three years, while the cooperative and mutual movement would invest $1.5 million during the given period (CQCM, 2007, p. 15).

By 2010, the cooperative and mutual movements seemed to have more tools at their disposal than ever. First, the weaker federations grew stronger. Second, when committees went into action, the vitality of the CQCM stood out in many areas: the life of the association, management, and administration (funding, the synergy created through various acquisitions, program management); the focus on young people

and cooperative education; communication; the content of the cooperative forum; and research and development (wind power, cooperative
identity formation, health, accounting standards, and multi-activity
cooperatives). Third, interest in conducting research on cooperatives
seemed to grow; the IRECUS, the Guy-Bernier Chair (UQAM), the Centre d'études Desjardins en gestion des coopératives financières, and the
Observatoire international des coopératives de services financiers at
the HEC Montréal have for several decades been focusing exclusively
on cooperatives; and the CQCM can now count on a partnership with
the UQO within the ARUC (CURA) framework. One topic covered by
this partnership is social innovation and community development. Another topic deals with the cooperative movement and territorial development. The CQCM and the CRDT co-direct this topic, which has
mobilized researchers from at least six universities. The CQCM is also a
member of CIRIEC Canada, which is headed by Léopold Beaulieu, and
the Groupe d'économie solidaire du Québec (GESQ), which is headed
by René Lachapelle. In addition, by taking into account the activities of
the Fondation pour l'éducation à la coopération and the financial tools
on which it draws, one can assume that the cooperative and mutual society movement now has the principal elements of a system for innovation (Lévesque, 2004a).

THE CHANTIER DE L'ÉCONOMIE SOCIALE AND GOVERNMENT SUPPORT

From 1996 to 1998, the Chantier de l'économie sociale monitored the
GTES development plan. Although it was made up of social economy
representatives, the Chantier came under the direct authority of the
Conseil exécutif (Executive Council) of the Government of Québec. In
1999, following consultation with all parties involved, the Chantier increased its power by becoming an NPO with its own board of directors. Because CCQ requests for clarification of this new organization's
mission and mandate were not met, they refused to join the Chantier.[35]
The Chantier continued to be financed by the Québec government and
to receive support from its own partners, in which the Mouvement
Desjardins figured prominently. Consistent with the GTES's mandate,
"the principal mission of the Chantier de l'économie sociale is to promote the social economy as an integral part of Québec's socio-economic
structure and, as such, to ensure recognition of our economy's plural
character" (Économie sociale Québec, 2012). It is working "to promote
and sustain the emergence, development and strengthening of social
economy enterprises and organizations in a specific set of economic

sectors" (ibid.). More specifically, its mandate is "promotion; representation at the national and international levels; providing support for consolidation; experimentation; development of new niches and projects; and encouraging consultation among the various social economy actors." As a forum for analysis and exchanging views on ways to help the social economy, the Chantier set up various working committees dealing, most importantly, with regional poles, communication and promotion, external relations, and youth issues.

The composition of the board of directors has changed somewhat from the time it was set up, since the Comités régionaux d'économie sociale (CRES) have given way to regional poles, while the services created through its initiatives (e.g., RISQ) are represented on the board. Nonetheless, social economy actors are still close to social movements, in a way that is reminiscent of their closeness to the Conseil supérieur de la coopération from 1940 to 1951. In late 2006, the board of directors of the Chantier had 32 members, seven of which represented social economy coalitions (Les services adaptés Transit [special needs services], the Fédération des coopératives paramédics, the Association des CPE [an association of day-care centres], Regroupement québécois des OSBL en habitation [a Québec coalition of housing NPOs], Confédération québécoise des coopératives d'habitation [a Québec coalition of housing cooperatives], Regroupement des entreprises d'économie sociale en aide domestique [a coalition of social economy enterprises providing housekeeping services], and the Collectif des entreprises d'insertion [a labour-market integration collective]). There were also five individuals representing 17 regional poles, five representatives of coalitions working to develop the social economy (the Association des CLD du Québec, the Réseau québécois du crédit communautaire, the Regroupement des CDEC du Québec, the Regroupement québécois pour la coopération du travail and the Association des GRT du Québec), six representatives of various movements (union, cooperative, women's, and community-based movements), four ex-officio members that were "subsidiaries" (the Fiducie du Chantier de l'économie sociale, the CSMO-ESAC [Comité Sectoriel de main d'oeuvre-Économie social, action communautaire], the ARUC en économie sociale, and the RISQ) and one appointed member from the university milieu. This board of directors was oriented towards an emerging social economy that was intellectually close to the new social movements, even though some of the organizations had worked for a long time in fields such as leisure and tourism.

In many respects, the objectives of the development plan developed within the framework of the 1996 "Sommet de l'économie et de l'emploi" were achieved and even surpassed, in terms of developing entreprises and employment as well as in obtaining new tools and recognition. For example, the number of CPEs increased from 600 to 1,000, while the number of spaces they could offer increased from 50,000 to 200,000. The number of day-care jobs increased from 10,000 to 40,000 (this figure included both the CPEs themselves and family-run day-care services), while government contributions increased from a few hundred million dollars to $1.3 billion (with parents paying $7 a day) (Lévesque, 2011). Over 100 home-care enterprises, 50 NPOs, and 51 co-operatives, together employing 5,088 people, now provide this service to 79,059 people in every region of Québec. It is funded through a combination of user fees, subsidies, direct grants, and a tax credit for home support services (Vaillancourt & Jetté, 2009; Vaillancourt, Aubry, & Jetté, 2003, p. 138).

The stock of community-based housing, which had about 45,000 housing units and represented assets of over $1.4 billion, increased in 2005 to about 55,000 units and accounted for assets of $3.1 billion (NPO assets of $2 billion and cooperative assets of $1.1 billion), not counting the 10,000 units under construction (Gouvernement du Québec, 2006, p. 13). Similarly, recycling, waste sorting and recovery centres, labour market integration enterprises, and cultural days also surpassed their objectives; also noteworthy were very dynamic sectors such as perinatal centres, communications and new technologies, youth services cooperatives, and social tourism.

Based on the development plan's second priority – creating tools and winning recognition for the social economy – the achievements clearly surpassed what had been hoped for in 1996. For example, the Chantier de l'économie sociale played an excellent leadership role here, especially in support of the Fiducie du Chantier de l'économie sociale (whose capitalization amounted to $52.8 million), not to mention the CLDs that were opening up to the social economy. Between 1998 and 2004, CLDs supported 3,765 social economy projects, or 537 projects per year (Sommet de l'économie sociale et solidaire, 2006c, p. 5). Similarly, the CSMO-ÉSAC made a significant contribution to social economy enterprises, whose diverse needs and organizational complexity were acknowledged. Lastly, the Chantier and academics from four universities have, since 2000, been co-managing an ARUC en économie sociale and a Réseau québécois de recherche partenariale en économie sociale

(RQRP-ES, the Québec regional partnership node on the social economy). The latter brings together academics from eight universities and is itself a stakeholder in a Canada-wide network, the Canadian Social Economy Hub headed by Ian MacPherson. In addition, the Chantier is also a member of CIRIEC-Canada and the GESQ.

In sum, the Chantier has made a very great contribution to setting up the various sectors of a Québec system for innovation in the social economy (Chantier de l'économie sociale, 2005b; Lévesque, 2004a). As well, the social economy summit held in autumn 2006 confirmed the mobilization capacities of the social economy (through the lines of action adopted)[36] and its influence in Québec and abroad (Sommet de l'économie sociale et solidaire, 2006c).

The ability of the Chantier to produce these positive results was due largely to the partnerships it formed with and the support it received from the Québec government and, more recently, the Canadian government. With the rise to power in 2002 of the Liberal Party of Jean Charest, this support could not be taken for granted, because the social economy could be considered a creation of the Parti Québécois (whence the importance to the social economy of obtaining recognition from the federal Liberals). Nonetheless, a conversion did in fact take place: in May 2004, the Chantier reached an agreement with the MDEIE, which guaranteed it $450,000 per year for three years, to be used for promotion and development. The total grant of $1.3 million represented 10 per cent of the sum granted to the CCQ, although the responsibilities of the CCQ are, admittedly, different from those of the Chantier.

While the non-market sector of the social economy did not seem to generate much interest in the MDEIE, it is clear that the funding provided by departments with a more socially oriented mission continues to grow: In fact, that funding exceeds $2 billion. The Ministère de la Famille, Aînés et Condition féminine alone allocated $1.3 billion for day-care services, most of which went to the social economy (Gouvernement du Québec, 2009). Similarly, for 2005 the Ministère de la Santé et des Services Sociaux allocated $350 million (around 1.9 per cent of this department's total budget) to approximately 3,000 NPOs (Santé et Services sociaux Québec, May 2010). For the same year, it expected to allocate $233 million to community-based, social housing. For fiscal year 2005–6, about 20 departments and organizations disbursed more than $634.7 million to nearly 5,000 community-based organizations in accordance with 63 measures and programs.[37]

To assess the total share of Québec government funding to the social economy, we must also take into account contributions made through all sectoral and regional policies[38] (D'amours, 2006, p. 97ff). Lastly, the proposals made by the Chantier to the federal government apparently bore fruit. For example, the government gave around $30 million to the Fiducie du Chantier d'économie sociale, not including its funding of academic research based on the social economy programs of the CURAs (Lévesque & Mendell, 2004). The public service even undertook an analysis of the nature of the social economy, although when the Conservative Party came to power there was a pause in policy-making (Bakopanos, in Gouvernment du Canada, 2005).

Conclusion

Institutional recognition of the social economy as a unifying and inclusive concept did not occur until 1996; the circumstances in which it occurred are well known. That being said, each sector of this economy existed well before coalitions – or even partial coalitions – of a social economy nature appeared. With the exception of the mutual aid societies movement (in the second half of the nineteenth century), it was not until the first third of the twentieth century that a genuine movement emerged. It was formed under the aegis of the cooperative movement and took the form of a social reform project inspired by Social Catholicism – a project tinged with nationalism and conservatism. For want of a real corporatist system, the "corporatist cooperative system" became the favoured approach. The establishment in 1940 of the Conseil supérieur de la coopération (CSC), however, a coalition of cooperative projects, would be based on a liberal view of cooperation (cooperation as an end in itself), one that was non-denominational, apolitical, and non-ethnic. This created tension among groups that supported a more corporatist approach. The other elements of the cooperative movement would not be able to join the CSC unless they went along with this particular cooperative model. While the Quiet Revolution facilitated a form of compromise between the two views of the cooperative movement, the rise of a new generation of cooperatives and associations supported by new social movements promoted a view of the cooperative movement as a means of implementing a particular social vision or blueprint. The latter view considered itself as an alternative approach and distrusted the compromise involving economic nationalism. Once again, this gave rise to much tension within the CCQ and other groups.

In the 1980s, the tension intensified because of an economic crisis and a stabilizing of economic nationalism, especially as it concerned the status accorded to the cooperative movement. This would result in a repositioning of the various forces of what is known today as the social economy.

The repositioning of social forces, which opened the way to institutional recognition in 1996, explains the progress made over the last decade by both cooperatives and associations with economic activities. Yet, in spite of these remarkable achievements, the founding compromise remained fragile and tensions persisted. To start, there were still tensions between, on the one hand, the approach that saw the social economy as a way of achieving a specific social vision or blueprint and, on the other hand, the cooperative movement, which saw the social economy as an end in itself. Furthermore, this tension manifested itself within particular cooperative sectors that were close to associations that had strong links to social movements. These tensions are not of great concern here, since they reflect the pervasive heterogeneousness of the social economy's various sectors, and of the enterprises within each sector. In any case, such tensions exist in most countries and regions, although not all forms of tension are creative. Sometimes the tensions were fostered by the presence of competing forms of incorporation, which cannot be ignored, particularly because cooperative status is, theoretically, more rigid and more rigorous in terms of governance. On the other hand, the defenders of the cooperative movement as an end in itself tend to have a strong mistrust of overly flexible legal forms, such as that of the NPO. Once again, it would be overly simplistic to explain all of the conflict between supporters of different legal statuses through the lens of competition. After all, disagreements over orientation still exist, just as they did in the past within the CCQ. Two of the greatest challenges facing the current social economy are (a) the quest for a form of unified governance that can identify converging viewpoints and potential avenues for joint action, and (b) making the social economy part of a social and economic blueprint that would be in tune with public interest in the era of globalization, and with sustainable development (including the role of social responsibility in economic endeavours).

Efforts to adopt institutional forms to govern the entire social economy have been too timid. At the same time, they may have been introduced too rapidly, despite a long process that led to recognition of various social economy sectors as stakeholders in the same grouping (there does not seem to be any argument over this point). The result was a bicephalous governance that gave rise to structural disputes over spheres of control and representativeness. On the one hand there is the CQCM, whose mission is to coordinate "consultation among cooperatives and mutual societies (and their partners), represent and defend the interests of Québec's entire cooperative and mutual society movement, foster the development of cooperatives and mutual societies to increase the benefits of cooperation for their members and the population as a whole" (Conseil québécois de la coopération et de la mutualité, 2012). On the other hand, there is the Chantier de l'économie sociale, whose mission is, in part, "to promote and support the emergence, development and support of social economy entreprises and organizations in a group of economic sectors," and, in part, "to promote the social economy as an integral part of Québec's socio-economic structure and, in so doing, ensure recognition of the fact that our economy is plural in nature" (Chantier de l'économie sociale, 2003). Viewed from the sole standpoint of the concept of inclusiveness in the social economy (as adopted in 1996), we are obliged to conclude that, by definition, the combination of the two forms of governance has been a source of conflict. To complicate matters, the administrative structure of the Government of Québec has been quasi-schizophrenic, since its cooperatives division functions as if the Bureau de l'économie sociale did not exist (and vice versa). Lastly, by helping to introduce development tools intended for both cooperatives and associations with economic activities, the government stirred up new tensions. Stated differently, even if the Chantier limited its membership to associations with economic activities, the conflicts would not disappear completely, since cooperatives and associations must share a large proportion of the existing resources and development tools. There is a need for dialogue between the Chantier and the CQCM, and a fortiori for joint action.

Since France's social economy inspired its counterparts in Québec and several other countries, it may be interesting to briefly re-examine that country's experience, so as to cast light on the specific characteristics of the Québec model. First, from the very beginning, France, unlike Québec, could rely on national, sector-specific, social economy coalitions, not only for its cooperatives but for its mutual societies and associations as well. Thus, overall coordination could be carried out by setting up a coordinating body with representatives from various coalitions. Second, in France, large cooperatives and large mutual societies headed up the process, resulting in recognition for the social economy, whereas in Québec, this role was assumed by small cooperatives, community groups, and women's groups. Third, France's solidarity-based economy saw itself as being at odds with the social economy, whereas in Québec it was perceived as a way to enrich the social economy. In Québec, therefore, the solidarity-based economy and the social economy formed a continuum, as was confirmed during the 2006 Sommet de l'économie sociale et solidaire. On the other hand, the refusal of some independent community action organizations to join the social economy, even though some of them did in fact participate in it, indicated the existence of a view in which partnership and compromise were rejected in principle.

It would be impossible for Québec to import the current French model of unified governance, since the coalitions of associations in the province are still too fragmented while the large cooperatives and mutual societies have not yet assumed enough of a leadership role to justify establishing a consultative body for all stakeholders. Clearly, associations with economic activities could provide themselves with bodies capable of better representing their common interests, although such initiatives would no doubt call for innovative approaches, such as the setting up of a coordinating committee that was non-centralized and working as a network. Moreover, even if this "multiple affiliation" led to innovative forms of management, it would still be necessary to create a body that brings together all social economy sectors or elements, if for no other reason than to improve consultation and negotiation with the government on issues of mutual interest. On a deeper level, one might think that a consultative body of this type would also be very useful in clarifying the contribution of all sectors of the social economy to major social and economic issues. Hence the second challenge: that of developing an original vision of society, which should be the first priority.

A lesson to be drawn from the history of the cooperative movement in Québec (and other societies) is that this movement was at its best when it was linked to a project that was meaningful to society as a whole. For example, Québec's major cooperatives, unlike their counterparts in France and elsewhere, were able to avoid trivialization because their broad integration into Québec society provided them with a new level of understanding: the collective interests they supported appeared to be consistent with the general interest. The social economy will not be able to further unite and mobilize all sectors of society unless it can also embrace an overall vision of society – not a rigid blueprint, but one with which we are already familiar, involving the challenges of globalization and the environment. There are two ways of broaching the challenges: one that is less democratic and one that views the challenges as providing opportunities for sustainable development and a form of globalization that would respect democracy and fairness, thereby converting the economy into an agent of social development. In tackling these challenges, the social economy is endangered by trivializing factors from two sources: the first, a desire to imitate capitalist enterprises whose most enlightened proponents cultivate a measure of social responsibility; the second, the belief that, in order to meet the above challenges, it is enough for the social economy to continue in its present path. A qualitative leap is required. Cooperatives and the new forms of association cannot achieve this leap by developing separately, as if they did not share resources and strengths that, while unique to their needs in some respects, are also highly complementary. They must combine their efforts in this veritable work in progress, which will require extreme foresight in anticipating new challenges and issues. In taking this path, the social economy will serve as a valid tool for those who look to the future, and as an end in itself for those whose day-to-day work includes deeply held convictions.

NOTES

1   We wish to thank our colleagues and members of this collective for their insightful comments, namely Marie J. Bouchard, Jean-Marc Fontan, Louis Jolin, and Yves Vaillancourt, as well as Martin St-Denis and Paulo Cruz Filho, assistants at the Canada Research Chair on the Social Economy. We take full responsibility for our viewpoints and for the eventual mistakes that may be found in this text. The research paper that forms the basis of this chapter has been published by CRISES and ARUC-ÉS and is available on their websites (http://www.crises.uqam.ca and http://aruc-es.uqam.ca). Finally, we wish to thank Stewart Anthony Stilitz for the translation of this text.
2   Patrick Develtere (2007) characterizes the form of cooperation that is viewed as an end in itself as "ideological cooperation"; this form has a strong foothold in England. By contrast, he sees the form of cooperation that is viewed as a tool as "corporatist cooperation," especially in Belgium, with its socialist and Christian–socialist mainstays, which include cooperatives as well as mutual societies, unions, and associations (Defourny, Simon, and Adam, 2002). Cooperation, especially of the *Boerendbond* type found in rural environments, was strongly influenced by the Belgian model, which is conservative,

Catholic, and associated with the Peasants' League (Kesterman, 1984, p. 30). In addition, since French-Canadians lacked a corporatist orientation, they would turn to cooperation, though without confusing the two approaches (Martel, 1987; Minville, 1980, p. 742).

3   As explained by Lester M. Salamon in his lecture "Putting Civil Society on the Economic Map of the World," given at the First International CIRIEC Research Conference on the Social Economy, 22–25 October 2007 (see Salamon, 2008).

4   In the American and European cases, but not as of yet in Québec.

5   The social vision could be conservative, as in the social doctrine of the Church (corporatist vision), or more progressive or socialist (neo-corporatist vision).

6   Apart from the fact that the Caisses populaires Desjardins would refuse to join this Council until 1957, the 12 founding members included only four cooperatives (Lamarre, 1991, p. 14).

7   It should be mentioned here that it was not until 2007 that the Conseil de la coopération du Québec (CCQ, the Quebec Cooperation Council) became the Conseil québécois de la coopération et de la mutualité (CQCM), thereby explicitly acknowledging the distinctiveness of mutual societies vis-à-vis cooperatives.

8   The Société de développement coopératif (SDC) was created in 1977 as a mixed enterprise (in collaboration with the Mouvement Desjardins) but became a public corporation in 1979, only to disappear in 1992, at which time Investissement Québec was placed in charge of the cooperative division.

9   This conference was organized jointly by the CCQ; the SDC; the Ministère des Consommateurs, Cooperatives et Institutions financières; and the Secrétariat permanent des conférences socio-économiques du Québec (1980). See also: Office de Planification et de Développement du Québec (1980).

10   In 1980, "of the 1,055 cooperatives in Québec (aside from savings and credit cooperatives) 730 are not grouped into federation" (Rioux, 1989, p. 176).

11   They criticized the Mouvement Desjardins for not treating cooperatives as a privileged clientele, pointing out that it had lent the Mouvement only about 0.5 per cent of its assets. With regard to the mature cooperatives, they questioned its practice of purchasing capitalist corporations without proposing that the latter be transformed into cooperatives (Larivière, 1980, p. 53). See also Laliberté, 1973, p. 325; Larivière, 1980, p. 54.

12   Pursuant to a 1964 review of previous laws, the Cooperatives Act stipulated that "in addition, the Minister may, after taking the opinion of the Conseil de la Coopération ... authorize the creation of cooperatives for educational, scientific, artistic, athletic, sports or recreational purposes"

(Article 4, cited in Angers, 1974, p. 172) thus giving rise to "cooperatives with a social purpose."

13 Thus, when in 1976 Tricofil workers took over their company, which had been threatened with closure, they chose the status of company rather than that of cooperative because "at this time, according to one of the founders, it was not at all certain they could become a producers' cooperative" (Boucher, 1982, p. 121). Before disappearing in 1982, Tricofil became a workers' cooperative in order to gain access to SDC funding (ibid., p. 306). At the time the application was made (and supported by the SDC), the CCQ took a neutral stand, providing neither a favourable nor an unfavourable opinion. In the end, the decision to grant cooperative status to Tricofil was taken not by the CCQ but by the department in charge of cooperatives.

14 It was inspired by two economics professors, Diane Bellemare (Université de Québec à Montréal) and Lise Simon-Poulin (Université Laval).

15 We hesitatingly started to employ this term in 1979, at a Université du Québec à Rimouski symposium bringing together community-based organizations and cooperatives (Lévesque, 1979).

16 Le local en action was organized in 1989 by the Programme économique de Pointe-St-Charles (later, by the CDEC du Sud-Ouest de Montréal, a community economic development corporation), and currently by the RÉSO (Regroupement économique et social du Sud-Ouest) (ANDLP & IFDEC, 1989); the second symposium, held in 1997, whose theme was "Stratégie locale pour l'emploi et l'économie sociale," was organized by the Institut de formation en développement économique communautaire (IFDEC, 1998).

17 The Fédération des travailleurs et travailleuses du Québec (FTQ) created the Fonds de solidarité and the Confédération des syndicats nationaux (CSN) created the FondAction.

18 Two issues of the CIRIEC-Canada journal, *Coopératives et Développement*, mirrored this analysis: Vol. 22, No. 2, under the heading "État de la coopération: I. le Projet coopératif"; and Vol. 23, No. 1, under the heading, "État de la coopération: II: les secteurs."

19 Its comparatively broad mandate included defining and obtaining recognition for the "Québec model of social economy," developing an action plan to promote job creation in the area of social economy, mobilizing material resources to start-up job-creation projects, and giving a boost to expanding the social economy so that it had a sound and sustainable foundation (Groupe de travail sur l'économie sociale, 1996).

20 The objective of creating 20,000 jobs in five years was very ambitious, since social economy sectors as a whole (cooperatives and associations) only accounted for 80,000 jobs.

21 Three-year, basic-funding agreements for the mission and funding for projects ratified through negotiated agreements.

22 Groupes de ressources techniques (GRT, technical resources groups) and Coopératives de développement régional (CDR, regional development cooperatives).

23 As is increasingly the case in Europe.

24 These are "sectors" as defined by the MDEIE, which considers manufacturing to be a single sector, whereas in fact it is made up of several sectors. Consequently, the number of sectors (as understood by Statistics Canada) is even higher.

25 From 2000 to 2009, 1,517 cooperatives were formed, while the total number of non-financial cooperatives increased from 2,117 in 2001 to 2,814 (active cooperatives) in 2009, which would prompt us to assume that a number of cooperatives (797) disappeared because of either consolidation or bankruptcy, or because they never began operating. The number of Coopératives de travailleurs actionnaires (CTAs, worker–shareholder cooperatives) increased from 58 registrants in 2000 to 62 in 2007, while between these two dates 121 CTA were formed; not counting departures, the total number should be 179 CTAs. Similarly, the number of worker cooperatives decreased from 190 in 2000 to 186 in 2007, and, during the same period, 338 cooperatives were formed (not counting departures, the total number for 2007 should be 528 worker cooperatives). Lastly, the number of solidarity-based cooperatives increased from 72 in the year 2000 to 202 in 2007, while during the same period 387 were formed; not counting departures, the total number should be 459 CTAs (see MDEIE, 2007).

26 Like workers' funds with an economic development mission, starting in 2006 this new company was supposed to invest 60 per cent of the average net assets of its previous exercise in Québec enterprises. Part of this amount (21 per cent of its average net assets), must be invested in cooperatives or enterprises located in resource areas. To fulfil these objectives, investors are offered a Government of Québec tax credit of 50 per cent. Its maximum value is $2,500 per year per investor. In addition, the fund received a start-up subsidy of $10 million, with the Government of Québec and the Mouvement Desjardins each contributing half. Lastly, over the next ten years, this company expects to raise $1.5 billion at a rate of $150 million per year (see Capital régional et coopératif Desjardins, 2010).

27 Five years would go by before a second workers' fund was founded. Since then, about 20 similar funds have been created in Canada, whereas there are none elsewhere in the world (Lévesque et al., 2000, p. 65).

28 Since its founding in 1920, the cooperative movement has been a concern of the CSN (known at that time as the Confédération des Travailleurs Catholiques du Canada) (Lévesque, 1998). In 1940, it was on the first board of directors of the Conseil supérieur de la coopération. In the 1980s, the CSN emphasized worker participation and sustainable development, first by promoting worker cooperatives, then by creating an advisory panel for this purpose, the MCE conseil (CSN, 1996). In a 1995 document, this central labour body did not hesitate to investigate the hypothesis of a solidarity-based economy (Aubry & Charest, 1995), and would follow it up with another document entitled Nos Outils Collectifs ("Our Collective Tools") (Confédération des syndicats nationaux, 1996).

29 This included $12 million for the Fonds de solidarité, $8 million for the FondAction, $22.8 million for Développement économique Canada, and $10 million for the Government of Québec.

30 Centre local de services communautaires (local community services centre).

31 Centraide of Greater Montréal (Centraids United Way Canada) is a coalition bringing together three organizations associated with religious groups (Catholic, Protestant, and Jewish) for the joint collection of funds to support the economically disadvantaged and, increasingly, those who provide them with care services.

32 This figure is close to the one provided by the Registraire des entreprises (2004, p. 13), which identified 46,519 associations, of which 84.6 per cent are incorporated under Part III of the Companies Act (Québec); there are also 1,500 special statutes affecting NPOs.

33 They identify themselves instead as community organizations or even as independent community action groups (Jetté, 2005).

34 In 1963, a service for cooperatives was created within the Secrétariat du Québec, while the Conseil de la Coopération received a $15,000 grant to, among other things, give its opinion on the creation of a new cooperative (Lamarre, 1991, p. 67).

35 A consensus was reached to continue the Chantier for a period of two years, and even to ensure its long-term survival. In 1998, "all partners consulted, coalitions of social economy organizations, the Confédération des syndicats nationaux (CSN), the Fédération des travailleurs et travailleuses du Québec (FTQ), the Conseil de la coopération du Québec (CCQ), the local development groups, and the Comités régionaux de l'économie sociale (CRÉS), ... expressed a desire to see the work of the Chantier continue,

while submitting proposals to have its mission, mandates and structure clarified" (Neamtan, 1999, p. 22). The clarifications made did not meet the requirements of the CCQ, which therefore withdrew.

36 These lines of action involved the following areas: alternative approaches, solidarity-oriented work, solidarity-based investments, solidarity-based territorial development, socially responsible consumption, and solidarity-based globalization (Sommet de l'économie sociale, 2006b).

37 Of this amount, $363.6 million was allocated to the overall mission in support of over 4,070 organizations, $229 million to service agreements, and $42 million to ad hoc projects. See Ministère de Emploi et Solidarité sociale, 2010.

38 This amount (nearly half a billion dollars) does not include the amounts disbursed by the Fonds de lutte à la pauvreté par la réinsertion par le travail, nor those committed to the following organizations: social economy enterprises (such as the centres de la petite enfance [CPE, day-care], waste sorting and recovery centres, etc.); social economy cooperatives; amounts paid to organizations funded by the Fonds de lutte contre la pauvreté par la réinsertion au travail (this fund was terminated in March 2004); Centres locaux de développement (CLD); Conseils régionaux de développement (CRD); conférences régionales des élus (CRÉ, regional conferences of elected officers); foundations whose sole objective is to collect and redistribute funds; organizations with a religious purpose; professional, union, or political associations; and salary subsidies (for individuals) conveyed by community-based organizations (Secrétariat à l'action communautaire autonome [SACA], 2006, p. 5).

REFERENCES

Association nationale pour le développement local et les pays (ANDLP) & IFDEC (Institut de formation en développement économique communautaire). (1989). *Le local en action.* Paris: Les Éditions de l'Épargne.

Angers, F.-A. (1974). *La coopération de la réalité à la théorie économique.* (Vol. I). Le monde vivant de la coopération. Montréal: Fides.

Aubry, F., & Charest, J. (1994). *Développer l'économie solidaire: Éléments d'orientation.* Montréal: Service de recherche, Confédération des syndicats nationaux.

Baribeau, C. (1981). Coopération et Autogestion au Québec. *Revue du CIRIEC, 13*(1–2), 101–16.

Beauchamp, C. (1981). La coopération au Québec: Évolution du projet et de la pratique au XXe siècle. *Revue du CIRIEC, 13*(1–2), 23–36.

Béland, C. (1987). Pour des États-généraux de la coopération québécoise. Paper given to the Conseil de la Coopération du Québec. In *Info-Giresq*, 4(1), 2.

Béland, C. (1991). L'état du mouvement coopératif au Québec: Rétrospectives et prospectives. Table ronde réalisée par B. Lévesque and D. Côté. *Coopératives et Développement*, 22(2): 123–57.

Béland, C. (1992). Message du président. In Conseil de la coopération du Québec (CCQ), *Rapport annuel. Réussir ensemble un développement de qualité.* Lévis: CCQ.

Bélanger, P.R., Boucher, J., & Lévesque, B. (2007). L'économie solidaire en Amérique du Nord: Le cas du Québec. In J.-L. Laville (Ed.), *L'économie solidaire. Une perspective internationale* (pp. 105–44). Paris: Hachette Littérature.

Bélanger, P.R., & Lévesque, B. (1992). Le mouvement populaire et communautaire: De la revendication au partenariat. In G. Daigle & G. Rocher (Eds.), *Le Québec en jeu. Comprendre les grands défis* (pp. 713–47). Montréal: PUM.

Bellemare, D., & Poulin-Simon, L. (1996). *Le défi du plein emploi.* Montréal: Éditions Saint-Martin.

Bond, L., Clément, M., Cournoyer, M., & Dupont, G. (1999). *Taux de survie des entreprises coopératives au Québec.* Québec: Ministère de l'Industrie et du Commerce.

Bouchard, M.J. (1991). *Le logement populaire au Québec entre l'État et le secteur coopératif.* Montréal: Cahiers du Centre de gestion des coopératives (École des H.É.C.), no. 91–6.

Bouchard, M.J., Bernier, L., & Lévesque, B. (2003). Attending to the general interest: New mechanisms for mediating between individual interest, collective interest and general interest in Québec. In *Annals of Public and Cooperative Economics*, 74(3), 321–47.

Boucher, P-A, in collaboration with J-L. Martel. (1982). *Tricofil, tel que vécu!* Montréal: Éditions du CIRIEC et des H.É.C.

Capital régional et coopératif Desjardins. (2010). Rapport Financier Intermédiaire, 30 Juin 2010. Montreal: Desjardin.

CDC des Bois-Francs. (1987). *Les Actes du colloque provincial sur le développement communautair. Fais-moi signe de changement.* Victoriaville: CDC des Bois-Francs.

Centre coopératif de recherche en politiques sociales. (1975). *Les coopératives ouvrières de production et la lutte des travailleurs.* Montréal: Centrale de l'enseignement du Québec, 3. Study edited by P. Vaillancourt with the collaboration of L. Beaudry, J. Sylvestre, and J.-P. Beaudry.

Chantier de l'économie sociale. (2001). *De nouveau, nous osons…* Document de positionnement stratégique. Montréal: Chantier de l'économie sociale. Accessed 10 July 2011. http://www.chantier.qc.ca/

Chantier de l'économie sociale. (2003). *Rapport annuel 2002–2003*. Accessed 10 July 2011. http://www.chantier.qc.ca

Chantier de l'économie sociale. (2005). *Bilan 2004–2005 et plan d'action 2005–2006*. Montréal: Chantier de l'économie sociale.

CIRIEC-Canada. (1998). *Appel pour une économie sociale et solidaire*. Montréal: CIRIEC-Canada. Published with financial help from the Fondation d'éducation à la coopération and CIRIEC-Canada.

CIRIEC International. (2000). *Les entreprises et organisations du troisième secteur: Un enjeu stratégique pour l'emploi*. Liège: CIRIEC.

CIRIEC International. (2006). *The social economy in the European Union*. Liège: CIRIEC No CESE/COMM/05/2005, The European Economic and Social Committee.

Cloutier, É. (1932). L'organisation professionnelle. In Semaines sociales du Canada, XIe session, *L'ordre social chrétien* (pp. 251–68). Montréal: Secrétariat des semaines sociales du Canada.

Confédération des syndicats nationaux (CSN). (1996). *Nos outils collectifs*. Montréal: CSN.

Conseil de la coopération du Québec (CCQ). (1992). *Rapport annuel. Réussir ensemble un développement de qualité* (p. 6). Lévis: CCQ. (Page 1 of this document contains the new manifesto of the Conseil de la coopération du Québec.)

Conseil de la coopération du Québec (CCQ). (2000). *Rapport annuel*. Lévis: CCQ.

Conseil de la coopération du Québec (CCQ). (2005a). *Rapport annuel. La coopération: Un projet de société en pleine éclosion!* Lévis: CCQ.

Conseil de la coopération du Québec (CCQ). (2005b). *Plan d'ensemble 2004–2007 du développement coopératif québécois*. Lévis: CCQ.

Conseil québécois de la coopération et de la mutualité (CQCM). (2007). *La coopération, des valeurs à transmettre*. Rapport d'activités 2006. Lévis: CQCM.

CCQM. (2012). *Notre mission*. Accessed 22 April 2012. www.coopquebec.coop/fr/mission-du-conseil.aspx

Conseil supérieur de la coopération. (1940). *Manifeste du Conseil supérieur de la coopération*. Québec: CSC série A.

Côté, D. (2000). Les coopératives et le prochain millénaire: L'émergence d'un nouveau paradigme. *Revue internationale de l'économie sociale (RECMA)*, 275–276, 150–66.

D'Amours, M. (2002). Économie sociale au Québec: Vers un clivage entre entreprise collective et action communautaire. *Revue internationale de l'économie sociale*, 284, 31–44.

D'Amours, M. (2006). *L'économie sociale au Québec*. Montréal: Édition Saint-Martin and ARUC en économie sociale.

Defourny, J., & Monzón Campos, J.L. (Eds.). (1992). *Économie sociale entre économie capitaliste et économie publique/The Third Sector: Cooperative, mutual and nonprofit organization*. Brussels: De Boeck Université/CIRIEC.

Defourny, J., Simon, M., & Adam, S. (2002). *Les coopératives en Belgique: Un mouvement d'avenir f?* Brussels: Éditions Luc Pire.

Deschênes, G. (1976). Associations coopératives et institutions similaires au XIXᵉ siècle. *Revue d'Histoire de l'Amerique Francaise, 29*, 539–54.

Deschênes, G. (1981). Le mouvement coopératif québécois: Guide bibliographique. In *Revue du CIRIEC, 11*(1–2). Montréal: Éd. Le Jour.

Deschênes, G. (1982). Le premier siècle du mouvement coopératif. *Revue du CIRIEC, 13*(1–2), 15–22.

Caisses Desjardins du Québec et caisses populaires de l'Ontario. (2009). *Rapport annuel du Movement des caisses Desjardins 2009*. Montreal: Caisses Desjardins du Québec.

Desroche, H. (1983). *Traité d'économie sociale*. Paris: CIEM.

Desroche, H. (1987). Postface [Quatre écoles d'économie sociale]. In *Communautés, Archives de Sciences sociales de la Coopération et du Développement, 82*, 121–6.

Draperi, J.-F. (2000). De l'économie sociale face à un siècle de pratiques coopératives. *Revue internationale de l'économie sociale, 275–276*, 124–35.

Économie sociale Québec. (2012). Accessed 22 April 2012. http://economiesocialequebec.ca/?module=directory&uid=4511

Evers, A., & Laville, J.-L. (Eds.). (2004). *The third sector in Europe*. Cheltenham, UK: Edward Elgar.

Favreau, L., & Lévesque, B. (1996). *Développement économique communautair: Économie sociale et intervention*. Québec: Presses de l'Université du Québec.

Fecher, F., & Lévesque, B. (2008). Le secteur public et l'économie sociale dans les Annales (1975–2007): Vers un nouveau paradigme. *Les Annales de l'économie publique, sociale et coopératives, 79*(3), 647–82.

Fecteau, J.-M. (1989). *L'émergence de l'idéal coopératif et l'état au Québec 1850–1914*. Montréal: Cahiers de la Chaire de coopération Guy-Bernier, 72: 39.

Fecteau, J.-M. (1992). État et associationnisme au XIXᵉ siècle québécois : élément pour une problématique des rapports État/Société dans la transition au capitalisme. In A. Greer & I. Radforth (Eds.), *Colonial Leviathan: State formation in mid-nineteenth-century Canada* (pp. 134–62). Toronto: University of Toronto Press.

Fondaction, fonds pour la coopération et l'emploi (CSN). (2006). *Premier rap-port de développement durable. Rapport annuel 2009–20.* Montréal: Fondaction. Accessed 10 July 2011. www.fondaction.com

Fondaction, fonds pour la coopération et l'emploi (CSN). (2010). *Rapport finan-cier 2009–2010.* Montréal: Fondaction. Acessed 10 July 2011. http://www.fondaction.com/?cat=28

Fonds de solidarité des travailleurs (FTQ). (2007). *Vous investissez, nous inves-tissons, le Québec s'enrichit.* Rapport annuel 2006, Montréal.

Girard, J.-P. (2004). Solidarity cooperatives in Québec (Canada): Overview. In C. Borzaga & R. Spear (Eds.), *Trends and challenges for cooperatives and so-cial enterprises in developed and transition countries* (pp. 165–82). Trento, Italy: Fondazione Cariplo.

Gouvernement du Canada. (2005). *Ce qu'il faut savoir sur l'économie sociale: Un guide pour la recherche en politiques publiques.* Ottawa: Gouvernement du Can-ada. Research project on policy.

Gouvernement du Québec. (2006). *Les coopératives d'habitation au Québec.* Qué-bec: MDEIE, Direction des coopératives, édition 2005 and RQOH.

Gouvernement du Québec. (2009). *Budget 2009–2010, La politique familiale du Québec, où en sommes-nous.* Québec: Gouvernement du Québec.

Gueslin, A. (1998). *L'invention de l'économie sociale.* Paris: Economica.

Gui, B. (1991). The economic rationale for the third sector: Nonprofit and other noncapitalist organizations. *Annals of Public and Cooperative Economics, 62*(4), 551–72. http://dx.doi.org/10.1111/j.1467-8292.1991.tb01367.x

Hall, M.H., de Wit, M.L., Lasby, D., McIver, D., Evers, T., & Johnson, C., et al. (2004). *Force vitale de la collectivité: Faits saillants de l'Enquête nationale auprès des organismes à but non lucratif et bénévoles.* Catalogue no 61-533-XPE. Ot-tawa: Statistics Canada.

IFDEC (Institut de formation en développement économique communau-taire). *Stratégies locales pour l'emploi et l'économie sociale.* Montréal: Les Publi-cations de l'IFDÉC, in collaboration with the OECD and Human Resources Development Canada.

Imagine Canada. (2005). *Enquête nationale auprès des organismes à but non lucra-tif et bénévoles.* Toronto: Imagine Canada and Social Development Canada. Accessed 10 July 2011. www.imaginecanada.ca

Investissement Québec. (2005). *Investissement Québec: Une organisation perfor-mante. Rapport annuel 2004–2005.* Québec: Investissement Québec.

Jetté, C. (2005). *Le programme de soutien aux organismes communautaires du Ministère de la santé et des services sociaux: Une forme institutionnelle struc-turante du modèle québécois de développement social (1971–2001).* Montréal: Doctoral thesis in Sociology (Department of Sociology, UQAM).

Joron, G. (1980). *La clôture du colloque*. Colloque sur l'entreprise coopérative dans le développement économique du Québec. Québec: Secrétariat permanent des Conférences socio-économique du Québec.

Kesterman, J.-P., in collaboration with Boisclair, G., & Kirouac, J.-M. (1984). *Histoire du syndicalisme au Québec. UCC-UPA, 1924–1984*. Montréal: Boréal Express.

Laliberté, R.G. (1973). *La culture politique du Conseil de la Coopération du Québec*. Sherbrooke: Chaire de la coopération du département d'économique de l'Université de Sherbrooke.

Lamarre, K. (1991). *50 ans d'avenir! 1939–1989*. Lévis: Conseil de la coopération du Québec.

Lamonde, Y. (2004). *Histoire sociale des idées au Québec, 1896–1929*. Montréal: Fides.

Landry, B. (1980). *Rapport: L'entreprise coopérative dans le développement économique*. Québec: Conférences socio-économique.

Larivière, C. (1980). *Le choix entre le conservatisme et le changement social*. Colloque sur l'entreprise coopérative dans le développement économique du Québec. Québec: Secrétariat permanent des Conférences socio-économique du Québec, 51–7.

Larocque, P. (1991). Dévitalisation rurale et créativité sociale: La Coalition Urgence rurale dans l'Est-du-Québec. In J. Chevalier, B. Jean, J.-L. Klein, & N. Sztokman (Eds.), *De la Loire au Saint-Laurent: Des régions rurales face aux recompositions socio-territoriales* (pp.125–34). Rimouski: Chicoutimi, GRIDEQ, GRIR, URA 915.

Laville, J.-L. (1994). *L'économie solidaire: Une perspective internationale*. Paris: Desclée de Brouwer.

Laville, J.-L., Lévesque, B., & Mendell, M. (2005). *The social economy: Diverse approaches and practices in Europe and Canada*. Paris: OECD.

Levasseur, R., with the collaboration of R. Boulanger. (1990). La dynamique des associations au Québec: Démographie et morphologie, 1942–1981. In M.-M.T. Brault & L. Saint-Jean (Eds.), *Entraide et associations* (pp. 153–80). Québec: Institut québécois de recherche sur la culture.

Lévesque, B. (Ed.). (1979). *Animation sociale et entreprises communautaires et coopératives*. Montréal: Éditions Albert Saint-Martin.

Lévesque, B. (1981). Coopératives et socialisme au Québec. *Interventions critiques en économie politique, 6*, 193–210.

Lévesque, B. (1989). Les coopératives au Québec, un secteur stratégique à la recherche d'un projet pour l'an 2000. *Annals of Public and Cooperative Economics [Université de Liège], 60*(2), 181–215. http://dx.doi.org/10.1111/j.1467-8292.1989.tb02000.x

Lévesque, B. (1991). Coopération et syndicalisme: Le cas des relations de travail dans les Caisses populaires Desjardins. *Relations Industrielles, 46*(1), 13–45.

Lévesque, B. (1998). La CSN et l'économie sociale: De promoteur à entrepreneur. In Y. Bélanger & R. Comeau (Eds.), *La CSN, 75 ans d'action syndicale et sociale* (pp. 239–45). Québec: PUQ.

Lévesque, B. (2004a). Les entreprises d'économie sociale, plus porteuses d'innovations sociale que les autres? In *Le développement social au rythme de l'innovation* (pp. 51–72). Québec: Presses de l'Université du Québec and Fonds de recherche sur la société et la culture.

Lévesque, B. (2007). *Un siècle et demi d'économie sociale au Québec: Plusieurs configurations en présence (1850–2007)*. Montréal: Cahier du CRISES (no. ET0703).

Lévesque, B. (2009a). *Le CIRIEC-Canada, 1966–2006: Quarante ans de recherche en partenariat sur les enterprises publiques et d'économie sociale.* Montréal: Éditions Saint-Martin/CIRIEC-Canada.

Lévesque, B. (2009b). Le repositionnement de l'économie sociale québécoise. In J.-F. Draperi (Ed.), *L'année de l'économie sociale et solidaire* (pp. 221–8). Paris: Dunod.

Lévesque, B. (in press). *Un service public de la petite enfance par l'économie sociale et solidaire: Le cas québécois.* Montréal: Cahiers du CRISES.

Lévesque, B., Bélanger, P.R., Bouchard, et al. (2000). *Le Fonds de solidarité des travailleurs du Québec (FTQ: Nouvelle gouvernance et capital de développement.* Montréal: CRISES.

Lévesque, B., Côté, A., Chouinard, O., and Russell, J.-L. (1985). *Profil socio-économique des coopératives de travail au Québec.* Montréal: UQAM/Comité provincial des coopératives de production, de travail et pré-coopératives.

Lévesque, B., & Fecher, F. (2008). The public sector and the social economy in the *Annals* (1975–2007). *Annals of Public and Cooperative Economics, 79*(3–4), 679–727.

Lévesque, B., & Malo, M.-C. (1992). L'économie sociale au Québec: Une notion méconnue, une réalité économique importante. In J. Defourny & J.L. Monzon Campos (Eds.), *Économie sociale – The third sector* (pp. 349–403). Brussels: De Boeck.

Lévesque, B., Malo, M.-C., & Girard, J.-P. (1999). L'ancienne et la nouvelle économie sociale: Le cas du Québec. In J. Defourny, P. Develtere, & Fonteneau, B. (Eds.), *L'économie sociale au Nord et au Sud* (pp. 195–216). Brussels: De Boeck.

Lévesque, B. & Mendell, M. (2004), L'économie sociale: Diversité des approches et des pratiques. Proposition pour la nouvelle ARUC en Économie sociale. Published in 2005 in *Interventions économiques, 32.* Accessed 10 July 2011. http://interventionseconomiques.revues.org/852

MacPherson, I. (2004). Remembering the big picture: The cooperative movement and contemporary communities. In C. Borgaza & R. Spear (Eds.), *Trends and Challenges for Cooperatives and Social enterprises in developed and transition countries* (pp. 39–48). Trento, Italy: Fondazione Cariplo.

Martel, J.-L. with the collaboration of D. Lévesque. (1986). Émergence du mouvement coopératif agricole au Québec: D'un mouvement populaire à une politique de développement. *Revue du CIRIEC, 18*(1): 13–39.

Martel, J.-L. (1987). L'organisation coopérative et les projets de restauration sociale des années '30 au Québec. *Revue du CIRIEC, 18*(2), 15–38.

Martel, J.-L. (1988). *L'évolution du Mouvement coopératif québécois, 1975–1985.* Montréal: Centre de gestion des coopératives, Cahier 88–10.

Ministère de Développement, économique, Innovation et Exportation (MDEIE). (2005). *Rapport annuel de gestion, 2003–2004.* Québec: Author.

Ministère de Développement, économique, Innovation et Exportation (MDEIE). (2007). *Coopératives du Québec, données statistiques 2001–2005.* Québec: Author.

Ministère de Développement, économique, Innovation et Exportation (MDEIE) and Conseil québécois de la coopération et de la mutualité (CQCM). (2006). *Entente de partenariat 2007–2008 à 2009–2010 entre le Ministre du développement économique de l'innovation et de l'exportation et le Conseil québécois de la coopération et de la mutualité relativement au développement des coopératives.* Québec: Author.

Ministère de l'Industrie et du Commerce (MIC). (2001). *Avant-projet de Politique de développement des coopératives.* Québec: Direction des coopératives.

Ministère de la Santé et des Services sociaux. (2010). *INFO-ORG.COM Bulletin d'information sur les montants accordés aux organismes communautaires subventionnés.* Québec: Service du développement de l'information. Accessed 10 July 2011. http://publications.msss.gouv.qc.ca/statisti/pdf/Info-ORG.COM-2010.pdf

Ministère de Emploi et Solidarité sociale. (2010). Statistiques sur l'action communautaire. Québec: Service du développement de l'information. Accessed 10 July 2011. http://www.mess.gouv.qc.ca/statistiques/action-communautaire

Ministère des finances, de l'économie et de la recherche. (2003). *Politique de développement des coopératives. Horizon 2005. La coopération, tout le monde y gagne.* Québec: Direction des coopératives.

Ministère du Développement économique, de l'Innovation et de l'Exportation (MDEIE). (2007). *Coopératives du Québec, Données statistiques (édition 2007).* Québec: Author.

Ministre du développement économique et régional et de la recherche (MDERR) and Conseil de la coopération du Québec (CCQ). (2005). *Entente*

*de partenariat entre le Ministre du développement économique et régional et de la
recherche et le Conseil de la coopération du Québec relativement au développement
des coopératives.* Québec: Author.

Minville, E. (1980). *La vie économique: Système et structure économique.* Montréal:
Fidès (edition of the complete works of François-Albert Angers).

Mouvement Desjardins. (2007). *Des millions de raisons d'être. Rapport annuel
2006.* Lévis: Desjardins. Accessed 10 July 2011. http://www.des
jardins.com/fr/a_propos/investisseurs/rapports-annuels/mouvement.
jsp?cm_sp=DESJ-_-RapportAnnuel2011-_-BlocPromo

Münkner, H. (2004). Multi-stakeholder co-operatives and their legal framework. In C. Borzaga & R. Spear (Eds.), *Trends and challenges for co-operatives
and social enterprises in developed and transition countries* (pp. 49–82). Trento,
Italy: Fondazione Cariplo.

Neamtan, N. (1999). Le Chantier de l'économie sociale poursuivra le travail
entrepris. *Economie et Solidarites, 30*(1), 18–23.

Office de Planification du Développement du Québec. (1980). *Les coopératives au
Québec: Problématique et potentiel de développement.* Québec: Éditeur officiel.

Pallard, J. (2005). Henri Desroche et ses réseaux québécois: Entre théorie de
l'utopie et pratiques maïeutiques. *Sociologie et Sociétés, 37*(2), 21–48.

Payette, M. (1992). Le forum pour l'emploi: Histoire et perspectives. *Interventions économiques pour une alternative sociale, 24.*

Petitclerc, M. (2005). *Une forme d'entraide populaire: Histoire des sociétés québécoises de secours mutuels au 19ᵉ siècle.* Montréal: Department of History (doctoral thesis). Published under the title *Nous protégeons l'infortune: Les origines
populaires de l'économie sociale au Québec.* Montréal: VLB Éditeur, 2007.

Rioux, A. (1989). L'État et la coopération. *Coopératives et Développement, 20*(2),
171–82.

Rocher, G. (1984a). Introduction. In G.-H. Lévesque, G. Rocher, J. Henripin
et al. (Eds.), *Continuité et rupture: Les sciences sociales au Québec* (pp. 7–22).
Montréal: Les Presses de l'Université de Montréal.

Rocher, G. (1984b). Le sociologue et le pouvoir ou comment se mêler des af-
faires des autres. In G.-H. Lévesque, G. Rocher, J. Henripin et al. (Eds.),
Continuité et rupture: Les sciences sociales au Québec (pp. 2, 369–83). Montréal:
Les Presses de l'Université de Montréal.

SACA (Secrétariat à l'action communautaire autonome). (2005). *État de situation de l'intervention gouvernementale en matière d'action communautaire.* Québec: Gouvernement du Québec.

SACA (Secrétariat à l'action communautaire autonome). (2006). *État de situation de l'intervention gouvernementale en matière d'action communautaire, Édition 2005–2006.* Québec: Gouvernement du Québec.

Salamon, L.M. (1987). Partners in public service: The scope and theory of government-nonprofit relations. In W. Powell (Ed.), *The nonprofit sector: A research handbook* (pp. 99–117). New Haven: Yale University Press.

Salamon, L.M. (2010). Putting the civil society sector on the economic map of the world. *Annals of Public and Cooperative Economics, 81*(2), 167–210. http://dx.doi.org/10.1111/j.1467-8292.2010.00409.x

Salamon, L.M., & Anheier, H.K. (1996). *The emerging nonprofit sector: An overview.* New York: Manchester University Press.

Salamon, L.M., Anheier, H.K., List, R., Toepler, S., Wojciech, S.S., & Associates. (1999). *Global civil society: Dimensions of the nonprofit sector.* Baltimore: Johns Hopkins Comparative Nonprofit Sector Project.

Secrétariat des conférences socio-économiques. (1980). *L'entreprise coopérative dans le développement économique.* Study paper submitted to the conference on cooperative enterprises in economic development, held in Montréal on 4, 5, 6, and 7 February 1980.

Solidarité rurale. (2011). *Solidarité rurale du Québec.* Accessed 10 July 2011. http://www.ruralite.qc.ca/

Sommet de l'économie sociale et solidaire. (2006a). *Le Québec affiche ses valeurs.* Rapport synthèse des travaux préparatoires. Montréal: Chantier de l'économie sociale. Accessed 10 July 2011. www.chantier.qc.ca

Sommet de l'économie sociale et solidaire. (2006b). *Entreprendre solidairemen: Bilan 1996–2006.* Montréal: Chantier de l'économie sociale.

Sommet de l'économie sociale et solidaire. (2006c). *Pistes d'action adoptées.* Montréal: Chantier de l'économie sociale. Accessed 10 July 2011. www.chantier.qc.ca

Vachon, B. (1993). *Le développement local. Théorie et pratique. Réintroduire l'humain dans la logique de développement.* Montréal: Gaëtan Morin.

Vaillancourt, Y. (2006). Le tiers secteur au Canada, un lieu de rencontre entre la tradition américaine et la tradition européenne. *Canadian Review of Social Policy/ Revue canadienne de politique sociale, 56*, 23–39.

Vaillancourt, Y., & Jetté, C., in collaboration with Leclerc, P. (2009). *Les arrangements institutionnels entre l'État québécois et les entreprises d'économie sociale en aide domestique. Une analyse sociopolitique de l'économie sociale dans les services de soutien à domicile.* Montréal: Éditions Vie Économique (EVE).

Vaillancourt, Y., Aubry, F., & Jetté, C. (Eds.). (2003). *L'économie sociale dans les services à domicile.* Québec: Presses de l'Université du Québec.

Vercamer, F. (2010). *Rapport sur l'économie sociale et solidaire – L'économie sociale et solidaire, entreprendre autrement pour la croissance et pour l'emploi.* Paris: Ministère de l'Economie et de l'Emploi. Accessed 10 July 2011. http://www.ladocumentationfrancaise.fr/rapports-publics/104000206/index.shtml

Vienney, C. (1994). *L'économie sociale*. Paris: La Découverte (in collaboration with Repères).

Vienney, C. (1998). Les rapports sur les coopératives et l'État. *Coopératives et Développement, 20*(1), 13–38.

Vienney, C. (2000). Qu'est-ce que l'économie sociale? *Revue internationale de l'économie sociale, 275–276*, 38–41 (excerpt of an article written in 1989).

2 Social Economy Research Partnerships: The Québec Experience

JEAN-MARC FONTAN

Introduction

The social economy is made up of established or emerging social organizations and collective enterprises belonging to the cooperative, mutual, or associative sectors. It differs fundamentally from the private and public economies. The social economy depends on citizen involvement, democratic management in the production of goods and services, and the pursuit of objectives that are both social and economic. It allows people to fulfil both their individual and collective aspirations, though in different ways. It promotes experimentation by fostering innovative socio-economic solutions for responding to social emergencies or socio-economic problems insufficiently considered by the private or public economies.

In its modern form, the social economy goes back to the nineteenth century. Essentially, the emergence of the sector is attributable to social forces that mobilized a set of human, financial, material, relational, and cognitive resources to facilitate the emergence, consolidation, and expansion of certain social and economic activities. There is a long-standing relationship between, on the one hand, academic educators and researchers and, on the other hand, social economy players.

Yet there has been little discussion on the historical relationship between academic circles and social economy circles. What can we say about this relationship? What types of coalitions and collaboration have been established between academic researchers and the leaders of social economy organizations and enterprises? What types of mechanisms did they employ? What work methods did they set up? If we take the example of partnership research, what can we say about the role and impact of the joint construction of knowledge in developing Québec's social economy? Finally, what political and ethical issues have emerged from these kinds of contacts?

This chapter examines the specific contribution of academic actors to the joint creation of Québec's contemporary social economy sector. We analyse their contribution from the standpoint of the different forms of collaboration, coalition, and partnership that have arisen over the last half-century.

Our presentation and analysis of the organic links between social economy sectors and academic research sectors is divided into three parts. The first part analyses the concept of the research partnership. Starting with the late 1960s, the discussion provides the context for the contemporary evolution of the concept and its employment on North American university campuses. The second part provides a recent historical overview of various mechanisms in Québec involving general collaboration between academic researchers and social economy actors. The third part describes the experience of social economy partnership research consortia and the process of jointly creating knowledge. This part also reveals the impact of this form of collaboration on the evolution of the social economy sector. It paves the way for our discussion about the main issues raised by this type of research and introduces theoretical considerations on the specific contribution of partnership research to the creation of knowledge.

Partnership Research: Developing the Process of Joint Knowledge Creation

As noted by Wiewel and Broski (1997) and Wilson (2004),[1] the involvement of North American universities in local communities goes back to the seventeenth century. A turning point in the long history of this involvement occurred at the turn of nineteenth century, when universities became the primary institutions supporting the creation and mobilization of knowledge for developing modern society:

> In 1636, when Harvard University was founded, and for the institutions that were established over the next two centuries, the primary function of higher education was to produce an educated class of leaders. It was not until 1862 – when Congress enacted the Morrill Act – that a different set of universities came into existence. Known as the Land-Grant Act, this

sweeping piece of legislation brought into existence a cadre of institutions whose raison d'être was to provide access to higher education for common folk, and to produce research that could help America develop as a nation. These institutions, which ranged from Penn State University to the University of Florida, exist in every state in the nation and, arguably, have made higher education in America the envy of the world. (Wilson, 2004, p. 17)

By the end of the nineteenth century, there was an organic link between university circles and civil society in a minority of universities in the Americas and Europe. In the 1960s – by which time this link was more than a hundred years old – it had become even stronger, more established, and more structured. Latin America had its extención, a system of cooperation between universities and local communities for training, research, and coaching. In Europe –in the Netherlands, to be precise (Neubauer, 2002) – the end of the 1960s saw the introduction of a new mechanism: science shops. These shops soon began to collaborate with an international network of organizations pursuing the same vision and similar objectives.[2] The Trent Centre for Community-Based Education, located at Trent University in Peterborough, Ontario, is affiliated with the European network of science shops. To a large extent, the Canadian program of the Alliance de recherche universités-communautés en économie sociale (ARUC-ÉS), developed by the Social Sciences and Humanities Research Council (SSHRC), drew its inspiration from the European program of the science shops (Commission européenne, 2004). In the early 1970s, an innovative intervention model was established in Québec: the Service aux collectivités (Community Support Service) of the Université du Québec à Montréal (UQAM). The Service liaises between organizations representing various social movements and university resources. The goal is to make these resources more accessible to social organizations.

The science shops fell within the sphere of influence of the countercultural movement of the mid-1960s. During that decade, a new approach to educational relationships emerged. Student movements questioned traditional teaching methods. There was an articulated desire to participate in managing university affairs and conduct research with social organizations:

"Science shops" are found at the crossroads of science and society. These grassroots research organizations deal with practical scientific problems at the local community level. Although they cater to the community, science shops are not really "shops" in the traditional sense of the word. They carry out scientific research in a wide range of disciplines – usually free of charge – on behalf of citizens and local civil society. Over the past 30 years, science shops have spread across Europe and beyond – to the USA, Canada, Israel, and South Africa. The concept arose in the student movement and counter-culture of the early 1970s when a group of Dutch chemistry students came up with ways to help not-for-profit associations solve scientific problems. (Commission européenne, 2005)

Starting in the 1980s, the challenges raised by the transformation of modern societies into knowledge-based societies virtually ensured that university involvement in the community would strike out in new directions. On the one hand, there was a strong trend within the United States to revive the civic vocation of the university (Soska & Butterfield, 2005; Vidal et al., 2002). On the other hand, there was a basic questioning of traditional ways of thinking about knowledge creation:

> In the past, universities generally operated on the deficit model: the community, or society at large, had certain needs, and the university, as the home of experts, would fill these needs. In other cases, the community was merely seen as laboratory, with more or less compliant "guinea pigs." In a partnership model, things are more equal. It is acknowledged that both parties have needs and that success requires a mutual recognition of needs, shared problem definition, and a joint search for solutions. (Wiewel & Broski, 1997, p. 2)

Hackney (1994) and Walshok (1995) maintain that partnership research has an innovative methodology that is based on a dynamic expertise bringing together academic circles and social groups. In such research, the work of experts is no longer detached from the knowledge acquired by social forces (Bussières & Fontan, 2003). On the contrary, it relies on comparing knowledge, both to jointly create new knowledge and initiate development activities (Benson & Harkavy, 2000; Fontan, 2006). Still, this form of collaboration raises questions, as Mayfield and Lucas note (2000) in their critical analysis of this method of joint knowledge production, because academics risk being trapped in the political agenda of the actors with whom they are collaborating.

In Canada, the idea of creating knowledge jointly – and especially of making sure that the research has concrete applications in collective action or social projects – has taken a different path. We can identify at least three major types of partnership in this country.

First, researcher-practitioners cooperate with academic researchers by introducing their knowledge-mobilization and knowledge-construction models. These are limited forms of partnership between academic researchers and researchers in a particular sector of the social economy. For example, in the early 1960s, several cooperative sectors established internal structures and other mechanisms to carry out research, training, observation, or transfer.

Second, partnership proposals bring together mainly academic researchers and group representatives to provide the latter with access to academic knowledge. Thus, the partnership is based on an academic apparatus designed to help social groups mobilize resources; this model was introduced in the early 1970s by UQAM's Community Support Service. A government may also wish to use a special resources program to provide certain economic sectors with research and knowledge-transfer capability. This is the model employed by Québec's Centres de liaison et de transfert (CLTs, liaison and transfer centres, which were started in the 1980s).

Third, some funding bodies for university research have programs providing academic research structures with financial resources to develop research activities in partnership with sector-based organizations. The partnership may be supported by a grant program of the concerted-action type (a model used extensively by the Government of Québec, through its Fonds québécois de recherche sur la science et la culture). The concerted actions introduced in the 1990s were based on a grant package that brought into play a number of organizations. The partnership is also based on shared coordination of (a) management and monitoring of the competitive process and (b) the funded research projects. It may be supported by a research-grant program designed specifically to encourage cooperation between community action groups and universities. Indeed, this is what occurred in the case of ARUC-ÉS funding (SSHRC), the grant program dedicated to the social economy (SSHRC), and the program to set up research partnerships between researchers and representatives of community action groups in Canada and their counterparts in developing countries (SSHRC in partnership with CIDA, the Canadian International Development Agency).

The typology above provides a very brief description of current practices. The task of systematizing knowledge based on the strategy of joint knowledge creation is still in its early stages. The objective of the Canadian research centre the Office of Community-Based Research (OCBR),[3] which was formed in January 2007, is to network researchers and centres that subscribe to this work philosophy. The OCBR intends to promote partnership research while developing knowledge creation and systematization projects.

A Contemporary Contextualization of the Collaborative Relationship between Québec's Academic Research Groups and Its Social Economy Groups

The post-war years foretold an important transformation in the political and economic landscape, both on the national and global levels. In Québec, the transformation took the form of a radical political rupture in which the Quiet Revolution, initiated in the early 1960s, began to emphasize the Keynesian state and state providentialism, rather than the interests of social corporatism and clerical providentialism.

For the social economy, the early 1950s revealed that the vast growth experienced by the cooperative sector of that era was running out of steam.[4] Concurrently, within the associative sector the number of groups incorporating through the legal form of organization known as the not-for-profit organization (NPO) continued to grow. Within the not-for-profit sector of that era, associations with an economic mission constituted an interesting legal form, since it was less restrictive and provided more flexibility than did the various legal forms of incorporation characterizing cooperatives of that period.[5] The NPO formula made the incorporating instrument accessible by allowing a single status to be used to set up different types of projects, including those designed to respond to emergencies (e.g., free health clinics and legal clinics, consumer associations), fulfil unmet needs (e.g., representing persons sharing the same identity or defending the same case), or give free rein to new aspirations (e.g., self-managed artist centres and spaces, community gardens).

Beginning in the 1950s, there was an upsurge of research on associations with a non-cooperative legal status. In due course, it complemented and strengthened a tradition of research on the cooperative sector that dated back to the early twentieth century. The context for this research on associations was the transformation of Québec society, where there was accelerated development of the educational sector, especially the higher-education sector. Thus, the social sciences in Québec were able to develop a structure very quickly. This structure encouraged a transfer of expertise from Europe to Québec, and attracted many European intellectuals. The latter either filled the numerous posts that were opening up or came to Québec to teach for short periods of time. Henri Desroches (1973, 1978) figured prominently among intellectuals contributing to thinking on the social economy. Over about a 15-year period, he took part in various teaching and research activities in Québec while supporting the development of different projects that provided a structure for action-research (Fournier, 1972; Pallard, 2005).

There were two major waves of research on the social economy in the 1960–2005 period. We will discuss the various mechanisms introduced in each period. We have selected experiences with an important impact on this historic period, and most of which still exist. The description provided below, however, does not fully convey the rich and highly complex experiences of this period.

1960 to 1980

The first wave covers a 20-year period (1960–1980). It was marked by thematic and sector-based research conducted by committed researchers and activists working with various social movements, including the union movement, community-based movements, and the feminist movement. During this wave, community initiatives emerged via new informal organizations known as Comités de citoyens (Citizen Action Movements) (McGraw, 1978). They gave rise, amongst other things, to free health clinics and legal clinics, and in the late 1960s led to the setting up of action-research groups, which were an experiment in bringing together researchers and social actors. For example, there was the work carried out in Montréal by the Institut Parallèle (1968–1978), an action research centre that a group of McGill University professors initiated in the Pointe-St-Charles district to provide social and economic leadership for district residents (Weiner, 1970).

Between 1965 and 1975, three different bodies or coalitions of researchers and practitioners were created to support the development of the collective economy: the Centre interdisciplinaire de recherche et d'information sur les entreprises collectives[6] (CIRIEC-Canada), the Université de Sherbrooke Cooperative and Mutual Research and Teaching Institute (IRECUS, Université de Sherbrooke) (1966)[7] and the Centre de gestion des coopératives (Centre for Studies in the Management of Cooperatives) (1975) at the École des Hautes Études Commerciales (HEC) of the Université de Montréal.

The idea of creating a Canadian section of the International Centre of Research and Information on the Public, Social and Cooperative Economy (CIRIEC International)[8] emerged in 1964. The work performed by CIRIEC International was a good illustration of how Québec could benefit from various types of idea and expertise transfer.[9] The project materialized in 1966 with the founding of this organization by three professors at Sir George Williams University.[10] CIRIEC-Canada brought together researchers and other representatives of social economy and public economy organizations. It was based on the networking of Canadian and European researchers, and it started a journal that still exists today.[11]

Towards the end of the 1960s, and in parallel with the launching of CIRIEC-Canada, a group of researchers and practitioners decided to develop an initiative at the Université de Sherbrooke to teach and conduct research on the cooperative economy. Over a 30-year period, this university made its mark as Québec's leading university in this area. The highlights of this period included the establishment in 1968 of the Chaire de coopération, IRECUS, in 1976, the Réseau des universités des Amériques en études sur les coopératives et les associations[12] (UniRcoops) in 1995, the Chaire Desjardins de coopération et développement du milieu[13] in 1999, and the university's cooperative training program.

The Université du Québec à Montréal undertook a similar initiative in 1970 with the creation of its Service aux collectivités. The goal of this service is to support the development of community, women's, labour, and cultural organizations by giving them access to university resources for their research, educational, or other activities (such as symposia, exhibitions, and publishing). Also noteworthy was the creation in 1975 of the Centre for Studies in Management of Cooperatives[14] at the HEC. By 2001, this centre was specializing in cooperative financial services, and was later transformed into the Desjardins Centre for Studies in Management of Financial Services Cooperatives.

1980 to 2005

The second wave of research on the social economy extended from 1980 to the mid-2000s. It was formed following the creation of governmental grant programs to support the introduction of new research structures. The financial support was provided by either the federal or provincial government. Beginning in 1977, support was provided for the Social Sciences and Humanities Research Council (SSHRC) and, beginning in

1979, by Québec for Québec's Conseil québécois de la recherche sociale (CQRS) and Fonds pour la formation de chercheurs et l'aide à la recherche (FCAR).[15] Thus, there was a portfolio of subsidies to support research by teams of researchers in a particular discipline – or by multidisciplinary teams – on either general or targeted topics.

At first, these programs supported the creation of small or medium-sized research teams (during the 1980s); later, they supported the creation of larger teams (during the 1990s). By 1984, Québec's Department of Education, by way of the Fonds des services aux collectivités (Community Services Fund), was the principal agency funding the development of partnership research in the humanities and social sciences – that is, facilitating the creation of research projects based on close collaboration between researchers and social groups in the design and management of research teams and research projects. A few years later, the CQRS followed suit when it launched a funding plan to establish research teams based on partnerships between researchers and practitioners.

In 1987, the Chaire de coopération Guy-Bernier[16] was created through the Fondation de l'UQAM with the financial support of the Fédération des caisses populaires Desjardins de Montréal et de l'Ouest du Québec. One year later, the Centre de recherche sur les innovations sociales (CRISES) was established.[17] The latter was the first research centre in Québec to develop, as part of its research program, a main line of research dealing exclusively with the social economy. In 1992, shortly after the creation of CRISES, two other initiatives were launched: the Laboratoire de recherche sur les pratiques et les politiques sociales (LAREPPS) at UQAM (Montréal)[18] and the Chaire de recherche en développement communautaire (Hull), which in 2002 became the Chaire de recherche du Canada en développement des collectivités[19] (CRDC-GERIS). In 1997, LAREPPS formed the Équipe de recherche en économie sociale, santé et bien-être (a research team on the social economy, health and welfare).

In 2000, the first consortium for partnership research on the social economy was set up at UQAM. Based on a partnership with the Chantier de l'économie sociale (the Social Economy Task Force),[20] other social economy organizations, and union circles, the consortium brought together researchers from the Université du Québec en Outaouais, the Université du Québec à Chicoutimi, and Concordia University. The Alliance de recherche universités-communautés en économie sociale (ARUC-ÉS)[21] is Québec's first interuniversity, interfaculty, and interregional research centre dedicated entirely to partnership research in social economy. Since then, various consortiums and centres have been established, including the Observatoire en économie sociale et en développement régional,[22] the Centre de recherche en intervention sociale (CERIS)[23] (Université du Québec en Outaouais), the Alliance de recherche universités-communautés en économie sociale (ARUC-ISDC) (Université du Québec en Outaouais), the Chaire de responsabilité sociale et de développement durable,[24] and the Chaire de recherche du Canada en économie sociale (UQAM).[25]

In 2005, the CRSH launched a research program at a cost of $15 million over five years (2005–10) and dedicated entirely to the social economy. This program funded the creation of six regional research centres on the social economy in Canada, including the Réseau Québecois de recherche partenariale en économie sociale (RQRP-ÉS).[26] This funding made it possible to create the Centre canadien de recherche partenariale en économie sociale.[27] In 2007, SSHRC, in partnership with CIDA, launched a new program of cooperation between Canadian and developing country universities to support transfer and training activities in a variety of sectors, including the social economy. A single project in which partnership research teams have access to two sources of funding is a rare occurrence in the field of humanities and social sciences: SSHRC will fund partnership research activities on Canadian soil and CIDA will support transfer and research activities managed by the developing country partners.

From the early 1990s to 2005, these Québec research structures, under the leadership of researchers working to jointly create knowledge with players in their field, came to form a "global pole of excellence" in basic research and dedicated partnership research in social innovation, social development and the social economy. The numerous networks of teams comprise over 250 Québec, Canadian, and international researchers working on a multidisciplinary, interfaculty, interuniversity, and inter-regional or partnership basis. In concrete terms, over a 40-year period the social economy sector has acquired tools for structuring the creation and mobilization of knowledge. These tools are used to convey the realities of this sector, including the conditions in which it emerges and grows, its strengths and limitations, and the challenges and issues it faces.

The Québec Model of Partnership Research in Social Economy

The preceding section allowed us to examine the increasingly institutionalized cooperation in Québec between social economy actors and university researchers and educators. In this section we will discuss the partnership research model employed in the research networks formed by the Alliance de recherche universités-communautés en économie sociale (ARUC-ÉS) and the Réseau québécois de recherche partenariale en économie sociale (RQRP-ÉS).

The ARUC-ÉS partnership research model was developed over a period of about 30 years. It is based on academic expertise involved in the mobilization of knowledge. Part of the knowledge to be mobilized consists of theoretical and methodological tools devised by academicians, while another part consists of empirical and theoretical knowledge created by social economy practitioners. The model mobilizes the expertise of social economy actors; this is called experiential knowledge,[28] which is formed from both practical knowledge of the social economy and an identity-based view and understanding of the role, status, and significance of this sector within the domestic economy.

This working model relies on a partnership between actors and researchers to develop and carry out each research activity. It facilitates the co-construction of collaborative people skills based on a culture of partnership research updated through action-research activities and education through action (Sutton, 2007a and b). The model favours the establishment of communities of practitioners of actors and researchers and the formation of "common worlds" among stakeholders supporting different cultures.

In this model of partnership research, both researchers and practitioners take part in all stages of the process of co-constructing and mobilizing knowledge. The preferred approach for managing the research program is based on co-management by a representative of university groups and a representative of social economy groups. The same applies to research projects or activities conducted within this type of work group: both the Chantiers d'activités partenariales (CAP) of the ARUC-ÉS and the Groupes régionaux d'activités partenariales (GRAP) of the RQRP-ÉS bring together researchers and practitioners under the co-management of two persons of authority from these groups.

How does a research project take root in these work environments? First, the knowledge mobilization stage is generated by a research requirement or a questioning initiated in social economy or research circles. In the working meetings of partnership groups there are sometimes participants who emulate the decisions of others concerning research planning. Once there is a developing consensus to carry out a research activity, resources are mobilized. This allows participants to clarify the research application, modify it, and come up with research specifications for the main questions, the major orientations, the schedule, the work methodology, and the strategy for mobilizing the results.

The initial stage is critical. Fundamentally, it differentiates this type of research from other types used in basic research or research used by consultation firms. The process of clarifying the research topic allows participants to compare the application or need with the realities of existing knowledge and appropriate methods for attaining their objective. The initial monologue characterizing the views of each stakeholder is gradually transformed into a dialogue. For the latter to take hold requires open-mindedness on the part of both researchers and practitioners. They must be able to modify their expectations, points of view, and approaches according to the new representation of the project the two parties have accepted to develop together.

Each project is unique, requiring a greater or lesser mobilization of resources, including:

- human resources (time available for joint work meetings);
- material resources (documents, databases);
- cognitive resources (experiential, tacit, and scientific knowledge);
- relational resources (networks of contacts); and
- financial resources (amounts invested directly in the project, or indirectly to support the project, e.g., travel, work time).

Resources are mobilized according to need and the ability to raise the required funds. Occasionally, the project requires a complex financial package. Thus, the amounts invested can come from different sources: research circles associated with the sector in question, as well as from governments. Once the project has been defined and resources mobilized, the research program's coordination committee approves it and formalizes the work process.

Starting up research activities involves the creation of a steering committee, which becomes the focal point for coordination and facilitating an exchange of ideas between researchers and practitioners. The steering committee includes a resource professional hired by the ARUC or the RQRP to provide support services for the work carried out by the partners. If students are hired, they too take part in committee meetings.

For researchers, working in a partnership provides them with access to information they would have found difficult to obtain using conventional research processes. The trust developed while the project is being set up makes it easier to collect key data. For social economy players, contact with researchers provides them with an opportunity to sort out their needs and expectations vis-à-vis the research project they wish to undertake. Lastly, for students, action research constitutes a critical part of their training and skill development in partnership research. This involvement allows them to participate in the production of research reports, co-author scholarly articles, and present research data.

Once the project has completed its research activities, it is ready for the final stage of the work: mobilizing the knowledge through dissemination, training, and transfer. This stage takes on even greater importance given that the project will have received funds and special attention for this purpose right from the time the project was formulated. These activities include producing working papers, writing articles (accompanied by a conventional dissemination of results), or organizing a seminar (for invited participants) or symposium for the public at large (accompanied by specialized or extended dissemination of results). They may lead to the production of specialized information capsules or perhaps the production of audio-visual documents (a more formative strategy). Lastly, they may be designed to disseminate information in specialized media or be used as (i) basic material or reference material for university courses or (ii) training sessions designed for a variety of publics (academic training or the updating of knowledge).

Not all projects have the same potential when it comes to mobilizing knowledge. For example, one team project designed to look into available paths for carrying out an industrial conversion activity in an urban environment had weak potential in terms of transferring knowledge, but strong potential for disseminating it. By contrast, another project was conducted in collaboration with a social economy sector to devise a tool that would allow organizations to evaluate the accessibility of the services they provide; it had strong potential for both disseminating results and transferring knowledge.

The distinction between the dissemination and transfer of knowledge involves the type of impact the mobilization process will have on actors. For example, when there is no pre-existing strategy in place, greater familiarity with ways to design intervention strategies in deindustrialized districts allows one to guide the work without having to transform attitudes. Having a tool to identify the extent to which one's organization is accessible to various populations allows the organization to transform behaviour that is less effective in terms of providing

accessibility to one that is more effective. The process must include follow-up action, however.

The Epistemological Contribution of Partnership Research

Researchers used to working in a classic fundamental research setting
may find it difficult to pursue joint knowledge creation on applied issues closely linked to the needs and interests of practitioners, and using
a form of questioning based on collaboration with a socio-professional
sector. Researchers are entitled to ask if it is relevant and legitimate to
perform the research in a work environment that is highly reliant on the
needs and interests to which these actors lend support. Thus, questions
regarding the scholarly objective need to be raised: Should the research
serve the needs of the actors? Should it be utilitarian? Can science be
sound when a political agenda is omnipresent? Do researchers involved
in partnership research give precedence to the social causes they support? Are they prisoners of the normative aspects of this commitment?

Of course, there is no cut-and-dry answer to all of these questions.
Experience with the research performed in our two networks clearly
indicates that research results will differ when practitioners are advocates of a social cause, though this is true for a variety of reasons.

First, we have to admit that when a partnership defines the research
topic, the latter may deal with matters that the researcher does not
necessarily support at the outset. Framing a set of problems for a research topic defined by a partnership may involve research interests –
and, consequently, cognitive dimensions – that are intrinsically different from those of a single researcher or research team. Since the partnership reflects a diversity of concerns, viewpoints, and experiential
knowledge, there is an increased benefit and a greater store of knowledge in the scholarly learning. It is true that this contribution steers the
problematization in a direction that may modify it. Yet, is this not precisely what happens when research problematics are based on a multidisciplinary approach? For some, there is another worrisome point: A
research topic investigated by two different researchers in the same discipline and using identical methods will not necessarily have the same
result in terms of knowledge created. Is this not a form of relativity,
since it raises the question of the absolute objectivity of basic research
in the social sciences and humanities?

Second, throughout the research activity, the exchange of ideas between practitioners and researchers permits validation of the way the

information is processed (collection and analysis). The processing of the information, as has been amply demonstrated by the anthropological research method using participant observation of medium or long duration, ensures that culture plays an important role in information collection, the meaning attributed to the latter, and, lastly, the analysis that follows from this. Of course, to process information one must first perform the research required to retrieve it. To be in a position to bring to light empirical, dynamic, procedural, or political information, it is important to foster debate on the meaning and impact of the information collected. Thus, the discussion group turns into a laboratory for mediating and interpreting the very content of the information collected. This type of activity is a learning experience for practitioners and students, as well as for researchers.

By way of illustration, research carried out on experiments to mobilize local unions following company shutdowns provided material for a dozen data-rich monographs whose meaning could be interpreted in different ways. The work of the steering committee created a dual transfer process. Researchers were able to advance a sensible mobilization strategy for several actions under consideration. Once they understood how relationships between the local unions and their central labour body were structured, interpreting the data collected for the monographs was very easy. Union representatives were able to clarify the importance of considering union struggles in their sector so that they could systematize the knowledge stemming from these struggles. As well, training materials for unions were designed with a view to transferring to the representatives of local unions a set of potential tools and actions for responding to company shutdowns or mass layoffs.

Special Issues to Consider When Developing Knowledge in the Social Economy

Several issues of relevance to partnership research and the development of knowledge in the social economy merit discussion.

The first issue falls within the purview of basic research and partnership research. It deals with the direct impact of producing and mobilizing new knowledge on the social economy sector, and on developing Québec and Canadian society. Neither the concept of social economy nor that of social economy initiatives is well known in Canada. While drawing a portrait of the social economy in England, Belgium, or France may not be particularly problematic, this is not true of Canada. Various studies have allowed us to describe several aspects of the social economy, especially the cooperative economy, the not-for-profit sector, and community economic development initiatives. On the other hand, we are unable to create a unified portrait of the social economy in Canada. There is no consensual definition of the term "social economy" among Canadian civil society groups. The definition requires further formulation. Canadian universities, via the six regional centres and the Centre national de recherche partenariale en économie sociale, could of course take an active part in this endeavour.

The ignorance surrounding Canada's social economy also applies to other countries and continents. Consequently, it is important on the one hand to support the development of social economy research structures in Canada, and on the other hand to link them up with those existing elsewhere. In this way, we can bring out their particular characteristics and their points of convergence.

The second issue is theoretical. It deals with the role played by the social economy in mediating relationships between the economic and social spheres (Lévesque, Bourque, & Forgues, 2001). This involves demonstrating the social economy's influence in developing methods for regulating society. The social economy has an impact on political environments and economic conditions wherever there is growing cooperation between the state (or the market) and civil society to mobilize a group of resources in an innovative way. It is important to evaluate both the specific contribution of the social economy to defining or redefining public policy and the impact of this economy on the Canadian development model. Over the last 10 years, some consideration has been given to these issues, although the effort has been half-hearted.

Partnerships need to consider the theoretical aspects of development approaches in modern societies whenever social, economic, environmental, and cultural objectives are involved. Some social economy actors have proposed extending the development model to include two new types of accounting: the environment (sustainable development; consideration given to ecological relationships) and culturality (interculturality and consideration given to cultural biodiversity law). This will involve considering the implications of these new cultural directions for the institutional system and the current world scene. These proposals involve new ways of living together.

The third research issue deals with the specific contribution of the social economy to territorial development, especially territories trying to come to grips with social and economic decay. Concretely, the issue speaks to the production of knowledge linked to the impact on community welfare of an expanding social economy.

The fourth research issue deals with the development of concrete policy instruments. The social economy is experiencing strong growth. This reality requires that we deepen our understanding of the mechanisms underlying social or collective entrepreneurship. Such entrepreneurship requires the introduction of tools and services to either strengthen existing social economy sectors or create integrated sectors, rather than sector branches, which are limited to market niches.

On this point, the actors' needs are clear. The survival and growth of social organizations and emerging collective enterprises will depend on cognitive advances in many fields, including those associated with democratic management, human resources development, work relations and conditions, new forms of funding, and evaluating the results and impacts of the social economy. Research is needed on the democratic functioning and ethical foundations of this economy. It must be analysed from the standpoint of collective management, social responsibility, and ethics, and in terms of community relationships and local development.

Conclusion

Partnership research raises key questions about the way knowledge is created, its impact on erudite supporters of this research, and science in general.

In essence, traditional portrayals of the production of scholarly knowledge associate this production with the work of a sage, a philosopher, or a major thinker who brings together important information, organizes summaries of a lesser order, and, above all, makes sense of reality. As a rule, the production of key fundamental knowledge – that is, the type of knowledge that allows us to fundamentally reorganize our perceptions, such as theories on the origin of the universe, the nature of collective action, or cybernetics, is presented as the work of enlightened individuals, specialists who develop a number of superlative intellectual abilities and skills. It thus involves special actors, trained in science and essentially striving to develop the latter.

A less traditional portrayal of the production of knowledge links the act of production to all individuals developing their intellectual abilities to think about reality. All actors in a society can participate in this process as long as they follow up their thinking with action. Not all actors who do this will necessarily receive recognition for their contribution, since they will not automatically have access to the mechanisms that make possible the dissemination of their ideas, nor will they have all the skills required to explain the new knowledge they have generated. Lastly, since their ideas may not circulate widely, or not at all, these individuals will not find it easy to substantiate their hypotheses or explanations textually – that is, to submit them for evaluation by the scientific or scholarly community.

The significance of partnership research becomes clear when one considers that the process of producing knowledge is a collective one that brings together a variety of actors and topics in specific locations over clearly defined periods. The work of Berger and Luckmann (1966) on the social construction of reality has allowed us to open up the discussion on the complex process of producing knowledge. The work of Latour and Woolgar (1988) and that of Callon (1992) has continued this line of thought by demonstrating how the research process brings together a variety of actors and topics; together, they form a testing ground and generate new knowledge. The essential point is to depersonalize and de-identify the process of knowledge production. Of course, we might also have to rely on the work of major thinkers, after the fashion of Amartya Sen's work (2000a, 2000b) or that of Saskia Sassen (2006). At the same time, we must establish cooperative think tanks, environments for intervention, and laboratories for analytical thinking and interpretation to provide recognition for and support the growing intellectual contribution of thinkers other than professionals (scientists and scholars).

Does this mean there is no longer a place for the traditional, more linear form of knowledge production? Not at all, since this realm has every reason to exist. It is important, however, to open up the realm of science to other players – intellectuals whose primary occupation does not consist of scholarly research. The act of taking into account the intellectual wealth of non-scientific actors and establishing mechanisms for joint knowledge creation constitutes a significant qualitative leap.

The preceding discussion on partnership research has allowed us to demonstrate the advantages of producing knowledge via the partnership method. The central argument deals with the potential for mobilizing knowledge and resources – a potential beyond the purview of traditional research. Yet what are the dangers associated with this outward-looking attitude?

The first danger is linked to the central role researchers must play in systems for joint knowledge creation. This role can simultaneously involve leadership, interpretation, mediation, determining non-negotiability, listening ability, and modesty:

- Leadership is needed to ensure that the research is carried out professionally, that the joint research does not lose its objectivity, and that there is always a place for criticism.
- Interpretation is needed to ensure that communication amongst the stakeholders is intelligible.
- Mediation facilitates the working out of compromises and negotiation.
- Non-negotiability refers to situations in which stakeholders retreat to consult amongst themselves; in such cases, the researcher must know when to terminate joint research activities.
- The ability to listen facilitates inclusion of what, at first sight, might seem to disconcert or threaten: Thus, it is important to remain open to criticism and alternative thinking.
- Modesty must be practised, in recognition of the fact that individuals who are not researchers may provide fresh insights and new knowledge.

If the researchers are unable to properly fulfil these roles, the process can easily veer off in different directions. At one extreme, partners may end up playing only a token role, by participating in a research process completely controlled by the researchers. At the other extreme, the researchers may be criticized by actors who control the subject matter and process information so that the knowledge created ends up dealing with very limited and inadequately collectivized interests.

The second danger is linked to the clear responsibility of the non-academic actors to learn the basics of university research culture when they accept to work in partnership. That said, the acculturation must work both ways. It is less likely to occur among non-scholars who have experienced contractual relationships. Consequently, the risk that the partnership research will exploit the research is related to the risk that the actors will use the partnership for highly specialized projects, meeting very specific needs. If the research deals with sensitive issues, they could ask to be excluded from this particular research activity. For other types of research, they could proceed differently: Some could work with individual researchers on a contractual basis, or, where control over the information is an important consideration, could work with consulting firms.

There are also three major challenges in ensuring that partnership research in social economy fully develops its potential.

The first challenge is to circulate the partnership research model and ensure that it receives recognition. The ARUC-ÉS and RQRP-ÉS research consortium is made up of a group of researchers whose work is often undervalued because it fails to meet the normative assessment criteria for scholarly creation. There is more prestige in organizing an international symposium consisting of academic researchers who are leaders in their field than one consisting of community actors. Similarly, research circles place greater value on publications submitted to peer-reviewed journals than on publications that popularize knowledge. In addition, there is a need to innovate in the academic area of cognitive production; this will allow the institutional arrangements of the state, private sector and social sphere – all of which shape the production and circulation of scholarly knowledge – to adapt to the world of partnership research. This involves reviewing the very foundations of research funding to facilitate the establishment of new types of research networks and partnerships. It also suggests a need to allocate resource envelopes with a view to allowing researchers to focus more on knowledge transfer. On this point, the current mindset is limited to a linear logic in which research requirements lead to a research activity, whose results are then published. Publication is viewed as a consumer good. A new mindset, relying on the circularity of the process and interactivity among stakeholders occurring at every stage of the process, would ensure a genuine and more dynamic transfer of knowledge.

The second challenge is to further develop partnership processes involving the co-management and circulation of research whenever it brings researchers and practitioners together. On the one hand, it entails the ability to involve practitioners in a qualitative problematization of research questions and methodological organization of data production, as well as in resulting data management analyses. Consequently, it involves transmitting the scholarly culture to practitioners. The culture is based essentially on linking together elements of empirical observation, critical analysis, and theoretical models. On the other hand, it entails explaining to researchers the culture of "emergency response," which constitutes an everyday reality of social players. Transmitting this strategic intervention culture raises the question of how researchers need to deal with subjectivity: how far to go, which boundaries to cross or not cross, and, above all, which safeguards to employ to ensure the scientific character of the research.

The third and final challenge is of a cognitive nature. It is difficult for scientific research to economize on its own assessment. How does investing in partnership research in social economy create knowledge that is appropriate to the world in which we live? Stated differently, science also has a work agenda – one with a mission whose contours are ill defined. The research community is a sector that must simultaneously endeavour to develop both itself and humanity. Partnership research in the social economy is pursuing a plan to make reality more transparent by giving it concrete expression, and to narrow the gap between subjective and objective truth. Thus, collaboration with other intellectuals must allow the research community to better affirm and present the role it plays – or is called upon to play – and the status it enjoys and seeks to develop in society.

NOTES

1 For an exhaustive English-language bibliography on university-community partnerships, see the article by Tracy Soska at: www.acosa.org/bib_soska.pdf. For an annotated bibliography including references (names and addresses and uploading locations) for each annotated entry, see the document created jointly by the Milwaukee Idea, University of Wisconsin–Milwaukee, and the Center for Healthy Communities, Department of Family and Community Medicine, Medical College of Wisconsin: www.uwm.edu/MilwaukeeIdea/publications/revised_amy_biblio.pdf.

2 See the network's website: http://www.livingknowledge.org/livingknowledge.

3 OCBR: www.uvic.ca/ocbr.

4 The golden age of cooperation occurred between 1930 and 1945. In that period, the number of cooperatives grew immensely and several new sectors emerged. After 1945, the process of diversification would proceed very slowly, and growth in the sector generally would be slow.

5 In 1946, there were about 3,000 not-for-profit associations. This number grew to 9,300 organizations in 1966, 34,000 in 1988, and 46,000 in 2003 (Fontan, 1992, p. 131; Imagine Canada, 2005; Bussières et al, 2006).

6 CIRIEC-Canada: http://www.ciriec.uqam.ca.

7 IRECUS: http://www.usherbrooke.ca/irecus.

8 CIRIEC International: http://www.ciriec.ulg.ac.be.

9 CIRIEC International is a European organization created in 1947 by Professor Edgard Milhaud, who taught political economy at the Université de Genève.

10 It was renamed Concordia University in 1974. The university has its origins in the popular education and training programs launched by the Montréal YMCA when it was created in 1851.

11 *Economie et Solidarités* is the journal of CIRIEC-Canada.

12 UniRcoops: http://www.unircoop.org.

13 Chaire Desjardins de coopération et développement du milieu: http://acpcol01.usherbrooke.ca/prod/recherche/USherbAdminweb.nsf/ContenuDesjardins/accueil?OpenDocument.

14 Desjardins Centre for Studies in Management of Financial Services Cooperatives: http://preprod.centredesjardins.hec.ca.

15 These funds have now merged within the Fonds québécois de recherche sur la société et la culture (FQRSC).

16 Chaire de coopération Guy-Bernier: http://www.er.uqam.ca/nobel/ccgb/index.html.

17 CRISES: http://www.crises.uqam.ca.

18 LAREPPS: http://www.larepps.uqam.ca/Page/default.aspx.

19 CRDC-GERIS: http://www.uqo.ca/crdc-geris.

20 Chantier de l'économie sociale: http://www.chantier.qc.ca.

21 ARUC-ÉS: http://www.aruc-es.uqam.ca.

22 Observatoire en économie sociale et en développement régional: http://www4.uqo.ca/observer.

23 CERIS: http://www.uqo.ca/crdc-geris.

24 Chaire responsabilité sociale et développement durable: http://www.ceh.uqam.ca.

25 Chaire de recherche du Canada en économie sociale: http://www.chaire.ecosoc.uqam.ca.

26 RQRP-ÉS: http://www.aruc-es.uqam.ca.

27 Canadian Social Economy Hub (CSEHub): http://www.socialeconomyhub.ca/?q=fr. The Internet addresses of the six regional centres in Canada are available at the CCÉS page.

28 "Scientific knowledge is knowledge that has been legitimated and validated through a process of systematic scientific research. The internal dynamics of science involves improving knowledge. Other forms of knowledge (experiential knowledge) also allow for action, but they are not recognized as having the same properties in terms of their reliability or the generality of their nature. Experiential knowledge can be traditional or modern. It is frequently specific to a local context and is

acquired through individual and collective learning. Experiential knowledge is rarely validated or tested systematically. Nonetheless, it is dynamic and used by everyone in our daily lives. This knowledge must not be confused with a pseudo-science that is very static (that changes solely in conflict with systematic science) and is of very benefit to society" (Foray, 2003, p. 2).

REFERENCES

Allaire, J.B.A. (1919). Catéchisme des sociétés coopératives agricoles du Québec. *La Tribune*. Saint-Hyacinthe.

Angers, F.A. (1970). Y a-t-il une théorie économique de la coopération? *Revue du CIRIEC, 3*(2).

Barbeau, V. (1940). Le coopératisme: Une solution au problème économique et social de notre province. *L'Actualite Economique, 16*, 1–20.

Benson, L., & Harkavy, I. (2000). Higher education's Third Revolution: The emergence of the democratic cosmopolitan civic university. *Cityscape, A Journal of Policy Development and Research, 5*(1): 47–57.

Berger, P.L., & Luckmann, T. (1966). *The social construction of reality*. New York: Doubleday.

Bussières, D., Chartrand, S., Cucumel, G., et al. (2006). *Le secteur sans but lucratif et bénévole du Québec, Faits saillants régionaux de l'Enquête nationale auprès des organismes à but non lucratif et bénévoles*. Toronto: Imagine Canada & Alliance de recherche universités-communautés en économie sociale.

Bussières, D., & Fontan, J.M. (2005). L'expérience de recherche de l'Alliance de recherche universités-communautés en économie sociale. In J.M. Fontan (Ed.), *L'économie sociale: Un bilan des recherches et des pratiques au Québec. Interventions économiques* (32). Accessed 10 July 2011. www.teluq.uquebec.ca/interventionseconomiques

Callon, M. (1992). Sociologie des sciences et économie du changement technique: L'irrésistible montée des réseaux technico-économiques. In *Les réseaux que la raison ignore* (pp. 53–78). Paris: L'Harmattan.

Checkoway, B. (2001). Renewing the Civic Mission of the American Research University. *The Journal of Higher Education, 72*(2 sp), 125–47. http://dx.doi.org/10.2307/2649319

Commission Européenne. (Ed.). (2004). *Les boutiques de sciences, les connaissances au service de la communauté*. Brussels: Commission Européene. Accessed 10 July 2011. http://ec.europa.eu/research/science-society/pdf/science_shop_fr.pdf

Commission européenne. (Ed.). (2005). *Sensibilisation à la science – Les "science shops."* Brussels: Commission Européene. Accessed 16 June 2011. http://ec.europa.eu/research/science-society/scientific-awareness/shops_fr.html

D'Amours, M. (2006). *L'économie sociale au Québec, cadre théorique, histoire, réalités et défis.* Montréal: Éditions Saint-Martin.

Déchêne Mingy, C., & Montplaisir, C. (1981). *Histoire du mouvement coopératif au Québec.* Québec: Ministère des institutions financières et coopératives.

Desroche, H. (1973). *Sociologie de l'espérance.* Paris: Calmann Lévy.

Desroche, H. (1978). *Education permanente et créativités solidaires: Lettres ouvertes sur une utopie d'université hors les murs (Apprentissage 2).* Paris: Ed. Ouvrières.

EU Science and Society. *Living knowledge: The international science shop network.* Accessed 22 April 2012. http://www.livingknowledge.org/livingknowledge

Fitzgerald, H.E. (2005). Connecting knowledge to serve society, scholarship focused outreach and engagement. PPT presentation, Michigan State University.

Foisy-Geoffroy, D. (2001). *Esdras Minville (1896–1975).* Québec: Université Laval. Accessed 16 June 2011. http://agora.ulaval.ca/~dofog1/

Fontan, J.M. (1992). *Les corporations de développement économique communautaire montréalaises: Du développement économique communautaire au développement local de l'économie.* Montréal: Doctoral thesis, Department of Sociology, Université de Montréal.

Fontan, J.M. (2000). De l'intellectuel critique au professionnel de service, radioscopie de l'universitaire engage. *Cahiers de Recherche Sociologique,* (34), 79–97.

Fontan, J.M. (2006). La recherche partenariale en économie sociale au Québec. *Horizons, 8*(2), 16–21.

Foray, D. (2003). Savoir et information. In *Optimiser le savoir dans le cadre de la société de l'information.* Paris: Conseil international des sciences sociales.

Fournier, M. (1972). De l'influence de la sociologie française au Québec. *Revue Francaise de Sociologie, 13,* 630–65. http://dx.doi.org/10.2307/3320723

Hackney, S. (1994). Reinventing the American university: Toward a university system for the 21st century. *Universities and Community Schools, 4*(1–2), 9–11.

Imagine Canada. (2005). *Le secteur sans but lucratif et bénévole au Québec, National survey on not-for-profit and voluntary organizations.* Accessed 10 July 2011. www.imaginecanada.ca

Lanctôt, M. (1872). *L'association du capital et du travail.* Montréal: J. Wilson.

Larose, C. (1991–92). *Jalons de l'histoire de l'éducation des adultes au Québec.* Cité éducative.

Latour, B., & Woolgar, S. (1988). *La vie de laboratoire: La production des faits scientifiques.* Paris: La Découverte.

Leclerc, A. (1982). *Les doctrines coopératives en Europe et au Canada.* Sherbrooke: IRECUS.

Lépine, A.T. (1887). *Explications de la déclaration des principes de l'Ordre des Chevaliers du Travail.* Montréal: Imprimerie du Trait-d'Union.

Lévesque, B., Bourque, G., & Forgues, E. (2001). *La nouvelle sociologie économique.* Paris: Desclée de Brouwer.

Lévesque, B., & Malo, M.C. (1991). Quel avenir pour la recherche universitaire sur les cooperatives: Une institutionnalisation fragile. *Revue des études coopératives, mutualistes et associatives, 39*(242): 87–99.

Lévesque, B., & Malo, M.C. (1995). Les études sur les coopératives: Base de données bibliographiques, centres de recherche universitaires. In M.-T. Séguin (Ed.), *Pratiques coopératives et mutations sociales* (pp. 246–67). Paris, L'Harmattan.

Louard, B. (1944). L'élément féminin dans les coopératives de consommation. In C.G.C. (Ed.), *Inventaire du mouvement cooperative* (pp. 241–2). Québec: CSC.

Lotz, J. (2005). *The humble giant: Moses Coady, Canada's rural revolutionary.* Ottawa: Novalis.

Mayfield, L., & Lucas, E.P. (2000). Mutual awareness, mutual respect: The community and the university interact. *Cityscape: A Journal of Policy Development and Research, 5*(1): 173–84.

McGraw, D. (1978). *Le développement des groupes populaires à Montréal (1963–1973).* Montréal: Albert St-Martin.

Neubauer, C. (2002). *Quelques réflexions autour de la notion de 'science citoyenne', l'exemple des boutiques de sciences aux Pays-Bas.* Paris: DESS CISTEM Paris VII.

Palard, J. (2005). Henri Desroche et ses réseaux québécois: Entre théorie de l'utopie et pratiques maïeuticiennes. In G. Fabre & P. Sabourin (Eds.), Le Québec et l'internationalisation des sciences sociales. *Sociologie et sociétés, 37* (2).

Pénault, H., & Senécal, F. (1982). *L'éducation des adultes au Québec depuis 1850: Points de repère, annexe 1.* Québec: Commission d'étude sur la formation des adultes.

Roby, Y. (1964). *A. Desjardins et les Caisses populaires, 1854–1920.* Montréal: Fidès.

Sassen, S. (2006). *Cities in a world economy.* Thousand Oaks: Pine Forge Press.

Sen, A. (2000a). *Repenser l'inégalité.* Paris: Seuil.

Sen, A. (2000b). *Un nouveau modèle économique.* Paris: Odile Jacob.

Soska, T.M., & Johnson Butterfield, A.K. (2005). *University-community partnerships: Universities in civic engagement.* Binghamton: The Haworth Press.

Soska, T. (2005). *University-community partnership bibliography.* Pittsburgh. Accessed 16 June 2011. http://www.acosa.org/bib_soska.pdf

Sutton, L. (2007a). *Guide de la recherche partenariale (Modèle consortium québécois de recherche partenariale en économie sociale).* Montréal: Alliance de recherche universités-communautés en économie sociale.

Sutton, L. (2007b). *Guide de la valorisation de la recherche partenariale (Modèle consortium québécois de recherche partenariale en économie sociale).* Montréal: Alliance de recherche universités-communautés en économie sociale.

Université du Québec à Rimouski. (1976). *L'opération CRAEQ (Coopérative de recherche-action de l'Est du Québec).* Québec: UQAR.

Université de Sherbrooke. (2009). *Bilan du siècle (Faculté des lettres et sciences humaines).* Accessed 16 June 2011. http://www.bilan.usherb.ca/bilan/pages/evenements/178.html

Vidal, A., Nye, N., Walker, C., Manjarrez, C., & Romanik, C. (2002). *Lessons from the Community Outreach Partnership Center Program.* Washington: The Urban Institute. Accessed 10 July 2011. www.oup.org/files/pubs/lessons_learned.pdf

Walshok, M. (1995). *Knowledge without boundaries: What America's research universities can do for the economy, the workplace and the community.* San Francisco: Jossey-Bass.

Weiner, A. (1970). *Pointe St. Charles: Rapport préliminaire de la situation économique.* Institut Parallèle, Pointe-St-Charles.

Wiewel, W., & Broski, D. (1997). University involvement in the community: Developing a partnership model. *Renaissance, University of Northern Iowa, 1* (1). Accessed 10 July 2011. http://www.qub.ac.uk/ep/research/cu2/data/bib_wiewel-broski_university-involvement.pdf

Wilson, D. (2004). Key features of successful university-community partnerships. In Pew Partnership (Ed.), *New directions in civic engagement: University Avenue meets Main Street.* Richmond: University of Richmond, Pew Partnership for Civic Change.

3 Governance and the Associative Sector of the Social Economy: The Partnership between the State and Civil Society in Question

LUC DANCAUSE AND RICHARD MORIN

Introduction

As noted in Chapter 1, the renewed interest in the social economy during the 1970s reflected civil society's reaction to the economic crisis of the times and to the challenges it posed to the welfare state. Projects emerged to meet new social needs and solve new social problems, namely social exclusion and new forms of poverty, within the social economy's associative (non-profit) sector. Associations cannot rely only on their own resources to produce goods and services. The state was experiencing a budgetary crisis, however, and a challenge to its overly centralized approach, and thus decided to review the way it was managing its affairs. It was also called upon to recognize and support non-profit organizations.[1] The upshot was that a new way of managing problems was established, one that linked the state to civil society organizations. The concept of governance evokes this form of public affairs management: it involves negotiation and cooperation between the state and several other actors, rather than simply state intervention alone, in an effort to redefine public policy. Governance constitutes a central issue for the social economy's associative sector inasmuch as the growth of the latter depends on recognition and support by the state, within a partnership based on the contribution and cooperation of each stakeholder.

In this chapter, we will deal, first, with the concepts of governance and partnership. We will then discuss the relationship between the social economy's associative sector and the state, using examples from outside of Québec, particularly in English-speaking Canada, the United

States, the United Kingdom and France. Lastly, we will examine the case of Québec. We first briefly look at the governance model employed in Québec (a theme that is explored in more depth in Chapter 4). We then highlight several issues facing the relationships between the non-profit sector and the state, as more and more of them take the form of partnerships. This chapter essentially deals with the associative sector of the social economy and not with mutual societies and cooperatives, both of which belong to the social economy and have a different type of relationship with the state.

The Theoretical Bearings

The concept of governance, which has been widely used in the social sciences since the early 1990s, is associated with the new forms of public policy restructuring the modern states that are opening up to input from market forces and civil society so as to provide services and regulate socio-economic processes. For Hamel and Jouve (2006, p. 35), "governance refers to the new mechanisms and processes in which public policy is formulated through cooperation between actors and institutions, and the mutualization of their resources and legitimacy" (Translator's translation [TT]). Thus, the concept is not far removed from that of partnership, which refers to a process of decision-making and action, and that is based on input from various partners who recognize each other, cooperate and invest resources in a common project. The recent history of the social economy in Québec shows many examples of partnerships, as examined in Chapter 1.

Governance

The contemporary concept of governance refers to an empirical phenomenon affecting forms of state intervention and the way the state is being transformed. It also stems from a new theoretical perspective that helps us to understand social system coordination processes, as well as the role of the state in these processes (Enjolras, 2005b). Thus, the concept is employed to better understand "the introduction of new methods for developing negotiation-based public policies, as well as new ways of implementing these policies, especially through partnerships" (Canet, 2004, p. 1; TT). The concept[2] allows us to rethink relationships among various economic, political, and social actors, as well as forms of public intervention. Its point of departure is that the state no longer plays the same role as in the past, while its critical feature is the nature of the links among the actors (Stocker, 1998). Hamel & Jouve (2006) also correctly note the ideological role played by governance, which has served to justify and legitimize the transition from Keynesianism to neo-liberalism.

It is possible to link the increasingly widespread use of the governance concept with the fact that the state has lost its central role in the formulation of public policy. This has occurred on three levels: international relations, economic regulation, and state relations with local powers (Canet, 2004). Some see the state as just one of several actors, acting in concert with other market and civil society partners (Duchastel & Canet, 2004). In terms of public policy and state regulation, hierarchical, vertical, and coercive relationships have gradually been replaced by horizontal relationships, incentives, negotiation, and co-operation, involving a variety of economic and social actors (Canet, 2004; Eme 2005; Lévesque, 2001). In the areas of economic development and social development (the social economy is located at the intersection of the two) the state no longer plays the leading role. It is, rather, a partner wielding numerous regulatory, human, and financial resources.

Partnership

The concept of governance is closely connected to that of partnership. Enjolras (2005b, p. 67) has also introduced the concept of "partnership governance," which suggests institutional arrangements in which the role of the government "is not one of a hierarchical, commanding authority in charge, but one of a facilitator who exercises leadership and collaborates as a partner within a network of actors" (TT). For Dommergues (1989, p. 242), partnership refers to "new forms of cooperation between the public sector and the private sector; between employers and work forms; universities and the business sector; and institutional actors and third sector actors" (TT). The partnership involves a relationship between parties who recognize and respect their respective contributions to a project. That said, the parties are not necessarily cast in the same mould. They may differ by culture, mission, operating methods, activities, resources, and interests (Caillouette, 2001; René & Gervais, 2001; Panet-Raymond & Bourque, 1991). Partnership relationships are characterized not only by collaboration but also by conflict, which, in the search for joint action, calls for negotiation among stakeholders.

Partnership can be asymmetric, since the actors do not have the same resources, or hierarchical, since one of the partners can exploit the power relationship to his or her advantage or for its private purpose (Lévesque & Mager, 1992). However, in a real partnership, each partner makes a contribution, in one form or another, which is recognized by the other partner, tries to benefit from the pooling of the various partners' resources, and agrees to deal with conflict by negotiating compromises (Dommergues, 1988). Thus, partnerships are different from strategic alliances because they constitute more than the sum of individual economic interests. Partnerships generate collective learning and a hybridization of the logics of the various actors involved (Bouchard, 2006).

The social economy, and especially its associative sector, refers to a form of partnership between the state and civil society (represented by the non-profit sector) that is designed to meet social needs. The two parties do not necessarily carry equal weight and their relationship may vary from one country to another, depending on, among other things, the degree of openness of the state and the dynamism of the civil society in the country in question. This explains our interest in the way the state and civil society interrelate, on matters involving the social economy, in various national contexts.

Governance and the Social Economy: Beyond Québec

A review of the historical trajectories and theoretical constructions of the social economy in Europe and Canada have been examined by Laville, Lévesque, and Mendell (2005). It reveals this sector's diversity from country to country:

> While cooperatives and mutual societies may be formed from the same mould as associations, countries like the United Kingdom have lost sight of this common origin. This explains why these countries refer not to the social economy but to the third sector, which consists of non-profit organizations (NPOs). In other words, the third sector consists only of non-profit associations and excludes both mutual societies and cooperatives; this approach is dominant in Anglo-Saxon countries. Consequently, not everyone in Europe refers to the social economy, a term used primarily in French-speaking countries. (Ibid., p. 8; TT)

Thus, the social economy's status and role vary from one country to another (for Europe, see also Chaves & Monzon, 2007) and, in Canada, even from one province to another. Various interpretations can be made of the particular contribution of the social economy, depending on the governance mode (Côté, 2003). In a liberal (or neo-liberal) mode, where the state holds a minimal role (laissez-faire), the social economy is seen as being instrumental to economic development. In a social-statist mode, where the state's intervention is institutionalized, the social economy strictly complements the public sector. In a partnership mode, the state takes an enabling role and supports the social economy, with the objective of democratizing the public services and opening their governance to participation from the civil society (see Chapter 4).

As a result, the relationship between civil society and the state in the area of social economy differs by country, giving rise to various models of governance. An examination of recent public policies outside of Québec will enable us to highlight the distinctiveness of the "Québec model," as well as general trends at the international level.

English Canada

The term "social economy" is not used to the same degree in different regions of the country, and is hardly used at all in English Canada. In fact, English Canada has preferred to employ terms such as "third sector," "civil society," and "volunteer work" (Leduc Browne, 2000; Laville, Lévesque, & Mendell, 2005). However, in 2004, the Government of Canada committed itself to promoting the "social economy," and in 2005 the federal Cabinet ratified a "social economy" pilot project "to implement targeted programs that would strengthen the ability of communities to develop social economy activities" (LeBlanc, Zeesman, & Halliwell, 2006, p. 4). Thus, in Canada the concept of social economy has only recently been institutionalized, and it lasted only for a very short while. The Conservative government, in power since 2006, has considerably reduced government support to these types of activities, preferring to call them "community development."

However named, the growing importance of the social economy concept in Canada can be traced to the fact that during the 1990s the federal and provincial governments decreased their expenses in order to lower their deficits. Thus, they sought alternative, less costly ways of providing services ("alternative service delivery") (Quarter, 2000). Nevertheless, Quarter (2000, p. 63) states, though without dealing directly with governance or partnership issues in the social economy, that, "over the past decade the neo-conservative agenda has eroded our social fabric and weakened, not strengthened, social economy organizations that depend upon government programs."

In Canada, the issue of partnerships between the state and the volunteer sector may be broached in the broader context of neo-liberal policy, the downsizing of the welfare state and a form of governance that some authors have described as the "new contracting regime," in which non-profit organizations (NPOs) end up serving as an alternative "for the unionized, better-paid public service" (Leduc Browne, 2000, p. 67). Although its contractual frameworks may benefit both parties participating in this type of governance, they often provide a way for governments to exercise greater control over the volunteer sector. They encourage organizations in this sector to professionalize and bureaucratize, and to abandon putting forward their claims, which are then usually replaced by service delivery (ibid.). The Ontario Works plan, advanced by the government of Ontario in the second half of the 1990s, is a good example of how NPOs are used in this way. Structured within a "workfare" perspective, the plan requires employable welfare recipients to work for a community project, failing which their benefits are cut off. Thus, the government subcontracts to volunteer organizations to provide work for these beneficiaries and report on their attendance. The organizations are encouraged to assume a role that may be characterized as "police workfare" (ibid., p. 70). They are reluctant to play this role, however: On the one hand, they wish to avoid playing into the hands of a government dealing with welfare beneficiaries; on the other hand, they need financial resources from this government. Thus, the partnership is under strain: The relations between the state and the volunteer sector are marked not only by cooperation and collaboration, but also by conflict and coercion (ibid.).

The question of partnerships between the state and civil society, as mediated by the social economy, may also be considered within the framework of progressive general policies, such as the one advanced in the early 2000s by the New Democratic Party government of Manitoba. The social economy concept is still not used very much in this province. Instead, the term "community economic development" (CED) is employed to refer to activities aiming for "broader social inclusion and greater socio-economic equity" (McKinnon, 2006, p. 26; TT). In 2001, the government of Manitoba adopted the CED Policy Framework. Its overall policy includes a definition of the objectives and principles underlying the CED approach in Manitoba, and its provincial departments must take them into consideration. These objectives and principles reflect those of the CED stakeholders who played a role in developing them. However, as there is no department in charge of this policy and no specific budget allocated for its implementation, few departments have introduced a CED policy and "within the government, there are still very few individuals familiar with the CED perspective, while those who are familiar with and support the approach do not have the power to use it to reshape policies and programs" (ibid., p. 28; TT).

The United States

Historically, the government of the United States has tended to avoid involvement in the creation of social services. It has relied to a great extent on non-profit organizations to provide these types of services. This way of responding to collective needs was at first based on pragmatic considerations, and then was gradually established on the basis of a conservative principle – non-intervention by the state (Salamon, 1997). Furthermore, during the period in which the American government was more interventionist, namely during the era of President Roosevelt's New Deal in the 1930s up until the rise to power of President Reagan in the 1980s, the non-profit sector did not figure prominently in political discourse. Nonetheless, in the 1960s and 1970s, this sector received substantial government funding, which gave rise to "a massive partnership between government at all levels and private non profit organizations that vastly extended the size and scope of non profit action" (ibid., p. 305). It was under the aegis of the Reagan and Bush-senior regimes that voluntary work rose to the top of the political agenda, under the pretext of "returning government to the people." This "concealed industrial deregulation, tax breaks for businesses, and the reduction in services and social programs intended for the very poor or persons of more modest means" (Rifkin, 1996, p. 330; TT).

Thus, in the area of social services, the United States has a long tradition of partnership between the federal government, state governments, municipalities, and social enterprises,[3] which have received financial support from these various levels of government (Martin, 2004). The form of partnership in the United States does not derive primarily from top-down public policy, but from adapting to the dynamism of the community sector, to hostility expressed towards bureaucratic government, and to the half-hearted support of the population to the services provided by the welfare state (Salamon, 1990). However, in the United States, as elsewhere, the crisis of the welfare state had a significant impact on the state-NPO partnership (Gidron, Kramer, & Salamon, 1992). In the 1980s, the American government, notwithstanding its favourable views regarding the volunteer sector, substantially reduced its financial support to non-profit organizations and increased its requirements in the area of accountability (Salamon, 1997).

At this point, another financial backer of NPOs began to grow in importance: major private foundations (Martin, 2004). Although they claimed that they did not intrude in community development, these organizations usually did more than simply respond to local demand. The differences separating the power of foundations and that of community organizations resulted in a hierarchical relationship in which foundations clearly had the most influence in decision-making, project selection, and methods of implementation (ibid.). At the same time, the NPOs increasingly abandoned activism in favour of providing personal services for a carefully targeted clientele with the means to acquire these services. A corollary of this new situation was that NPOs increasingly found themselves in direct competition with private-sector businesses.

The public sector continues to be the most important source of funding for the community sector. The relationship between these two sectors is changing, however (Salamon, 1997). An important government reform introduced in 1996 (National Welfare Reform Legislation and Policies), which transferred social responsibilities to sub-national levels of government, had a direct impact on this relationship. The relationship was contractual, which meant that the authorities would have new and more complex expectations towards NPOs. For example, welfare recipients would now have to participate in workfare programs providing services to the community (Austin, 2003).

NPOs performing service contracts became key actors in the operations of public agencies responsible for social services. According to Austin (2003, p. 103), "the relationship is more of a partnership than a traditional 'low-bid contract service provider.'" However, continues the author, "it is not clear how effectively these newly structured partnerships will be in addressing the shared goals of the collaborators" (ibid.). NPOs benefit from assignments in social services, especially because these assignments increase NPO resources and legitimacy; this in turn has a positive effect on their reputation in the community and on their ability to obtain additional resources. The relationship also has some disadvantages: inadequate financial resources to meet demand; pressures to professionalize; and the fact that the services provided do not always correspond to the needs of the community or to the historical mission of the organization. We may well ask to what extent this partnership constitutes real collaboration between public authorities and NPOs, or is it simply a marriage of convenience? (ibid.)

President Obama, at the beginning of his administration, made two important moves regarding the community sector: First, the amounts invested in the Community Finance Development Institutions that support community development initiatives were doubled (Neamtan, 2009); second, he created, within the White House, the Office of Social Innovation and Civic Participation, which uses new government investments as way to obtain more funds from foundations, businesses, and individual donors in order to finance non-profit organizations' projects, but with a heavy emphasis on measuring results (Perry, 2009).

The United Kingdom

In the United Kingdom, the Conservative government of the 1980s retreated from public services and gave greater prestige to the "voluntary sector," a term already used more widely than "social economy" (Moulaert & Ailenei, 2005). One immediate consequence of this move was greater involvement in these services on the part of NPOs, whose government funding (subsidies and service contracts) would more than double in the area of supply of services linked to employment, health, and social problems. However, this state of affairs stirred up debate on the role of the voluntary sector and its relationship with the government, because the sector's independence was questioned (Plowden, 2003).

When the Labour Party came to power in 1997, it promoted the voluntary sector without hesitation, judging that this sector's organizations had a comparative advantage over governmental agencies. However, it also saw its support as reflecting a partnership, which from that point forward was intended to characterize relations between the state and this sector (ibid.; Craig & Manthorpe, 2005). As Amin notes (2006), the "new governance in the social sphere," part of the approach promoted as the so-called Third Way, which sought to differentiate itself from approaches employed by previous Conservative governments, was based on this form of partnership with "social economy organizations." The state, which considered the voluntary sector (via the latter's development of social capital and citizen involvement) to be a key factor in strengthening social cohesion at the local level (Fyfe, 2005), sought to give it a broader role in producing services but continued to control the rules governing this role.

The enhanced status of the third sector through the establishment of partnerships was part of a trend in local government reform throughout the United Kingdom. From 1995 to 1998, new municipal structures were set up to improve the effectiveness of local governments (Craig & Manthorpe, 1999). The role of these governments as service providers declined. Consequently, the supply of some services became the responsibility of forms of local governance in which municipalities served as facilitator for the voluntary sector. However, since some of the new municipal entities had been scaled down and thus had fewer resources, they were unable to fund community organizations (ibid.).

In 1998, following this restructuring, national compacts were signed in the four jurisdictions of the United Kingdom (Wales, Scotland, England, and Northern Ireland). Today, they constitute the centrepieces of the state's commitment to the third sector, and are intended to consolidate existing links with it. As well, local compacts concluded between local authorities and voluntary organizations constitute an important element in the government–community partnership. They do not have the force of law, but constitute statements of principles designed to guide the partners. They define the way the government will recognize and support the independence of the third sector while supporting it financially, in return for which third sector organizations must collaborate with the public sector in promoting the work, champion good management of financial resources, and recognize that the public funding is granted on the basis of furthering government priorities in the area of public policy (ibid.; Fyfe, 2005).

An evaluation of the various local compacts reveals that differences exist from one jurisdiction to the next. For example, in Wales, Scotland, and Northern Ireland – but not in England – greater emphasis is placed on government obligations towards local organizations (ibid.). Overall, these compacts have played a role in reorganizing the third sector into two major branches. Thus, some organizations are truly voluntary and separate from the government, whereas others maintain close ties to it by way of the compacts. Consequently, the latter are subject to numerous controls and rules, thereby casting doubt on their autonomy. Several of these organizations are aware that they are moving away from their traditional mission, namely, defending people's rights, developing the community, and representing citizens (Craig & Manthorpe,

1999). This explains why, over the last few years, some of them have increasingly been trying to have the nature of the relationship between the community sector and local governments clarified. Plowden (2003) calls attention to the fact that compacts have little concrete effect and that the issue remains one of changing the culture of the relationship between the government and the voluntary sector.

The National Compact was renewed in 2010 under the newly elected coalition of Conservatives and Liberal Democrats (*Compact Voice*, 2010). It was accompanied by a document entitled *The Compact Accountability and Transparency Guide* (Cabinet Office, 2010). The subtitle of this document, *Helping to build a stronger partnership between the Coalition Government and civil society organisations*, underlines the coalition's will to carry on the partnership with voluntary organizations, but as was done in recent years by the Obama administration in the United States, with more control from the state. Moreover, this new National Compact occurred in the context of the "Big Society" agenda of the Coalition Government, which "is about helping people to come together to improve their own lives. It's about putting more power in people's hands – a massive transfer of power from Whitehall to local communities" (Cabinet Office, 2011). And, just as the Obama administration created the Office of Social Innovation and Civic Participation within the White House, the Coalition Government put in place the Office for Civil Society within the Cabinet Office, which "works across government departments to translate the Big Society agenda into practical policies, provides support to voluntary and community organisations and is responsible for delivering a number of key Big Society programmes" (ibid.). This Big Society agenda goes along with massive cuts in governmental expenditures, including in the financing of voluntary and community organizations (National Council for Voluntary Organisations, 2011). On the one hand, the government promotes a stronger state–civil society partnership; on the other hand, the government reduces its financial investments in this partnership.

France

As Archambault notes (1995, p. 191), "France did not base the development of its social services on the principle of subsidiarity" (TT). Unlike the American government, the more "Jacobinical" French system would provide these services in a highly centralized way. The associative sector was consigned a stopgap role (ibid., p. 192) in the welfare state: taking over tangential social problems, such as loneliness, drug dependency, and potential delinquency. During the 1980s, however, two important policies changed the relationship between the state and the associative sector: decentralization and the establishment of contract-based links. Decentralization signified a rupture with the centralized approach, since new responsibilities were given to the municipalities and regions. As for the setting up of contract-based links, it constituted a new way for authorities to provide social services: namely, through service contracts with other actors. The latter included associations that now began competing for invitations to tender not only with other associations, but also with profit-oriented enterprises. To these two policies, we must add the creation in 1981 of the Délégation à l'économie sociale, which was given the role of facilitating dialogue and joint action in the social economy and giving an impetus to the sector, in consultation with the ministries involved. According to Maillard (2002), starting in the 1980s associations became "partners" in public policy by participating in consultative meetings at the local level. They did this by serving as a link between public institutions and sponsors of projects funded by these institutions. As with similar situations at the national level, however, the relationship between associations and government authorities was not one of perfect symmetry. It involved "one of the fundamental ambiguities in the rhetoric of partnership" that "overlooks possible asymmetries in the relationship of the two types of actors with regard to their highly dissimilar statuses, legitimacy and resources" (ibid., p. 60; TT).

According to Warin (2002, p. 35), the "associative partnership" is increasingly establishing itself in France as a "way of making public policy." Relationships between associations and governments are given official status and standardized. In the 1990s and early 2000s, the associative partnership became the focus of renewed interest. This was exemplified by the re-establishment of facilitating bodies, such as the Délégation interministérielle à l'innovation sociale et à l'économie sociale (DIISES), which was set up in 1995; the prime minister's formal recognition in 1999 of the Conférence permanente des coordinations associatives (CPCA), which represents associations; the holding in 1999 of the Premières Assises nationales de la vie associative (the first national conference on non-profit organizations and associations) under the auspices of Prime Minister Jospin; the introduction in 2000 of a Secrétariat d'État à l'Économie solidaire (secretary of state for the solidarity-based economy); the creation in 2000 of a circular on long-term pacts between the state and associations, concerning their objectives; and the signing in 2001 of a charter of common principles for the state and associations regarding their reciprocal commitments. In this way, there emerged a "process for supervising and standardizing the activities of associations" (Warin, 2002, p. 42; TT). For the socialist prime minister, associations "testified to the extraordinary vitality of the 'other economy' henceforth referred to as the social and solidarity-based economy" (Jospin, 2001, p. 8; TT). Thus, governments were prompted to "rely on associations to implement social policies targeting populations with difficulties" and "discover the economic potential represented by the social and solidarity-based economy as a whole, especially in the area of job creation" (Warin, 2002, p. 42; TT).

Associations became stakeholders in public policy through the frameworks, rules, and norms defined by governments, and by way of the services funded, for the most part, by the state. However, governments do not necessarily control the policies of associations, since the relationship is "dominated by constant tension, conflict and arrangements between actors driven by different logics" (Maillard, 2002, p. 63; TT). According to Eme (2005), while the authorities applying various forms of governance use civil society to implement social policy, civil society for its part utilizes the authorities to introduce social innovations. Warin (2004, p. 201–2) is in complete agreement, referring to a "trend toward exploitation and interdependence between public services and private initiatives (whether or not the latter are profit making)" (TT). That said, and following the position taking by Eme (2005), one cannot ignore the fact that while the actors in the social and solidarity-based economy help generate public policy, their independence is relative and their actions dependent on governments, which largely determine the rules of the game and control the purse strings.

Comparing Governance Models

We have examined three modes of governance vis-à-vis social economy: the neo-liberal, the social-statist, and the partnership. In Ontario, the United States, and the United Kingdom, where the term "social economy" is not generally used, the mode of state–civil society governance is neo-liberal: non-profit or voluntary organizations deliver social services while the intervention of the state in this sector is minimal, as in the United States, or becomes less important under Conservative governments (as in Ontario and the United Kingdom). Even though these governments are less interventionist, the organizations are mainly financed by government funds, more and more by contracts, and with greater control from the state. Unlike the Obama adminstration, which has increased its investments in the community sector, the new Coalition government in the United Kingdom has decreased its expenditures in this sector.

In France, the mode of governance vis-à-vis the social economy is social-statist, in which the state used to play an important role until the beginning of the 1980s, at which time a decentralization policy took effect. Nevertheless, the growing importance of associations is still mainly a top-down process in which the government mainly defines the rules and controls the financing.

In these four cases, the state is promoting a kind of partnership with civil society organizations. Thus, we could associate these cases with the partnership mode of governance, mentioned above, in which the state supports the social economy and aims to democratize public services and encourage greater participation from the civil society in public affairs. Government discourse would suggest that this is indeed true, but the reality is somewhat different from the discourse. In all four cases, tensions between the state and community organizations continue to affect the financing and the autonomy of these organizations.

Governance and the Social Economy in Québec

The Québec model of governance (Hamel & Jouve, 2006) is different from its counterparts in North America and Europe. As Favreau notes (2006, p. 13), "Québec may be viewed as an unique laboratory for research on new approaches, owing to several institutional innovations demonstrating the potential for creating new bridges between civil society, the state and the market" (TT). The opening up of the state (in this case, of the provincial government) to dialogue and partnerships that make a place for representatives of community-based organizations, and that recognize the contribution of the social economy to the social and economic development of Québec, constitute the principle features of Québec's originality (Bernier, Bouchard, & Lévesque, 2003; Lévesque & Ninacs, 1997). As described in Chapters 1 and 4, the model is marked by partnerships between the state and civil society actors, namely in the coconstruction of public policies. We summarize, in the following pages, elements that have to do to governance in the Québec model.

We then outline the issues raised in Québec vis-à-vis governance in the area of social economy.

The Québec Model of Governance

With the onset of the Quiet Revolution, Québec went through a period of accelerated modernization from the early 1960s to the mid-1970s. The period was characterized by the emergence of Fordism (1945–75), the rise of the welfare state, and the creation of major state corporations in the financial, industrial, and energy sectors. There was a transition from a minimalist state to one that was much more interventionist (Morin, 2006): not simply a welfare state, but also an entrepreneurial state (Bernier, Bouchard, & Lévesque, 2003) that initiated development projects. In the 1960s, the government combined modernization with planning; while it may have sought to include the population in the development of Québec, as in the case of the Bureau de l'aménagement de l'Est du Québec (BAEQ), the approach proved to be very hierarchical and technocratic (Simard, 1979; Côté, 2003). The approach gave rise to social demands for development "from below" and real citizen participation in public affairs (Lévesque & Mager, 1992; Hamel & Jouve, 2006).

Thus, in the 1970s, the Québec government began paying attention to regional actors via various sector-based consultative organizations, such as the Conseils régionaux de la culture (CRCs, regional culture boards), the Conseils régionaux des loisirs (CRLs, regional recreation boards), and Conseils régionaux de la santé et des services sociaux (CRSSs, regional health and social services boards). It also lent an ear to users of these local services through, for example, their participation on boards of directors of Centres locaux de services communautaires (CLSCs). The late 1970s witnessed the beginning of a challenge to the welfare state in Québec. In the years that followed, the state was less interventionist, viewing its role as one that would guide local and regional actors. It tried to link these actors to the social and economic development of the province. From 1983 to 1989, the government organized 15 regional summits on social and economic cooperation.

In social services, the government relied increasingly on civil society (Favreau & Lévesque, 1997). No longer able to act alone, it had to find partners, especially among community organizations. In the 1980s and 1990s, these organizations would diversify their fields and, supported by public funding, increasingly move towards the delivery of services. Thus, new forms of public affairs governance would be implemented.

For instance, in 1991, the Act respecting health services and social services would establish community organizations as "partners" of the state in managing social problems.

As noted in Chapter 1, in the 1990s, following the Women's March on Poverty (Bread and Roses), one of whose demands dealt with the introduction of "social infrastructure," events were organized by the government at the request, in particular, of the unions: the Conférence sur le devenir social et économique du Québec (conference on the social and economic future of Québec) and the Sommet sur l'économie and l'emploi (summit on the economy and employment), held respectively in March and October of 1996. Those events brought together social forces representing the state, the market, and civil society (including unions, women's groups, and community-based organizations) and gave rise to the Groupe de travail sur l'économie sociale (Working Group on the Social Economy), which was transformed in 1999 into the Chantier de l'économie sociale. This became the apotheosis of the state's recognition of the social economy as a focus for job creation.

These major meetings also led to the establishment of the Groupe de travail Régions-Municipalités pour l'entrepreneurship local et régional, whose report would be considered by the government in developing its Politique de soutien au développement local et régional (policy for support of local and regional development), which was made public in 1997. The law that ensued from this policy strengthened the role of the Conseils régionaux de développement (CRDs) as regional governance bodies, and gave new local governance organizations, the Centres locaux de développement (CLDs), a mandate to support both profit-oriented enterprises and social economy enterprises (Morin, 2006). It should be emphasized that this law made provision for participation of community-based representatives on these two governance bodies.

The Québec model is characterized by partnerships that include civil society. These partnerships are involved in "the hybridization of the solidarity-oriented logic of the community-based movement and the administrative logic of government authorities" (Bouchard & Chagnon, 1998, p. 47; TT). In Québec, such partnerships are at the heart of several achievements by collective social forces, including community-based organizations, that have linked up with union and employer groups to advance the cause of a form of development capable of providing an alternative to neo-liberalism (Bernier, Bouchard, & Lévesque, 2003; Côté, 2003). In sum, the new governance that emerged in Québec during the

1980s and 1990s, which included the rise of social actors acquiring an ever-greater number of responsibilities, moved away from the hierarchy and centralization characterizing the model of the 1960s and 1970s. As we have noted, some authors (see, especially, Chapter 4) even refer to a "co-construction" of public policy, with civil society actors playing a role in the development of policy.

However, the partnership between the state and civil society is not without its tensions. "The partnership is essentially paradoxical, since it simultaneously belongs to different logics" (Bourque, 2007, p. 300; TT). On the one hand, there is top-down logic (administrative) – that of the state, which relies on the flexibility and versatility of community-based organizations but which also seeks to control the behaviour of these organizations. On the other hand, there is a bottom-up logic (community-based) – that of civil society organizations, which want to preserve their autonomy but find themselves playing a role that complements state policies with which their actions have been integrated. This clash results in a form of collaboration that is not always harmonious and is often marked by conflict. Evaluations of the social economy have demonstrated these different logics (see Bouchard, 2009).

To a certain extent, the government elected in 2003 broke with the model of governance open to civil society by placing greater emphasis on elected representatives assuming more responsibility, and on partnerships between the state and private enterprise. Nonetheless, to different degrees civil society organizations have maintained their links with governance bodies, such as the Conférences régionales des élus (CREs, regional bodies that comprise mainly local elected officials) and Centres locaux de développement (CLDs). In addition, the government continues to support the social economy, while community-based organizations carry on their mission with the support and recognition of the state. However, the law creating the Centres de santé et de services sociaux (CSSS) "repositioned" the partnership between the state and community-based organizations (Bourque, 2007). It gave the CSSS the role of "coordinator of community resources"; it did this through "new relationships" of the "contracting type" that "are based on service agreements" and establish "relations of a more hierarchical nature" with community-based organizations (ibid., pp. 302–3). However, aside from the service agreements, the CSSS must also cooperate with community groups in taking action regarding social and health issues (ibid., p. 304). Thus, as noted by Bouchard, Lévesque, and St-Pierre (2005, p. 24), "the odds are that the gains made through the partnership model will not disappear. Once civil society has won recognition, it is difficult to turn back the clock" (TT).

Issues of Governance in Québec's Social Economy

Over the last 20 years, the partnership in Québec between the state and civil society has increased in importance. This partnership, which has links with the social economy, does not only receive support: It arouses interest and hope among some individuals, and fear and mistrust among others. Among the issues raised are the danger of a technocratic management of social problems, the risk of treating the social functions of the state as commodities, and the possibility of democratic deficits.

THE DANGER IN TECHNOCRATIC MANAGEMENT OF SOCIAL PROBLEMS
For community-based organizations, partnership represents an opportunity to win recognition and obtain funding for their activities, and to participate in the development of policies and projects. However, there is also a more negative side.

While partnerships may constitute a lever of development, they can also provide a new form of control (René & Gervais, 2001). This raises the entire issue of the independence of social economy actors. The issue has proved to be very important – especially as concerns the job creation with which the state strongly identifies the social economy – since the ministry in charge of employment is the one that leaves community-based organizations with the least room to manoeuvre in this area, as well as the one that most often requires a high level of accountability (Fontan et al., 2007).

Some associate this governance with a form of social neo-corporatism that feeds on specific issues (Lamoureux, 1999). This neo-corporatism calls attention to an issue and then de-contextualizes it and gives it an existence of its own. The danger is that the complexity of the individuals involved is eclipsed by the problem they represent. According to Parazelli and Tardif (1998, p. 65), the "ideology of partnership masks the fact that the state tries to turn community action into merely a specialized service designed exclusively for a group of individuals targeted by State experts on the basis of certain of their dysfunctional characteristics" (TT). From this standpoint, the objective of the state is to appease people's demands by including the specialized groups in the issue-management process. The state creates the illusion that the process comprises a multiplicity of independent wills, but the room for manoeuvring that is available to the organizations is in fact rigorously charted through a series of norms that nullify its impact (Lamoureux, 1999). One direct effect of the state's recognition of the social economy was the transfer of bureaucratic constraints typical of state intervention to spheres in which they had previously been absent (Le Bel, 1998). In sum, one of the risks of state support, regardless of its form, was "the use of the social economy by the government for its own purpose, in the form of subcontracting the delivery of public services or workfare" (D'Amours, 2007, p. 124; TT).

The asymmetrical character of the partnership between the state and civil society also constitutes a major obstacle to genuine partnership practices. The ability of the parties to undertake or maintain real partnership relationships is not that easy if they occupy unequal positions, and if the relationship is one of domination (René and Gervais, 2001). However, the dominated parties generally have some leeway that stems from the existence of areas of uncertainty: that is, that derives from the fact that each party has areas of expertise. Moreover, the expertise of community-based organizations is winning increased recognition from the authorities. The partnership between the state and community-based organizations involves a type of cooperation marked by conflict and relies more on compromise than on consensus, since the parties involved have neither the same interests nor the same resources. However, Shragge (2006, p. 133) has raised the following question (TT): "[W]hat sort of compromises does the community sector make when forming partnerships with more powerful partners, be they economic or social?" Graefe (1999) strongly questions the real influence wielded by community organizations, as well as their independence, in their relationship with the state. In this author's view, in spite of attempts to diversify their sources of revenue, these organizations remain dependent on government programs. He states that much of the research dealing with the social economy presents an "idealized view of the ... political abilities of the community sector" (ibid., p. 137; TT). The launch in 2006 of the Fiducie du Chantier de l'économie sociale (social economy trust fund), which is based on a partnership involving the Chantier de l'économie sociale, the provincial and federal governments, and the development funds of the two central labour bodies (FTQ and CSN), represents a new opportunity to capitalize social economy, thereby diversifying its sources of revenue. This trust fund has proven to be highly dependent on public funds, however.

THE RISK OF COMMODIFYING THE SOCIAL FUNCTIONS OF THE STATE

Governance in the area of social economy comes down to a new division of responsibilities between the state and civil society, with the latter assuming responsibility – with assistance from the government – for meeting certain social needs.

The partnership causes social economy enterprises to run the risk of contributing to the commodification of the social functions gradually being offloaded by the state, however. Bourque (2007) notes the danger of commodifying community services found in service agreements concluded between the CSSS and community-based organizations. Lamarche (1998) denounces the entrepreneurial logic being adopted by the social economy, and also criticizes the government of Québec for the withdrawal of certain services, which are then replaced by those provided by local authorities that are allegedly better equipped both to manage the diverse public policies and distribute resources. She maintains that this view of power without the state promotes "anarchic partnerships," both in terms of the norms guiding them and the actors involved, and with respect to "the economic and social arrangements favouring competitiveness" (ibid., p. 154; TT).

Lamoureux (1999) is in complete agreement, stating that the new links developed between the state and social economy organizations are leading to a shift, inspired by a market mentality, away from militancy and towards management of social problems (which are often created by the state itself). In a study on non-profit social economy enterprises providing Montréal with various services (recreation; toy recycling and lending services; housekeeping; home adaptation; catering and meal delivery), Morin and Rochefort (2006) also emphasize the fact that several of them have a relationship with the state that encourages them to adopt the logic of profitability. Profitability is associated with (a) less democratic forms of management; (b) operations that go beyond the local neighbourhood territory, in order to maximize potential demand; (c) a shift from the membership concept (for organizations that are closer to their users) to a client concept (for organizations who view the recipients of their services only as consumers); and (d) the quest for a clientele that includes more solvent sectors of the population, rather than simply low-income individuals. As concerns the social economy, Lévesque and Ninacs (1997, p. 15) also discuss:

the danger of commodifying every facet of human existence with, as a corollary, reducing the concept of the common good and redefining the operations of the state and mutual individual assistance as mere commercial transactions, thereby relegating citizenship to commercial activities involving the consumption of public services. (TT)

THE POSSIBILITY OF A DEMOCRATIC DEFICIT

Governance "is taking on an aura of democratic virtue; it is becoming the symbol of fashionable participative democracy" (Canet, 2004, p. 6; TT). The partnership between the state and civil society is providing community-based organizations with an opportunity for greater involvement in the management of public affairs. However, in his discussion of the social economy, Le Bel (1998) brings to light the danger of a drift towards corporatism when partnerships consider only the interests of social economy organizations recognized by the state as representative of these organizations. Referring to the governance model, Duchastel and Canet (2004, p. 39) touch on a form of democracy associated with it: namely, corporate democracy, which may be viewed "as an ideology of legitimation that, under the pretext of inviting all the concerned parties to the discussion, merely conceals a power relationship favouring the more structured organizations" (TT). In the case of the partnership between the state and civil society, the latter's organizations would fall within the remit of the state. Lamoureux (1999) states that the way major social movements are structured seems to lead to the development of a new elite among new groups (unions, women's movements, etc.). In his view, this involves a movement towards elitism, as well as a professionalization in social representation (ibid., p. 13). He gives the example of the October 1996 "Sommet sur l'économie et l'emploi," for which the government did not ask social movements to delegate freely nominated representatives to participate in the discussions, but instead chose the guests themselves from a list drawn up by the Office of the Premier.

Parazelli and Tardif (1998) criticize the way some community managers and professionals seeking legitimacy use both the ideology of partnership and the social economy model when battling poverty. While this is done in good faith, a pragmatic truth is imposed that can negatively affect the innovative capability of community actors. These authors come to a harsh conclusion regarding the hopes of certain social economy supporters for democratic inclusion: "Lacking a democratically debated vision of society, it is as if some actors were content with a

limited social economy model and, failing to tackle exclusion and dual-
ization, have accepted – using the social economy – to abandon the idea
of a democratic form of sharing and redistribution of wealth" (ibid., p.
89; TT).

Bourque (2007) also raises the question of citizen participation that
is not necessarily taken into account by partnership bodies, such as
community economic development corporations or centres locaux de
développement (local development centres) in which community organizations or associations are involved. These bodies can come to decisions without consulting the people represented by the community
organizations or associations and are often accountable to no one but
themselves.

Lévesque and Mendel (1999) make reference to partnership relationships established between, on the one hand, governments that rely on
the social economy to reduce their expenses, create jobs, and implement public policy and, on the other hand, social economy actors who
wish to obtain resources to carry out their activities or who seek recognition – from the state or society as a whole – for their accomplish-
ments. They conclude: "we are thus faced with compromises that are
still a long way from clearly defining the contours of a development
model likely to help the social economy bloom, in the sense of democratizing production and collective services" (ibid., p. 114; TT). D'Amours
(2007, p. 125) refers to the democracy issue "within organizations and
social economy enterprises as well as within economic and social governance" (TT). The first part of this reference concerns the participation
of workers, members, and users in the strategic decisions of organizations. The second part concerns participation by representatives of the
social economy on coordination and partnership bodies set up by the
government: Since 2003, the parameters of this form of participation
have changed within the Conférences régionales des élus (CREs) and
the Centres locaux de développement (CLDs), with local elected officials – who have been given greater responsibility by the state – often
having the preponderant influence (Morin, 2006).

Conclusion

Governance refers to new forms of public policy that are based on collaboration between multiple actors within the framework of a partnership. In the area of social economy, governance is associated with
a form of partnership between the state and civil society that aims to

produce goods and services meeting social needs. The type of partnership implemented depends, among other things, on the degree of openness of the state and on the dynamism of the civil society.

In English Canada, state recognition of the social economy (and the reference to it as such), is very recent. However, cooperatives, the voluntary sector, and community-based economic development organizations are much older. During the 1990s, the need to reduce government expenses led to various forms of alternative service delivery, especially those relying on non-profit organizations. The government of Ontario, in particular, entered into agreements with these organizations to provide social services and participate in workfare policy. These organizations were highly ambivalent about their role, since they were caught between the need to obtain resources and their desire to avoid playing the government's game. In the United States, the social economy concept is seldom used. Nonetheless, its governments, which historically have been less interventionist, have relied on NPOs to provide social services. That said, the government is still the principal NPO backer. The reform of welfare assistance policy in the mid-1990s changed relationships between the state and NPOs. As in Ontario, the latter were entrusted with the integration of welfare recipients into the workfare policy, and with service contracts. During the Obama administration, government investments in the community sector have increased, but more control is exerted over the results.

In the United Kingdom, some researchers are beginning to employ the concept of social economy, although the expression "voluntary sector" is still more common. The sector became more important during the 1980s under a Conservative government that was withdrawing from the delivery of public services. The Labour government, which came to power in 1997, promoted the sector within a partnership perspective. This partnership was formalized through the signature of national and local compacts setting out the principles the partners were expected to respect, although it did not make compliance compulsory. In many cases, the voluntary organizations were subject to various rules and forms of control, however. Moreover, in 2010, the National Compact was renewed by the new elected Conservative–Liberal coalition, but with reductions in national government financing of volunteer organizations.

In the 1980s, associations in France began playing a greater role as stakeholders in public policy. The social economy was recognized as a source of services and jobs. Relationships between governments and their partner-associations were established through national and local compacts, and by way of service contracts through which the governments defined the rules of the game while controlling the financial resources. Thus, the relationship was asymmetrical and eventually reduced the independence of the associations involved.

As we have noted, the Ontario, the United States, and the United Kingdoms represent a neo-liberal mode of governance over the nonprofit or voluntary sector, while in France the social-statist mode is the norm. In all four cases, the state is the main funder of civil society organizations and tends to have a greater control over these organizations through the implementation of accountability and assessment measures. The official discourse promotes a partnership between the state and the civil society organizations, but this partnership is asymmetric and creates tensions between the state and these organizations.

In Québec, the model of governance during the 1980s and 1990s was characterized by an openness of the state towards various market and civil society partners at the national, regional, and local levels. In the mid-1990s, the state formally acknowledged that the social economy played a role in creating jobs and providing services. Since 2003, social economy actors have continued to play a role in certain bodies of governance, although they no longer wield the degree of influence they once had on these bodies. Meanwhile, the relationship between the state and community-based organizations is increasingly making use of service contracts, which are nibbling away at the independence of these organizations. At the same time, within the framework of this relationship, the organizations are calling for action with a view to the social development of their communities – a call that is predicated on recognizing their independence. Thus, the issue of the independence of social economy organizations, both in Québec and elsewhere, is central to the dynamics of the partnership.

The other major issues facing Québec's social economy with regard to the state/civil society partnership – namely, the threats of technocratic use, commodification, and a democratic deficit – are not specific to the Québec context. The social economy remains dependent on public funding, while the rationale for this dependence is the fact that the state must not be allowed to abandon its social responsibilities and must continue to redistribute wealth. Thus, the main challenge facing social economy organizations in overcoming the dangers noted above is to work towards successfully influencing the formulation of public policies and the programs to which these policies give rise. This could be accomplished within the framework of a governance dealing with both daily operations and strategic directions, and that might include certain forms of participation on the part of the citizens involved – either as workers or members of these organizations, or as beneficiaries of these organizations' activities, a governance that corresponds to the partnership mode noted above.

NOTES

1 These "non-profit organizations" correspond, in large measure, to what are known in Québec as "community organizations."
2 Several authors have pointed out the polysemous nature of the concept of governance. Pierre (2000) differentiates between five usages of the concept in the fields of economic development, international institutions, corporate governance, public management strategies, and the new coordination and networking practices. Rhodes (2000, in Enjolras, 2005a) identifies as many as seven different meanings.
3 The United States and Europe are the countries that use the concept of social enterprise most frequently; among comparable concepts, the concept is probably closer in meaning than any other to that of social economy. It allows us to account for the existence of NPOs, which are increasingly involved in commercial activities (Laville, Lévesque, & Mendell, 2005).

REFERENCES

Amin, A. (2006). Le soutien au local au Royaume-Uni: Entre le recul politique et l'engagement solidaire. In J.-L. Klein & D. Harrisson (Eds.), *L'innovation sociale* (pp. 293–8). Sainte-Foy: Presses de l'Université du Québec.

Archambault, E. (1995). La gestion privée des services sociaux en France: Production déguisée ou partenariat innovant? In J.-L. Klein & B. Lévesque (Eds.), *Contre l'exclusion repenser l'économie* (pp. 187–98). Sainte-Foy: Presses de l'Université du Québec.

Austin, M.J. (2003). The changing relationship between nonprofit organizations and public social service agencies in the era of welfare reform. *Nonprofit and Voluntary Sector Quarterly, 32*(1), 97–114. http://dx.doi.org/10.1177/0899764002250008

Bernier, L., Bouchard, M.J., & Lévesque, B. (2003). Attending to the general interest: New mechanisms for mediating between the individual, collective and general interest in Quebec. *Annals of Public and Cooperative Economics,* 74(3), 321–48. Accessed 18 June 2011. Retrieved from http://www.blackwell-synergy.com/doi/abs/10.1111/1467-8292.00226

Bouchard, M.J. (2006). De l'expérimentation à l'institutionnalisation positive, l'innovation sociale dans le logement communautaire au Québec. *Annales de l'économie publique, sociale et coopérative, 77*(2), 139–66. http://dx.doi.org/10.1111/j.1370-4788.2006.00301.x

Bouchard, M.J. (2009). *The worth of the social economy.* Ciriec collection, Social Economy and Public Economy. Brussels: Peter Lang.

Bouchard, M.J., & Chagnon, L. (1998). Le développement des communautés locales à la croisée des partenariats. *Economie et Solidarites, 29*(2), 42–50.

Bouchard, M.J., Lévesque, B., & St-Pierre, J. (2005). *Modèle québécois de développement et gouvernance: Entre le partenariat et le néolibéralisme?* Co-publication: CRISES, collection Études théoriques, No. ET0505, and Cahier de recherche du Canada en économie sociale.

Bourque, D. (2007). Les partenariats dans le développement des communautés. In D. Bourque, Y. Comeau, L. Favreau, & L. Fréchette (Eds.), *L'organisation communautaire – fondements, approches et champs de pratiques* (pp. 297–309). Québec: Presses de l'Université du Québec.

Cabinet Office. (2010). *The compact accountability and transparency guide.* United Kingdom. Accessed 27 July 2011. http://www.cabinetoffice.gov.uk/sites/default/files/resources/The%20Compact%20Accountability%20Guide.pdf

Cabinet Office. (2011). *Big society.* United Kingdom. Accessed 27 July 2011. http://www.cabinetoffice.gov.uk/big-society

Caillouette, J. (2001). Pratiques de partenariat, pratiques d'articulation identitaire et mouvement communautaire. *Nouvelles Pratiques Sociales, 14*(1), 81–96.

Canet, R. (2004). *Qu'est-ce que la gouvernance?* Conférences de la Chaire MCD. Accessed 18 June 2011. http://er.uqam.ca/nobel/ieim/IMG/pdf/canet-mars-2004.pdf

Chantier de l'économie sociale. (2009). *Chantier de l'économie sociale.* Accessed 22 March 2007. http://www.chantier.qc.ca/

Chaves, R., & Monzon Campos, J.L. (2007). *L'économie sociale dans l'Union européenne.* Commission européenne: Comité économique et social européen (CESE), No. CESE/COMM/05/2005.

Côté, L. (2003). L'étude des modèles nationaux de gouvernance: Le cas québécois. *Economie et Solidarites, 34*(2), 95–117.

Craig, G., & Manthorpe, J. (1999). Unequal partners? Local government reorganization and the voluntary sector. *Social Policy and Administration, 33*(1), 55–72. Accessed 18 June 2011. Retrieved from http://onlinelibrary.wiley.com/doi/10.1111/1467-9515.00131/pdf

D'Amours, M. (2007). *L'économie sociale au Québec: Cadre théorique, histoire, réalités et défis*. Montréal: ARUC-Économie sociale/Éditions Saint-Martin.

Dommergues, P. (1988). *La société du partenariat: Économie-territoire et revitalisation régionale aux États-Unis et en France*. Paris: Anfor-Anthropos.

Dommergues, P. (1989). Quelles leçons tirées de l'exemple américain? In P. Dommergues & N. Gardin (Eds.), *Les stratégies internationales des métropoles regionals* (pp. 233–44). Paris: Syros.

Duchastel, J., & Canet, R. (2004). Du local au global – Citoyenneté and transformation de la démocratie. In B. Jouve & P. Both (Eds.), *Démocraties métropolitaines, Collection Géographie contemporaine* (pp. 20–41). Sainte-Foy: Presses de l'Université du Québec.

Eme, B. (2005). Gouvernance territoriale et mouvements d'économie sociale et solidaire. *Revue internationale de l'économie sociale* (299): 42–55.

Enjolras, B. (2005a). Le nouveau discours normatif sur la société civile. *Cahiers de l'ARUC-Économie sociale*, No. C-14-2005.

Enjolras, B. (2005b). Économie sociale et solidaire et régimes de gouvernance. *Revue internationale de l'économie sociale* (296): 56–69.

Favreau, L. (2006). Économie sociale et politiques publiques: L'expérience québécoise. *Horizons*, 8(2), 7–15.

Favreau, L., & Lévesque, B. (1997). L'économie sociale et les pouvoirs publics: Banalisation du "social" ou tremplin pour une transformation sociale? *Nouvelles Pratiques Sociales*, 10(1), 71–80.

Fontan, J.-M., Hamel, P., Morin, R., & Shragge, E. (2007). *Action collective et développement local en région métropolitaine: Le cas de Montréal*. Collection Études, matériaux et documents, No. 22. Montréal: Département d'études urbaines et touristiques, UQAM.

Fyfe, N.R. (2005). Making space for "neo-communitarianism"? The Third Sector, state and civil society in the UK. *Antipode*, 37(3), 536–57. Accessed 18 June 2011. Retrieved from http://onlinelibrary.wiley.com/resolve/doi?DOI=1 0.1111/j.0066-4812.2005.00510

Gidron, B., Kramer, R.M., & Salamon, L.M. (1992). Government and the Third Sector in comparative perspective: Allies or dversaries? In B. Gidron, R.M. Kramer, & L.M. Salamon (Eds.), *Government and the Third Sector: Emerging relationships in welfare states* (pp. 1–30). San Francisco: Jossey-Bass Publishers.

Graefe, P. (1999). Repenser l'économie sociale face à l'État. *Lien Social et Politiques – RIAC*, 41, 129–41.

Hamel, P., & Jouve, B. (2006). *Un modèle québécois? Gouvernance et participation dans la gestion publique*. Montréal: Les Presses de l'Université de Montréal.

Jospin, L. (2001). Preface. In C. Fourel (Ed.), *La nouvelle économie sociale: Efficacité, solidarité, démocratie* (pp. 7–9). Paris: Alternatives Économiques/Syros.

Lamarche, L. (1998). L'économie sociale: Un modèle de développement au service de l'État désétatisé. In L.L. Boivin & M. Fortier (Eds.), *L'économie sociale: L'avenir d'une illusion* (pp. 137–60). Québec: Fides.

Lamoureux, H. (1999). *Les dérives de la démocratie: Questions à la société civile québécoise.* Montréal: VLB Éditeur.

Laville, J.-L., Lévesque, B., & Mendell, M. (2005). L'économie sociale: Diversité des trajectoires historiques et des constructions théoriques en Europe et au Canada. *Cahiers de l'ARUC-Économie sociale,* No. C-12–2005.

Le Bel, G.A. (1998). La reconnaissance de l'économie sociale, ou l'étatisation du communautaire. In L. Boivin & M. Fortier (Eds.), *L'économie sociale: l'avenir d'une illusion* (pp. 101–33). Québec: Fides.

Leblanc, A., Zeesman, A., & Halliwell, J.E. (2006). Le gouvernement du Canada et l'économie sociale. *Horizons, 8*(2), 4–6.

Leduc Browne, P. (2000). The neo-liberal uses of the social economy: Non-profit organizations and workfare in Ontario. In E. Shragge & J.-M. Fontan (Eds.), *Social Economy – International Debates and Perspectives* (pp. 65–80). Montréal: Black Rose Books.

Lévesque, B. (2001). Le partenariat: Une tendance lourde de la nouvelle gouvernance à l'ère de la mondialisation. Enjeux et défis pour les entreprises publiques et d'économie sociale. *Annals of Public and Cooperative Economics/ Annales de l'économie publique, sociale et coopérative, 72*(3).

Lévesque, B., & Mendell, M. (1999). *L'économie sociale au Québec: Éléments théoriques et empiriques pour le débat et la recherche.* Cahiers du CRISES, No. 9908.

Lévesque, B., & Mager, L. (1992). Vers un nouveau contrat social? Éléments de problématique pour l'étude du régional et du local. In C. Gagnon & J.-L. Klein (Eds.), *Les partenaires du développement face au défi du local.* Collaboration, Développement régional. Chicoutimi: Groupe de recherche et d'interventions régionales (GRIR), Université du Québec à Chicoutimi.

Lévesque, B., & Ninacs, W.A. (1997). *L'économie sociale au Canada: L'expérience québécoise.* Issues paper for the colloquium "Stratégies locales pour l'emploi et l'économie sociale." Montréal: Les Publications de l'IFDÉC.

MacKinnon, S. (2006). L'économie sociale au Manitoba: Concevoir une politique publique d'inclusion sociale. *Horizons, 8*(2), 26–9.

Maillard, J. de, (2002). Les associations dans l'action publique locale: Participation fonctionnalisée ou ouverture démocratique? *Lien Social et Politiques-RIAC:* 53–65.

Martin, D.G. (2004). Nonprofit foundations and grassroots organizing: Reshaping urban governance. *Professional Geographer, 56*(3), 394–405. Accessed 18 June 2011. Retrieved from https://www.clarku.edu/departments/geography/pdfs/Deb%20Martin/Martin_2004_PG_nonprofitfoundationsandgrassrootsorganizing.pdf

Morin, R. (2006). *La régionalisation au Québec: Les mécanismes de développement et de gestion des territoires régionaux et locaux 1960–2006.* Montréal: ARUC-Économie sociale/Éditions Saint-Martin.

Morin, R., & Rochefort, M. (2005). Services de proximité et proximité sociospatiale: Les rapports aux usagers et au territoire des services communautaires. In A. Bourdin, M.-P. Lefeuvre, & A. Germain (Eds.), *La proximité: Construction politique et expérience sociale* (pp. 259–72). Paris: Anthropos.

Moulaert, F., & Ailenei, O. (2005). Social economy, third sector and solidarity relations: A conceptual synthesis from history to present. *Urban Studies (Edinburgh, Scotland), 42*(11), 2037–54. http://dx.doi.org/10.1080/00420980500279794

National Council for Voluntary Organisations. (2011). *Sustainable funding and the Big Society.* Accessed 27 July 2011. http://www.ncvo-vol.org.uk/sfp/bigsociety

Neamtan, N. (2009). Économie sociale: Concepts et défis. *Universitas Forum, 1* (3). Accessed 27 July 2011. http://www.universitasforum.org/index.php/ojs/article/view/31/160

Panet-Raymond, J., & Bourque, D. (1991). *Partenariat ou pater-nariat? La collaboration entre établissement publics et organismes communautaires oeuvrant auprès des personnes âgées à domicile.* Québec: Conseil québécois de la recherche sociale.

Parazelli, M., & Tardif, G. (1998). Le mirage démocratique de l'économie sociale. In L. Boivin & M. Fortier (Eds.), *L'économie sociale: l'avenir d'une illusion* (pp. 55–99). Québec: Fides.

Perry, S. (2009). White House officials discuss plans for Social Innovation Office. *The Chronicle of Philanthropy.* Accessed 28 May 2011. http://philanthropy.com/article/White-House-Officials-Discuss/63099/

Pierre, J. (2000). *Governance beyond state strength.* Oxford: Oxford University Press.

Plowden, W. (2003). The compact: Attempts to regulate relationships between government and the voluntary sector in England. *Nonprofit and Voluntary Sector Quarterly, 32*(3), 415–32. http://dx.doi.org/10.1177/0899764003254909

Quarter, J. (2000). The social economy and the neo-conservative agenda. In E. Shragge & J.M. Fontan (Eds.), *Social Economy – International Debates and Perspectives* (pp. 54-80). Montréal: Black Rose Books.

René, J.-F., & Gervais, L. (2001). Les enjeux du partenariat aujourd'hui. *Nouvelles Pratiques Sociales, 14*(1), 20–30.

Rhodes, R.A.W. (2000). Public administration and governance. In J. Pierre (Ed.), *Debating Governance* (pp. 54–90). Oxford: Oxford University Press.

Rifkin, J. (1996). *La fin du travail*. Paris/Montréal: Éditions La découverte/Éditions du Boréal.

Salamon, L.M. (1997). The United States. In L. Salamon & H.K. Anheier (Eds.), *Defining the nonprofit sector: A cross-national analysis* (pp. 280–319). Manchester, New York: Manchester University Press.

Salamon, L.M. (1990). The nonprofit sector and government: The American experience in theory and practice. In H.K. Anheier & W. Seibel (Eds.), *The Third Sector: Comparative studies of nonprofit organizations* (pp. 210–40). Berlin & New York: Walter de Gruyter.

Shragge, E. (2006). *Action communautaire: Dérives et possibilités*. Montréal: Les Éditions Écosociété.

Simard, J.-J. (1979). *La longue marche des technocrates*. Laval: Éditions coopératives Albert Saint-Martin.

Stoker, G. (1998). Cinq propositions pour une théorie de la gouvernance. *Revue internationale de sciences sociales* (155): 19–30.

Warin, P. (2002). La politique associative en construction: Enjeu économique, enjeu démocratique. *Lien Social et Politiques – RIAC*: 35–52.

4 The Co-construction of Public Policy: The Contribution of the Social Economy[1]

YVES VAILLANCOURT,
WITH THE COLLABORATION OF PHILIPPE LECLERC

Introduction

In this chapter, we look at the contribution of the social economy to the democratization of public policy. To that end, we have set up a dialogue between two research approaches. On the one hand, we have taken into account the results of conceptual and empirical research that we have conducted on social policy and public policy, with a particular focus on certain reforms that have occurred since the 1980s in the areas of health and social services and of social housing. On the other hand, we have conducted literature reviews on the participation of stakeholders from civil society and the market in the democratization of public policy in societies in both the North and the South. This led us, from summer 2007 onward, to make a clearer distinction between co-production and co-construction of public policy, two concepts that until then we had tended to see as one and the same.

To highlight the underlying thread of our thesis, it may be helpful to indicate at the outset the point at which the two concepts differ. "Co-production" refers to participation by stakeholders from civil society and the market in the implementation of public policy; "co-construction" refers to participation by those very stakeholders in the design of public policy. Thus, co-construction stands upstream from the adoption of public policy, whereas co-production lies downstream, at the moment of its implementation.

To analyse the processes of co-construction and co-production of public policy, we use a conceptual framework that is responsive to the multiple configurations arising from the tangible evolution of interactions among three main spheres – the state, the market, and civil society. By definition, public policy always involves participation by the state sphere and public authorities. But the questions to be considered are the following: Does state intervention in the development and application of public policy occur with or without participation by stakeholders from the market and civil society? And, when it does, what pattern does this participation take? To answer these questions, we will put forward the idea that the democratization and enhancement of public policy requires participation by collective and individual stakeholders from the market and civil society in its creation (co-construction) and its application (co-production). To have good public policy, however, it is not enough merely to pay lip service to co-construction and co-production; hence our focus on pinpointing the features and conditions of the configurations we find most compatible with the enhancement and democratization of public policy. In addition, in these configurations, it will be no surprise to find a degree of participation by social economy stakeholders.

This chapter comprises four main sections. In the first section, we clarify some concepts, in particular public policy and civil society. Then we look in turn at the co-production (section 2) and co-construction (section 3) of public policy, with a view to identifying the features of more democratic configurations that are imbued with the social economy's contribution. Finally, in the fourth section, we use actual cases taken from social housing policy to highlight the fact that the most democratic, solidarity-based form of co-construction and co-production of public policy is to be found in certain social policy reforms that have occurred in Québec over the past 20 years.

Some Theoretical Clarifications

To grasp more clearly, in theoretical and practical terms, the scope of the similarities and differences between co-production and co-construction of public policy while being attentive to the social economy's contribution, it is important to agree on the meaning we give to certain key concepts used in our conceptual framework, which come up frequently in our analyses. Cases in point include the concepts of state, market, civil society, third sector, social economy, and public policy. We will do so without losing sight of the fact that our chapter is part of a collective work, and that certain concepts – notably that of the social economy – have been benchmarked in the introductory sections of the work.

The State, Market, Civil Society, Third Sector, and the Social Economy

In order to tackle the phenomena of co-construction and co-production of public policy, we refer to a tripolar approach that is responsive to the evolution of shared responsibilities among individual and collective stakeholders associated with the state, the market, and civil society (Olvera, 1999, p. 20; Laville & Nyssens, 2001; Lévesque, 2003; Vaillancourt & Laville, 1998). In this way, we distance ourselves from two sorts of binary approaches prevalent in the literature, whether those interested solely in the interaction between the state and the market or those focusing exclusively on interaction between the state and civil society.

State players may belong to a variety of political scenes (local, regional, national, continental, or global). We make a distinction among the conventional branches of political power, namely, the executive branch (or the elected members of the political party running the government), the legislative branch (or all elected members from the various political parties), and the judiciary. Of course, we distinguish the political level, including those with a mandate under representative democracy, from the administrative level, comprising those involved in public administration.

As for the market, we see it as a sphere distinct from that of civil society. This clarification is an important one, since much of the literature on civil society remains confused in this regard. For us, the market refers to the individual and collective stakeholders in the labour market or the market economy (businesses, owners and executives, managers, employees and the self-employed, unemployed, etc.). It also refers to representation structures, including management and labour organizations.[2]

As for the concept of civil society, we recognize that it is not a uniform reality. In the tradition of CRISES and CIRIEC International (Lévesque, 2003; Lévesque & Thiry, 2008; Enjolras, 2006) and along with a number of Latin American researchers (Dagnino, 2002; Olvera, 1999; Marinez, 2007; Garretón, 2007; Cunill, 2004; Oszlak, 2007), we refuse both to embellish or to demonize it; instead, we focus on its potential for democratization (Côté, Lévesque, & Morneau, 2009). We have clearly noted theoretical debates currently under way, for instance in the journal *Voluntas*, as to the advantages and disadvantages of definitions of civil society that are exclusively normative (concerned with differentiating between "good" and "bad" organizations), or solely descriptive (embarrassed at the possibility of including such organizations as al-Qaeda within civil society) (Munck, 2006). We opt for a definition that is pre-dominantly descriptive while retaining some elements put forward by Anheier: "Global civil society is the sphere of ideas, values, institutions, organizations, networks, and individuals that are ... located between the family, the state, and the market" (2007, pp. 10–11).[3] In this defini-tion, we find it helpful to differentiate the sphere of civil society not only from the state and the market, but also from the family.

As to the concept of the third sector, we have used it for the past 15 years or so, and have been influenced by a current of European litera-ture that is interested both in social policy and in the possibly innova-tive input of third-sector organizations in the democratization of social and public policy (Defourny & Monzón Campos, 1992; Means & Smith, 1994; Lewis, 1999, 2004; Evers & Laville, 2004). This concept is narrower than that of civil society. But it is broader than that of the social econ-omy even if, in our earlier writings, we often treated them as one and the same (Vaillancourt et al., 2004), a little like Defourny and Monzón Campos (1992) and Evers and Laville (2004).

Concerning the concept of social economy, we subscribe to the inclu-sive definition put forward in the Introduction to this collective work. It makes room not only for the market components but also for non-market components, such as community and cooperative organizations that offer collective services without charging for them (Vaillancourt et al., 2004; Vaillancourt, 2006, 2008). As a result, stakeholders from the social economy can be anchored in both civil society (in particular for the non-market social economy) and the market (in particular for the market social economy).

Public Policy

The concept of public policy[4] encompasses that of social policy.[5] At the same time, it shares many of the features of social policy. At the outset, we stand apart from a reductionist vision of public policy that is inter-ested only in the activities of state organizations viewed as being pub-lic property in terms of legal status. In such a context, should a housing and institutional care policy for elderly people experiencing a decrease in autonomy, for instance, not be interested solely in public municipal housing bureaus and long-term care residential facilities? Such a policy would ignore, however, other housing and accommodation resources, such as for-profit private residences, and social economy housing, such as cooperatives and housing non-profits.

"Policy" refers to intervention by the state or public authorities in order to foster the general interest that is jeopardized when one relies merely on the operation of market laws or the resources of family solidarity. The pursuit of the general interest then involves functions of de-marketization and de-familialization, to use the expressions formulated by Esping-Anderson (1999). By relying solely on state intervention, however, it is difficult to obtain adequate social and public policy; this is where the distinction between co-construction and co-production of policy starts to be helpful.

In recent writings devoted to the definition of social policy with implications for the definition of public policy (Vaillancourt & Ducharme, 2000; Vaillancourt, in Tremblay, Tremblay, & Tremblay, 2006, pp. 25–8), we have applied ourselves to reconciling two goals: to value state intervention, and to find a way of doing so without erasing stakeholders' input from civil society and the market, in particular from the social economy. This work is more necessary than ever since the end of the golden age of welfare state policy. In fact, in the 1970s and 1980s, we had often acquired the habit, in left-wing intellectual circles, of valuing intervention by the state in defining its role as if the state were the sole architect of social and public policy. With the hindsight gained by following the welfare state and the employment crisis of the 1980s, however, some progressive circles tried to adjust their focus so as to tighten the links between that policy and the needs of the communities concerned (Jetté et al., 2000; Vaillancourt, Aubry, & Jetté, 2003; Vaillancourt et al., 2004).

To break down the various stages involved in the genesis of public policy, we often refer to six components: (1) identification of the main goals for attaining the general interest;[6] (2) the choice of regulation standards to foster quality; (3) a determination of funding means (state, private, mixed, etc.); (4) the definition of responsibility sharing with respect to management; (5) the arrangement of responsibility sharing with respect to the delivery of services belonging to public policy; and (6) the establishment of the policy for evaluating public policy. These components can help us examine the processes of co-construction and co-production in a detailed, precise manner, as we shall see in the following sections.

Co-production of Public Policy

The international literature on co-production is extensive, and has existed for the past 30 years or more. It looks at the co-production of services of public interest, as well as at the co-production of public policy. In this section, we will be focusing specifically on the co-production, or implementation, of public policy.[7]

Co-production involves the participation of both state and non-state stakeholders, the latter being associated with the market and/or civil society (third sector). The co-production of policy is deployed at an organizational level (in the organization of products and services), whereas co-construction (see "Co-construction of Public Policy and the Contribution of the Social Economy," below) is deployed at an institutional level (in the establishment of the general direction and underlying elements of the policy).

In the literature reviewed on the co-production of public policy, two meanings may be distinguished. In this regard, Pestoff, Osborne, and Brandsen, in their conclusion to a report devoted to co-production in an issue of *Public Management Review*, stated that:

> The concept of co-production was initially developed in America in the late 1960s to describe and delimit the involvement of ordinary citizens in the production of public services. It had a clear focus on the role of individuals or groups of citizens in the production of such services, although their involvement also had clear ramifications for both the meso and macro level of society. More recently, it has been given a normative angle. Co-production, according to some proponents, could play a significant role in the renewal of democratic political systems and the welfare state. (Pestoff, Osborne, & Brandsen, 2006, p. 593)

We note that the first meaning of the notion of co-production summarized by Pestoff and his colleagues concerns "public services," which we prefer to call "services of public interest" (Vaillancourt, 2008). It does not formally concern the co-production of public policy, but rather that of services. This is why we have mentioned it without examining it further in this chapter.

The second meaning of the word "co-production" mentioned in the quotation – that of involving a more "normative" perspective – is of great interest to us here. This kind of co-production concerns policy, and public policy in particular, insofar as it "could play a significant role in the renewal of democratic political systems and the welfare state" (Pestoff, Osborne, & Brandsen, 2006, p. 593). Co-production aims to foster the democratization of the state and public policy. To that end, it builds on the organization of public services and public policy, in which public authorities seek input from non-state stakeholders, particularly from the third sector. This understanding is limited, however, to the organizational dimension alone – the operationalization of policy, rather than its conception and institutionalization.

Among researchers interested in examining the new forms of co-production in the reconfiguration of public services or services of public interest, a number are looking at the changes in practices and policy being deployed in local areas, and municipalities in particular (Rich, 1981; Brito, 2002; Kliksberg, 2007). In these changes, new arrangements are appearing, both formal and informal, both hierarchical and cooperative in nature, between local governments and private-sector and third-sector organizations. These new forms of participation by non-state organizations in the production of collective services, also known as the "welfare mix" or "mixed economy of welfare" (Evers & Laville, 2004, pp. 14–17, 137, 169; Pestoff, 2006, pp. 511–13), often arise in the field of local services: transportation, garbage collection, waste recycling, food distribution, social housing, the development of parks and public spaces, social services, etc. (Bresser & Cunill, 1998; Batley, 2007; Ndiaye, 2005; Oszlak, 2007).[8] Thus, the concept of co-production, in the sense expressed here, refers to configurations involving a partnership between the state and private-sector for-profit organizations.

Other authors refer to partnerships between the state and third-sector organizations, including those belonging to the social and community economy family. The latter case gives rise to a variety of socio-economic practices that abound in the societies in both the South (Bresser & Cunill, 1998; Bifarello, 2000; Ndiaye, 2005; Vitale, 2005; Batley, 2007) and the North (Vaillancourt & Laville, 1998; Lewis, 1999, 2004; Pestoff, 2006; Proulx, Bourque, & Savard, 2007). It also gives rise to a great variety of theoretical and political configurations that we began studying some time ago in our research teams (at LAREPPS, for instance), although at that time we were not using the concept of co-production.

Some of these configurations are in line with neo-liberal perspectives concerned with arranging the disengagement or non-engagement of the state, particularly with the rise of public–private partnerships (PPPs) (Rouillard et al., 2004; Rouillard, 2006). Other configurations are in line with progressive perspectives, seeking greater democratization of the economy and society (Favreau & Salam Fall, 2007; Cunill, 2004; Pestoff, 2006). A number of authors are especially interested in configurations that promote progressive forms of co-production based on cooperation between the state and the third sector. Among them is Nuria Cunill (2004), whose contribution we have underscored else-where (Vaillancourt, 2007b).[9]

In an article reporting on comparative research under way in eight European countries concerning childcare services, Victor Pestoff (2006) looks at the configuration of responsibility sharing among the state, the private sector, and the third sector. He displays his preference for ser-vices provided by the third sector, emphasizing that parents' participa-tion is easier there than in public or private, for-profit services (Pestoff, 2006, p. 515). He expresses his interest in a co-production framework in which the role of the state concerns funding and regulation, while that of the third sector focuses on the management and delivery of wel-fare services (ibid., p. 517). He argues that third-sector organizations have a capacity to broaden and deepen the democratic governance ex-ercised by the public authorities. The forms of governance that are open to participation by the third sector are often deployed, in Sweden, for instance, in local areas under the aegis of municipal public authorities. The issue then becomes the sharing of power and responsibility (fi-nancial, political, educational, and social) among a variety of collective stakeholders (including the parents of children in child-care centres and child-care centre personnel) and the public authorities concerned in the local area (ibid., pp. 511–13).

For Pestoff, it is third-sector organizations that are the best placed to foster this plural participation with a "democratizing" reach – under certain conditions, obviously, such as being able to count on adequate public funding (ibid., p. 515) and appropriate regulation (ibid., p. 517). The contribution of Pestoff and other authors in the same theoretical vein is important for the democratization of public policy. This contri-bution appears to be limited, however, to the organizational dimension of public policy. Third-sector participation appears to be valued at the moment when policy is applied, but not at the moment when it is ad-opted. With such a viewpoint, we find ourselves close to the boundary between co-production and co-construction of public policy, but we do not cross it, and to our mind that is regrettable.

Co-construction of Public Policy and the Contribution of the Social Economy

Unlike the concept of co-production, that of co-construction of public policy receives little mention in the literature, hence the importance of benchmarking it clearly. In this section, we look at the co-construction of public policy, trying to pinpoint its various configurations and seeking the features of a democratic configuration in which the social economy provides input.

As we mentioned earlier, co-construction is deployed upstream: in other words, when public policy is being conceived. We suggest that the democratization of such policy would gain from this, at least in some societies, at certain moments in certain specific policy areas, if the state worked to co-construct it by partnering with stakeholders from the market and civil society, not to mention from the social economy.

To distinguish the conditions of the co-construction model that interests us, it is enlightening to set out a variety of scenarios in which the state constructs policy on its own or co-constructs it with other socio-economic agents.

The Mono-construction of Public Policy

To grasp the concept of the state as a partner in the co-construction of policy, it is helpful to distinguish it from its opposite, illustrated here by an authoritarian, hierarchical, entrepreneurial state that emerged in several Northern countries during the Trente Glorieuses, the 30 years following World War Two (Enjolras, 2005, 2006; Vaillancourt, 2007b).[10]

Examples include the French state, the Canadian federal state of 1945–75, and the Québec state of the Quiet Revolution and the Castonguay reform era of the 1960s and 1970s, respectively. In these scenarios, the classic conception of accountability in representative democracy makes elected officials solely accountable. It is based on lessons drawn from historical periods prior to 1945, during which the state was tossed at will by market forces, the family, and civil society. This leads directly to the shortcomings of the hierarchical state, however, which, to stand out more clearly from the laissez-faire attitude in vogue during the economic depression of the 1930s, sometimes found itself at the other end of the pendulum. In fact, the interventionist state often fell into other bureaucratic biases by seeing itself as a referee above the fray, like a great planner, entrepreneur, and operator. It acted in an authoritarian manner, seeing itself as solely responsible for public policy. This is all compatible with the recourse to co-production in one form or another. There is nothing to prevent the state from constructing its policy on its own, while using the private sector and third sector to implement that policy.

Neo-liberal Co-construction

For there to be co-construction of public policy, it is necessary for the state to favour open forms of governance that make room for participation by social stakeholders from non-state sectors – that is, the market and civil society. Before examining the benefits of this form of co-construction, it is important to remember that, in the recent evolution of capitalist societies in both various Northern and Southern countries, much co-constructed public policy was created as a result of special links established between the state and socio-economic elites anchored in market forces. Without returning to simplistic representations borrowed from the Marxist structuralism made popular during the 1970s, which suggested that the state is an instrument at the service of the dominant classes,[11] it must be recognized that the state is not neutral. It leans towards certain social forces rather than others, and is anchored in inegalitarian social relationships marked by class, gender, intercultural, and other divisions. In short, it should be recognized that co-construction can be conceptualized and operationalized in various ways, some of which may be less compatible than others with the pursuit of the general interest.

In neo-liberal co-construction, in vogue in the past few years in several countries (in particular with the popularity of the dominant managerial current of new public management [NPM] and the fashion for public-private partnerships [PPPs]), the state is encouraged to construct public policy by cooperating with the private sector – that is, with the dominant socio-economic agents in the market economy. In neo-liberal policy co-construction, there are institutional arrangements that favour competitive regulation, often described as "quasi-markets" in the United Kingdom literature on social policy. This quasi-market regulation may be recognized by the fact that the state opens up the construction and production of policy to participation by organizations from the public, private, and third sectors, while inviting those organizations to compete with one another for contracts (Le Grand & Bartlett, 1993; Means & Smith, 1994; Lewis, 1999, 2004). It embodies the logic of market-driven instrumentalization, for instance through performance-related contractual clauses or reporting methods built into service agreements. Finally, it can also tie in with a logic of "shedding the load" of public responsibilities onto other stakeholders, at lower cost and with a fragile guarantee as to quality of services.

Corporatist Co-construction

The corporatist co-construction model was in vogue in Québec in more traditional forms during the 1940s and 1950s, and in more modern forms during the 1970s and 1980s with the formula of sectoral socio-economic summits. In these two variants of the model, there was a form of cooperation between stakeholders from political society, the labour market, and civil society. These relations were deployed, however, along lines that remain associated with unequal representation. Some sectors of socio-economic activity and stakeholders associated with labour and management circles are included in the dialogue and deliberation with the state, whereas others are excluded. The result is that certain groups of stakeholders have more weight than others, and that the co-construction of public policy is monopolized by special interests (Bresser Pereira & Cunill, 1998; Cunill, 2004; Brugué, 2004; Oszlak, 2007; Enjolras, 2006; Thériault, 2003; Garretón, 2007).[12]

Democratic, Solidarity-Based Co-construction

The democratic, solidarity-based co-construction that interests us is consistent with the pursuit of the general interest and keeps its distance from the neo-liberal and corporatist configurations. We will identify four features of this configuration.

First, the state remains a partner like no other. The thesis of co-construction suggests that the state co-constructs policy by cooperating with co-architects from the market and civil society. As mentioned in our work on the État stratège (strategic state) (Vaillancourt, 2007b), the thesis of co-construction does not mean that the state stands on exactly the same footing as the other non-state stakeholders with which it co-constructs. Ultimately, the state has to rule alone on disagreements and makes the final decisions (Pierre & Peters, 2000). Certainly, it develops policy in close cooperation with stakeholders from the market economy and civil society. It dialogues, interacts, and deliberates with non-state stakeholders. It remains both above and close to them. In this way, it avoids becoming enclosed in a position of self-sufficiency and omnipotence.

Second, democratic co-construction builds on a reform of the state that enables it to become a partner of civil society without ceasing to be a partner of stakeholders from the market economy. This differs from an anti-capitalist co-construction, in which the state would be the partner of civil society and stand against the stakeholders from the market economy.[13] It ties in with a plural economy perspective (Lévesque, Bourque, & Forgues, 2001, pp. 59–65), having drawn lessons from the failures of real socialism in the former Communist countries since the fall of the Berlin Wall. Thus, it seeks a break with neo-liberalism, but not with the market economy (Julliard, 2007). It targets a reform of the state that Jon Pierre (2005) calls "participatory reform." This reform refuses to remain focused on either the state or the market. Instead, the "state's strength derives from its capacity to call on the resources of all segments of society with a view to achieving collective goals and meeting the collective interest" (Pierre, 2005). This vision is timely in the countries of both the South and the North (Salam Fall, Favreau, & Larose, 2004, pp. 1–43; Ndiaye, 2005).

Third, democratic co-construction involves a deliberation between the best of representative democracy and the best of participatory democracy (Thériault, 2003; Cunill, 2004; Enjolras, 2006). This perspective differs from certain trends that encourage the demonization of representative democracy (on the grounds that all politicians are dishonest) while discrediting participatory democracy (on the grounds that it immobilizes the state by holding it hostage to interest groups). While acknowledging that representative democracy ultimately has the last word, the co-construction promoted here implies that elected officials establish open, inclusive forms of governance in which dialogue is favoured between the officials and the leaders of participatory democracy. This supposes the existence of interfaces, forums for mediation, and deliberation encouraging gateways (Enjolras, 2006; Dagnino, 2002) and requires that leaders of state and political parties, and of civil society, possess qualities of democratic facilitation. Competent, democratic political facilitation here involves the ability to recognize and manage conflict, and foster the broadening of forms of governance by including socio-economic and socio-political stakeholders that are often excluded, or rarely listened to (Brito, 2002; Brugué, 2004; Vaillancourt, 2007b).

Fourth, the democratic, solidarity-based co-construction of quality public policy involves recognition of the participation by stakeholders from the social economy as well as a partner-type relationship. It is not a case of asking for a privileged status for the social economy. Rather, it is a case of enabling the social economy to express its voice among those of other stakeholders at the moment when public policy and programs are defined. The issue is to have the social economy move beyond the status of a mere instrument of the state in the application of public policy plans co-constructed without it. A partnership interface differs from an instrumental relationship insofar as stakeholders from the social economy retain a degree of autonomy in relation to the state (Proulx, Bourque, & Savard, 2007; Lewis, 1999, 2004; Vaillancourt & Laville, 1998; Thiry & Lévesque, 2008).

In short, solidarity-based co-construction is not a luxury but a necessity for democracy. In fact, when stakeholders from civil society and the social economy are forgotten or instrumentalized in the relationship with the state, public policy is impoverished, because it reproduces the downside of competitive or bureaucratic regulation. Hence the criticism addressed by the social economy at the institutional arrangements most often found in PPP-style initiatives. This criticism blames PPPs for often being similar to a binary co-construction calling exclusively on the state/market pairing and depriving itself of input from the social economy (D'Amours, 2006; Conseil de la coopération du Québec, 2004, 2006; Chantier de l'économie sociale, 2001, 2005; Lévesque, 2003; Vaillancourt, 2007b).

Thus, after maintaining our distance both from the mono-construction model and from the neo-liberal and corporatist co-construction models, we have underscored our preference for a democratic co-construction model that builds both on participation by stakeholders from the market and civil society and on participation by the social economy that promises social innovation based on successful experiments.

Illustration of the Democratic Co-construction Model (Using the Example of Social Housing)[14]

To facilitate a better understanding of the scope of our theoretical positions, we will illustrate our thesis using actual cases of social policy reform. This will show that the democratic model of co-production and co-construction of public policy presented above constitutes more than a conceptual device. It is a model that has tangibly left its mark in certain recent social policy reforms. To document this statement, we will briefly recount the history of social policy, with emphasis on the craeation of social housing.

Background to Social Policy, in Three Stages

In light of the subject of study chosen for this chapter, we can "re-read" the history of social policy by distinguishing three stages.[15]

In the first stage (1920–60), the Québec state was very reluctant to intervene in social policy, and, when it did so, it favoured co-production, not co-construction, of public policy. In the health and welfare field,.for example, third-sector organizations largely dominated by the Church were favoured. One thinks, for instance, of the (non-profit) social service agencies of the 1950s and 1960s.

In the second stage (1960–80) corresponding to the onset of the Quiet Revolution and the Castonguay reform, the Québec social state intervened, mostly on its own, to construct and produce welfare state–type social policy (Jetté et al., 2000). This led to a period of mono-construction of public policy, along with a moderate dose of co-production. In this co-production, stakeholders from the third sector and the social economy had a real but marginal presence and a low profile (Jetté, 2008).

In the third stage (1980–2008), which arose in a context of crisis and the transformation of the welfare state, more co-production and co-construction of social policy is to be found, with, in some fields, participation by stakeholders from the market and civil society within which the social economy is present and recognized, particularly in certain social policy reforms from the mid-1990s onward (Vaillancourt, 2003; Jetté, 2008; Ulysse & Lesemann, 2007).

Specifically, it was during this third stage that certain innovative reforms made their appearance, and these clearly illustrate the democratic, solidarity-based configuration of co-construction of public policy presented in the last section. In these reforms one finds, to varying degrees, partnership-based relations between the state and the social economy. In short, the social economy, often in alliance with other stakeholders from civil society and the labour market, including social movements, cooperates with the state to develop (co-construct) and operationalize (co-produce) policy that tends towards the general interest.

To illustrate this, let us take the example of social and community housing.[16]

Contextual Elements to Outline the Evolution of Social Housing

If one takes into account the theoretical clarifications provided above, we can see that social housing practices and policy evolved from a mode comprising elements of co-production (up to the late 1980s) to a mode resolutely focused on the co-production and co-construction of public intervention in social housing, along with strong participation from the social economy. In that regard, the social housing field in Québec is a fascinating laboratory with respect to social innovation. Let us look at the context.

Paradoxically, these social innovations occurred in difficult budgetary conditions. Canada's provinces and territories have little fiscal leeway for creating social housing. As well, from 1993 onward, there was a brutal withdrawal of joint funding by the federal state, which since the 1950s had made it possible to share the cost of new social housing programs put forward by the provincial and territorial governments.[17] In this difficult context, Québec was, along with British Columbia and Manitoba, one of the few Canadian provinces to develop new social housing programs (Vaillancourt & Ducharme, 2000; Dansereau, 2005, pp. 22–3).

Social innovations often occurred first through the social practices that emerged in a local or regional area, without even the benefit of a public policy that contributed to supporting them. Once these innovative social practices proved their worth and were recognized as successful experiments, they began to be publicized and become points of reference for encouraging public decision-makers to develop new public policy to support such practices. In this way, public policy helped disseminate and perpetuate timely innovations tested in conclusive experiments. That is what we call the transition from experimentation to institutionalization.

The main protagonists in social housing innovation include stakeholders from the social economy and the third sector. Among them are housing cooperatives and non-profits, as well as their regional and province-wide federations (Confédération québécoise des coopératives d'habitations [CQCH], Réseau québécois des OSBL d'habitation [RQOH], Fédération des OSBL d'habitation de Montréal [FOHM], etc.). There are also technical resources groups (Groupes de ressources techniques [GRT]); the urban movement Front d'action populaire en réaménagement urbain (FRAPRU); public housing's tenants' federation, the Fédération des locataires de HLM du Québec (FLHLMQ); and so on.

There are also stakeholders from the public sector, since the social economy does not hold a monopoly on housing innovations. The contribution of public-sector stakeholders was documented in an inventory of community-action practices in low-income housing (Morin, Aubry, & Vaillancourt, 2007; Morin, 2007). Among stakeholders from the public sector,[18] there are of course the elected officials responsible for housing issues in the Québec state. There are also managers and practitioners from the municipal housing bureaus, the Québec housing agency Société d'habitation du Québec (SHQ), and other provincial, regional, and local public agencies called upon to work with stakeholders from the housing sector, including, for example, those from the health and social services network.

In fact, the social innovations that have led to advances in public practices and policy in social housing have often been the outcome of close cooperation between social economy and public sector stakeholders. This has occurred on several occasions over the past 20 years at the local, regional, and provincial levels in Québec.

Four Examples of Co-production and Co-construction

The Québec community housing sector offers a very good example of how social economy actors become involved in co-constructing social policy as well as in co-producing its implementation. This can be shown in the following four illustrations, where we can see that (1) the idea of co-production in this area goes back as far as the 1960s, and travelled from the Québec arena to the federal government; (2) specific agents were involved in support of co-production; (3) new institutions were born from it; and (4) new institutionalized practices that crossed the traditional divide between public agencies also arose.

The first example is proof positive of the participation by the social economy in the co-production of public policy.[19] This participation began in Québec as early as the 1960s, in particular when the Québec government set up the Société d'habitation du Québec (SHQ) in 1967 and launched the Coop-Habitat program. From 1967 to 1970, that program fostered the growth of rental housing cooperatives supported by Québec public funds. Because of certain difficulties, the program was short-lived, but it nevertheless put the idea of co-production in the public mind. During the 1960s, the Québec government took advantage somewhat timidly of the federal state's public housing policy, managed on a cost-sharing basis by the Canada Mortgage and Housing Corporation (CMHC), to build low-income housing units. During the 1950s and 1960s, federal housing policy favoured the mono-production model of public policy. As a result, the provinces taking advantage of it were encouraged to promote the low-income housing formula rather than the housing cooperative and non-profit formula. Consequently, the new social housing units developed by the provinces in the 1950s and 1960s with a contribution from federal programs were most often publicly owned and managed.[20] During the 1970s, however, the federal government amended its national housing policy so as to enable provinces wishing to take advantage of it to develop new social housing units that were not only low-income housing units coming under the public sector, but also housing cooperatives and non-profits belonging to the social economy sector. During the 1970s and 1980s, Québec used federal cost-sharing housing programs to develop social housing units coming under both the public sector and the third sector. During the 1990s, particularly following the announcement of the federal government's financial disengagement from 1993 onward, the Québec government, in its own public housing policy, exhibited an even stronger preference for the social economy sector. Thus, the place of the social economy in the total number of social housing units, over the years, became greater than in the other provinces. In Québec in 1997, there were 64,500 social housing units coming under the public sector, compared with 47,000 under the social economy sector (Vaillancourt & Ducharme, 2000; Ducharme, 2006). The trend in favour of the social economy grew much stronger from 1997 to 2008 with the AccèsLogis program, which had been tried out since 1995 under the name of PARCO, through the influence of government employees working in alliance with representatives from the community housing field. This program notably involved the financial contribution of local stakeholders. Of the 20,000 new housing units developed through this program since 1997, housing cooperatives and non-profits accounted for the vast majority. Thus, over the past 40 years, the Québec government's public housing policy has increasingly featured co-production, building on the contribution of the social economy.

The creation of technical resource groups (Groupes de ressources techniques, or GRTs) in the late 1970s is a second example of innovation that contributed to consolidation of the participation by the social economy in the co-production of public policy on housing in Québec. GRTs developed from 1976 onward through community architecture clinics and university social service departments (AGRTQ, 2002). Their efforts focused on mobilizing resident populations to fight the deterioration of their living environments (Bouchard, 2006). Their recognition and the support of GRTs by the Québec state, as early as 1977, meant the appearance of a new tool that favoured the emergence of several innovations in housing. The GRTs are themselves non-profits – that is, organizations coming not under the public sector but, instead, under the third sector. They have been entrusted with a significant role within the application of Québec public housing policy over the past 25 years. They share the values of participation, democratization, accessibility, and local development specific to the social economy (Bouchard & Hudon, 2008), and are essential partners with the housing cooperatives and non-profits.

Québec's community housing fund (Fonds québécois d'habitation communautaire, or FQHC) is a third example that testifies to participation by the social economy, not only in the co-production but also in the co-construction of public policy. The FQHC was set up in 1997 with the mission of promoting the development of social housing in the social economy sector. Created by the Québec state in response to a need expressed by social economy stakeholders at the 1996 "Summit on the Economy and Employment," the FQHC has a structure consisting of a majority of stakeholders from various components of the social economy. It plays the role of gateway between the public sector, third sector, and private sector. It is an intermediary institution that favours a reconciliation between the input from representative democracy and that from participatory democracy in public policy decision-making (Ducharme & Vaillancourt, 2000, 2006; Dansereau, 2005; Bouchard & Hudon, 2008). The FQHC symbolizes and promotes the partnership between the third sector and the public sector in social housing, as three researchers explain:

> In Québec, groups of non-profit organizations (NPOs) and cooperatives also play a major role as partners of the public authorities, with which they regularly negotiate the application of policy and programs. These organizations have become front-line players on the social housing scene; notably, they were associated with the creation, in 1997, of the Fonds québécois de l'habitation communautaire (a mediating and advisory body called upon to monitor the application of community-type social housing programs) and are among its managers. (Divay, Séguin, & Sénéchal, in Dansereau, 2005, p. 37) [Our translation]

This quotation draws attention to the participation by the FQHC and the third sector not only in the co-production of housing practices and policy, but also in their co-construction. This is what the researchers from the INRS are talking about when they point out that stakeholders from the third sector were "associated with the creation of the FQHC" or that they "regularly negotiate the application of policy and programs." The FQHC is an original device that arose from co-construction, and that fosters it in return. It played a key role in particular in the development of the AccèsLogis and Affordable Housing programs in Québec (Ducharme and Vaillancourt, 2006; Bouchard and Hudon, 2008).

Social housing with community support is a fourth example of co-production and co-construction. This example clearly illustrates the contribution of the social economy to the co-production of new innovative practices, which often end up opening the way to the emergence of public policy co-produced and co-constructed with input from the social economy. This issue has been closely monitored by LAREPPS since 1995. In a first exhaustive research project on the topic, conducted on the practices of the Montréal federation of housing NPOs (Fédération des OSBL d'habitation de Montréal, or FOHM), LAREPPS showed that these innovative practices contributed to improving the living conditions of the FOHM's lessees (single people, the homeless, people with mental health or drug addiction problems, etc.) (Jetté et al., 1998; Thériault et al., 1997, 2001; FOHM, 1997). LAREPPS emphasized above all that the lack of long-term funding of these practices was a problem, since it constantly depended on local and regional stakeholders' resourcefulness. Consequently, the LAREPPS researchers recommended, as early as 1998, that the Québec government adopt a clear, sustainable funding policy for the community support part in social housing practices, with community support for socially and socio-economically vulnerable individuals (Jetté et al., 1998, pp. 198–9). These recommendations were often repeated in subsequent work on residential resource needs for a broader vulnerable clientele, in particular for elderly people experiencing a slight decrease in autonomy and for disabled persons (Vaillancourt & Ducharme, 2000; Ducharme & Vaillancourt, 2002; Ducharme, Lalonde, & Vaillancourt, 2005; Vaillancourt & Charpentier, 2005; Vaillancourt, 2007a; Proulx et al., 2006, pp. 140–5). They were taken up again by other researchers (Dansereau, 2005, pp. 38–9) and stakeholder groups, in particular the Québec housing NPO network (Réseau québécois d'OSBL d'habitation) (RQOH, 2004, 2007; Roy, 2007). They were repeated by concerned public agencies, such as the Société d'habitation du Québec, municipal housing bureaus, and the Québec Ministry of Health and Social Services (Ministère de la Santé et des Services sociaux, or MSSS) (MSSS & SHQ, 2007). In November 2007, the Québec government announced a new public policy to institutionalize funding of the community support component in the social-housing-with-community-support formula (MSSS & SHQ, 2007). This example is striking, but it is not the only one.[21]

In conclusion, we can summarize our thesis by saying that, in social housing as in other areas of practice and policy, the presence of the social economy contributes to a triple democratization. In fact, it fosters the democratization of practices, policy development (co-construction), and operationalization of new policy (co-production). The growing presence of stakeholders from the social economy in social housing practices and policy responds to the aspiration of the population groups targeted by these interventions to exercise greater control over their living and housing conditions. The flexibility of the cooperative and association-based formulas leads to innovations, such as lessees' participation in management, and targeting of population groups that are marginalized or have special problems (women, Aboriginal communities, disabled persons, the homeless, etc.).

Conclusion

This chapter, which is based both on literature reviews and on analyses of certain recent social policy reforms, clearly differentiates between the co-production and the co-construction of public policy. We observed that the social economy could participate in both the development and the application of this public policy. Finally, we saw that this participation by the social economy could contribute to the democratization of public policy, depending on the specific configurations in which the social economy operates.

In the co-production of public policy, participation by third-sector or social economy stakeholders is to be found, as much as participation by stakeholders from the private, for-profit sector. This participation is described as co-production insofar as it cohabits with participation by the state and the public sector. In other words, the state is not alone in being involved in the production of policy. The co-production of policy at issue here is clearly differentiated, however, from co-construction insofar as it is deployed solely at the operational or organizational level. Co-production refers to the implementation of policy, which can indeed very well have been constructed by the state all by itself. Historically and empirically, this type of policy co-production, sometimes known as the welfare mix, is not a rare commodity. It has long existed in many Northern and Southern societies, so it is not surprising that some of the scientific literature should refer to it. Yet in that literature and in public debate, a larger number of writings deal with PPP formulas. Fewer papers refer to scenarios that interest us more – that is, to partnership formulas in which the social economy is supported by the public authorities. Hence the interest in the writings of Pestoff (2006) and Cunill (2004), for instance, who studied and conceptualized the benefits of partner-type practices between the state and the third sector. In these scenarios, which offer alternatives to privatization, the co-production promoted by the state favours a partnership with stakeholders from civil society and the third sector, rather than a partnership with the private sector, as advocated by the dominant current of new public management.

As to the co-construction of public policy, its originality lies in the fact that it arises not at the moment of implementation, but at the moment when the policy is drawn up (i.e., the moment of construction). Thus, it is concerned with the institutional dimension of public policy, and not merely its organizational dimension. Throughout this chapter, we have highlighted the characteristics of policy co-construction in which the state, while retaining the last word, does not construct policy by itself. On the contrary, the state associates with this construction the active participation of stakeholders from the labour market and civil society, those from the social economy among them. In this regard, the social economy, through its ability to experiment and to reflect on its experiments, is particularly attractive as both a breeding ground and a lever for fostering the development of policy that does not ignore the general interest and is open to democratic governance.

To illustrate the fruitfulness of the theoretical distinctions presented in the first three sections, the final, more empirical section was devoted to the examination of certain social policy reforms appearing in Québec over the past 20 years, particularly in social housing. In building on the research results on this topic, we have highlighted social innovations in which stakeholders in the social economy played a leading role by being closely associated with the co-production and co-construction of public policy. Over the years, these innovations were to be found in both practices, the management and organization of policy (organizational dimension), and the negotiation and construction of policy itself (institutional dimension). The genesis and development of the Accès-Logis program and the Fonds québécois d'habitation communautaire are good illustrations of this.

In short, based on both our theoretical and empirical observations, we have seen that a great conceptual and practical partnership can and must be established between co-production (of services of public interest and policy) on the one hand, and co-construction (of policy) on the other. This partnership stems from the fact that the two concepts are used more often than not by researchers and stakeholders concerned with the democratization of services, organizations, and public policy. To deliver its analytical potential, the concept of co-construction of public policy has to be clearly differentiated from that of co-production of services and policy. That being said, the lessons drawn from the literature on co-production are an essential reference point for moving reflection and action forward with respect to the concept of policy co-construction carried out in partnership with the social economy. In any case, when co-production cohabits with co-construction, it may be deduced that the interfaces between the state and the social economy are less instrumental and more partnership-oriented. The result is then added value for the democratization of public policy, both at the time of its implementation and its definition.

NOTES

1   This chapter is a by-product of broader research on which we have re-
    ported in a research note (Vaillancourt, 2008). It was made possible
    through support from LAREPPS, CRISES, ARUC-ÉS (Community-Univer-
    sity Research Alliance; CURA in Social Economy) and the CURA in Social
    Innovation and Community Development. We thank five individuals who
    read and commented on earlier versions: Marie J. Bouchard, Marie-Noëlle
    Ducharme, Jean-Marc Fontan, René Lachapelle, and Benoît Lévesque.
2   Labour and management organizations represent stakeholders anchored in
    the labour market, but, as associations safeguarding their members' rights
    and interests, they are also located in civil society.
3   In this quotation, we have omitted the words "based on civility" as added
    by Anheier, in an effort to revise an earlier definition so as to take into ac-
    count criticisms from a current of literature that sought a more normative
    definition. We do not follow Anheier's path because his addition of a quali-
    tative criterion such as "based on civility" generates more problems than it
    solves. Indeed, how does one go about differentiating organizations based
    on civility from those that are not?
4   A number of ideas on public policy developed in Vaillancourt and Char-
    pentier (2005, pp. 111–17) are restated here.
5   Owing to our more extensive research experience in the social policy field,
    one specific component of public policy among others, it is clear that we
    spontaneously base our work on our theoretical, historical, and empirical

knowledge developed in the field of social policy to address the concept and reality of public policy.

6 We acknowledge that the general interest is never totally attained at a given moment in a given society. It is an ideal type that societies may come close to achieving provided they work towards it with all their strength by the appropriate means.

7 In another paper, we took a close look at the literature on the co-production of services of public interest, in particular the literature from administrative sciences and sociology of work (Vaillancourt, 2008, Section 1.1).

8 Thus, Argentinean political scientist Oscar Oszlak states that: "NGOs can play a crucial role in the co-production and co-management of socially valuable services" (2007).

9 Nuria Cunill, in making the distinction between two forms of private realities – namely, the for-profit private sector "guided by market logic" and the "private sector guided by the logic of solidarity," including cooperatives and certain NGOs – takes a position, implicitly at least, in favour of a tripolar conceptual framework favouring co-production based on the logic of solidarity (Cunill, 2004, pp. 26–8) and involving the specific contribution of third-sector stakeholders.

10 In the countries of the South, the form of authoritarian state that constructs – or mono-constructs – public policy on its own prevailed under military dictatorships, such as that ruling Chile from 1973 to 1989 (Garreton, 2007, pp. 77–82).

11 Consider the representation of the state in the working paper produced by the CNTU (CSN) in 1971, *Ne comptons que sur nos propres moyens* ("Let us rely on our own means alone"). In that paper, the Quiet Revolution was presented as having been brought about completely by the dominant classes.

12 In Latin American countries such as Mexico and Argentina, corporatism led to highly split, clientelist social policies that offer advantages to certain social groups (unionized civil servants, for instance) while leaving large segments of society without any social protection.

13 Along with other authors (Favreau, 2005; Julliard, 2007), we feel it is important to differentiate clearly between the break from capitalism and the break from neo-liberalism, which lets us speak of capitalism and its alternatives in the plural, not just the singular.

14 Marie-Noëlle Ducharme's comments and suggestions were very helpful to us in writing this section.

15 For a more detailed presentation of this historical re-reading, see Vaillancourt, 2008, pp. 16–18, and 2007b, pp. 14–19.

16 In another paper on the État stratège as a partner of civil society, we examined other examples of social policy reforms giving rise to participation by
the social economy in the co-construction and co-production of policy (see
Vaillancourt, 2007b, pp. 18–22).

17 Since 2000, the federal government has begun to participate once again in
the funding of certain provincial initiatives. But it has done so timidly in
reference to provincial programs concerning narrowly targeted clienteles
(such as the homeless), whose benchmarks remained fixed by the federal
government (Vaillancourt & Ducharme, 2000, p. 18).

18 As we focus on Quebec innovations in social housing, we draw the reader's attention to certain Quebec stakeholders in the public and third sectors. Clearly, a more comprehensive inventory of stakeholders would
identify others whose role is important in Canada as a whole, including
the Canada Mortgage and Housing Corporation (CMHC).

19 To pinpoint clearly the historical evolution of public policy concerning
the development of social housing in Quebec, two types of initiatives
have to be distinguished: those from the federal state, often (but not always) following the path of cost-sharing programs that had a structuring
effect on the policies of the provincial states that decided to take advantage of them; and those exclusively under the responsibility of the provincial state, such as Quebec's AccèsLogis program, which was launched
in 1997.

20 Until the mid-1960s, housing cooperatives targeted the working class
but were developed without any public support. Housing non-profits
were founded primarily by religious congregations or other charitable
organizations.

21 Among the other public policies on housing that were co-constructed
with participation by the social economy and other stakeholders from
civil society is the reform, introduced in 2002, of the rules of governance
for municipal housing bureaus. In fact, among the provisions of Bill
49 amending the Act respecting the Société d'habitation du Québec, a
number led to formal recognition of lessees' right of association and encouraged participation by low-income housing lessee association representatives on the municipal housing bureaus' boards of directors (Morin,
2007, p. 149). The democratization of the form of governance of public
social housing institutions stems from the dissemination in the public
sector of certain innovations in governance practices previously tested in
housing cooperatives and non-profits (Vaillancourt & Charpentier, 2005,
Chapter 4; Ducharme, 2006).

REFERENCES

Anheier, H.K. (2007). Reflections on the concept and measurement of global civil society. *Voluntas: International Journal of Voluntary and Nonprofit Organizations, 18*(1), 1–15. Accessed 30 April 2012. http://dx.doi.org/10.1007/s11266-007-9031-y

Association des groupes de ressources techniques du Québec. (2002). *Manuel de développement de projet.* Joint publication of AGRTQ and CSMO-ÉSAC, 01–2002.

Batley, R. (2007). Governments and non-state service providers: Engaged or divorced? *Capacity.ORG, A gateway for capacity development,* 30. Accessed 30 April 2012. http://lencd.com/data/docs/58-Partnerships%20for%20service%20delivery.pdf

Bifarello, M. (2000). *Public-third sector partnerships: A major innovation in Argentinian social policy.* Paper presented to ISTR Fourth International Conference, Dublin.

Bouchard, M.J. (2006). De l'expérimentation à l'institutionnalisation positive, l'innovation sociale dans le logement communautaire au Québec. *Annals of Public and Cooperative Economics, 77*(2), 139–66. Accessed 30 April 2012. http://dx.doi.org/10.1111/j.1370-4788.2006.00301.x

Bouchard, M.J., & Hudon, M. (2008). L'histoire d'une innovation sociale. In M.J. Bouchard (Ed.), *Se loger autrement au Québec* (pp. 15–53). Montréal: Éditions Saint-Martin.

Bresser, P., Carlos, L., & Cunill Grau, N. (Eds.). (1998). *Lo Público no estatal en la Reforma del Estado.* Buenos Aires, Barcelona, and Mexico City: Paidós and CLAD.

Brito, M. (2002). Buen gobierno local y calidad de la democracia. *Instituciones y desarrollo, 12–13,* 249–75.

Brugué, Q. (2004). Modernizar la administración desde la izquierda: Burocracia, nueva gestión pública y administración deliberativa. *Reforma y Democracia. CLAD.*

Chantier de l'économie sociale. (2001). *De nouveau, nous osons...* Strategy document. Montréal: Chantier de l'économie sociale. Accessed 30 April 2012. http://www.ccednet-rcdec.ca/?q=en/node/885

Chantier de l'économie sociale, in collaboration with the Canadian Community Economic Development Network (CCEDNet) and Alliance Recherche Universités-Communautés en économie sociale (ARUC-ÉS). (2005). *Social economy and community economic development in Canada: Next steps for public policy.*

Comité sectoriel de la main d'oeuvre (CSMO) en économie sociale et en action communautaire. (2006). *Travailler solidairement: Pour des emplois durables et de qualité. Défis et projets.* Summary of the Comité travailler autrement report. Accessed 30 April 2012. http://www.csmoesac.qc.ca/uploads/documents/actualites/les_enjeux_et_les_defis-synthese_12_juillet_final.pdf

Conseil de la coopération du Québec (CCQ). (2004). *Vers un réel partenariat public/coopératif.* Québec: CCQ.

Conseil de la coopération du Québec (CCQ). (2006). *La voie coopérative pour les citoyens à la gouverne de leur santé!* Brief submitted to the Parliamentary Committee on Social Affairs concerning the White Paper, *Guaranteeing access: Meeting the challenges of equity, efficiency and quality.* Québec: CCQ.

Côté, L., Lévesque, B., & Morneau, G. (Eds.). (2009). *État stratège et participation citoyenne.* Québec: PUQ.

Cunill Grau, N. (2004). La democratización de la administración pública: Los mitos a vencer. In Bresser Pereira, N. Cunill Grau, L. Garnier, O. Oszlak, & A. Przeworski (2004), *Política y gestión pública.* Buenos Aires: Fondo de Cultura Económica, CLAD.

D'Amours, A. (2006). Renouveler le système de santé grâce à la voie coopérative. *Le Devoir,* 18 April 2006, p. A7.

Dagnino, E. (Ed.). (2002). *Sociedad civil, esfera pública y democratización en América Latina: Brasil.* Mexico City: Editora Unicamp, Fundo de cultura económica.

Dansereau, F. (Ed.). (2005). *Politiques et interventions en habitation: Analyse des tendances récentes en Amérique du Nord et en Europe.* Québec: Presses de l'Université Laval and Société d'habitation du Québec.

Defourny, J. & Monzon Campos, J.L. (Eds.). (1992). *Économie sociale: Entre économie capitaliste et économie publique / The Third Sector: Cooperative, mutual and nonprofit organizations.* Brussels: CIRIEC and De Boeck Université.

Divay, G., Séguin, A.-M., & Sénéchal, G. (2005). Le Canada. In F. Dansereau (Ed.), *Politiques et interventions en habitation: Analyse des tendances récentes en Amérique du Nord et en Europe* (pp. 13–44). Québec: Presses de l'Université Laval et Société d'habitation du Québec.

Ducharme, M.-N. (2006). Les habitations à loyer modique publiques destinées aux aîné-e-s: Portrait sectoriel. *Cahier du LAREPPS, 06–05.*

Ducharme, M.-N., & Vaillancourt, Y. (2000). Le logement social, une composante importante des politiques sociales en reconfiguration: État de la situation au Québec. *Cahier du LAREPPS, 00–08,* Montréal.

Ducharme, M.-N., & Vaillancourt, Y., in collaboration with Aubry, F. (2002). Portrait des organismes sans but lucratif sur l'île de Montréal. Montréal:

LAREPPS in collaboration with the Fédération des OSBL d'habitation de Montréal (FOHM), UQAM, *Cahiers du LAREPPS*, 02–05.

Ducharme, M.-N., Lalonde, L., & Vaillancourt, Y. (2005). L'économie sociale au cœur des pratiques novatrices en logement social, l'expérience du Québec. In A. Amintas, A. Gouzien, & P. Perrot (Eds.), *Les chantiers de l'économie sociale et solidaire* (pp. 157–69). Rennes: Presses universitaires de Rennes.

Ducharme, M.-N., & Vaillancourt, Y. (2006). À l'orée d'une gouvernance associative? L'expérience du Fonds québécois d'habitation communautaire. *Economie et Solidarites*, 36(1), 110–25.

Enjolras, B. (2005). Économie sociale et solidaire et régimes de gouvernance. *RECMA: Revue internationale de l'économie sociale, 296*, 56–69.

Enjolras, B. (2006). *Formes institutionnelles et changements institutionnels: Le cas de la marchandisation des associations*. Doctoral thesis. Montréal: UQAM.

Esping-Anderson, G. (1999). *Les trois mondes de l'État-providence: Essai sur le capitalisme moderne*. Paris: PUF, coll. Le lien social.

Evers, A., & Laville, J.-L. (Eds.). (2004). *The third sector in Europe*. Cheltenham, UK: Edward Elgar.

Favreau, L. (2005). Économie sociale et politiques publiques: La question du renouvellement de l'État social au Nord et de sa construction au Sud. Montréal: UQAM, *Cahiers du LAREPPS*, 05-17.

Favreau, L., & Salam Fall, A. (Eds.). (2007). *L'Afrique qui se refait: Initiatives socioéconomiques des communautés et développement en Afrique noire*. Québec: PUQ.

Fédération des osbl d'habitation de Montréal (FOHM). (1997). *Évaluation de l'intervention du logement social avec support communautaire pour des personnes seules, à faible revenu et à risque de marginalisation sociale dans les quartiers centraux de Montréal*. Montréal: LAREPPS-UQAM, FOHM, CLSC Plateau Mont-Royal, SHQ.

Garretón, M.A. (2007). Del postpinochetismo a la sociedad democrática: Globalización y política en el bicentenario. Debate, Santiago, Chile.

Jetté, C. (2008). *Les organisations communautaires et la transformation de l'État-providence: Trois décennies de coconstruction des politiques publiques dans le domaine de la santé et des services sociaux*. Québec: Presses de l'Université du Québec.

Jetté, C., Thériault, L., Mahieu, R., and Vaillancourt,Y. (1998). *Évaluation du logement social avec support communautaire à la Fédération des OSBL d'Habitation de Montréal (FOHM). Intervention auprès des personnes seules, à faibles revenus et à risque de marginalisation sociale dans les quartiers centraux de Montréal*. Montréal: Final report on research conducted in partnership with the FOHM, the SHQ, and CLSC du Plateau Mont-Royal.

Jetté, C., Lévesque, B., Mager, L., & Vaillancourt, Y. (2000). *Économie sociale et transformation de l'État-providence dans le domaine de la santé et du bien-être: Une recension des écrits (1990–2000)*. Sainte-Foy: Presses de l'Université du Québec.

Julliard, J. (2007). Réinventer la gauche. *Le nouvel observateur* (2219), 20–1.

Kliksberg, B. (2007). Cómo avanzar la participación en América latina, el continente más desigual? Anotaciones estratégicas. *Reforma y Democracia, 37*, 37–80.

Laville, J.-L. (2005). *Sociologie des services: Entre marché et solidarité*. Paris: Érès.

Laville, J.-L., & Nyssens, M. (Eds.). (2001). *Les services sociaux entre associations, État et marché: L'aide aux personnes âgées*. Paris: La Découverte / MAUSS / CRIDA.

Le Grand, J., & Bartlett, W. (Eds.). (1993). *Quasi-markets and social policy*. London: Macmillan.

Lévesque, B. (2003). Fonction de base et nouveau rôle des pouvoirs publics: Vers un nouveau paradigme de l'État. *Annals of Public and Cooperative Economics, 74*(4), 489–514. Accessed 30 April 2012. http://dx.doi.org/10.1111/j.1467-8292.2003.00232.x

Lévesque, B. (2007). *Un siècle et demi d'économie sociale au Québec: Plusieurs configurations en présence (1850–2007)*. Montréal: Joint publication, CRISES/ÉNAP/ARUC-ÉS.

Lévesque, B., Bourque, G.L., & Forgues, É. (2001). *La nouvelle sociologie économique*. Paris: Desclée de Brouwer.

Lévesque, B., & Thiry, B. (2008). Conclusions: Concurrence et partenariat, deux vecteurs de la reconfiguration des nouveaux régimes de la gouvernance des services sociaux et de santé. In B. Enjolras (Ed.), *Gouvernance et intérêt général dans les services sociaux et de santé* (pp. 227–61). Brussels: Peter Lang (Collection Économie sociale & Économie publique).

Lewis, J. (1999). Reviewing the relationship between the voluntary sector and the state in Britain in the 1990s. *Voluntas: International Journal of Voluntary and Nonprofit Organizations, 10*(3), 255–70. http://dx.doi.org/10.1023/A:1021257001466

Lewis, J. (2004). The state and the third sector in modern welfare states: Independence, instrumentality, partnership. In A. Evers & J.-L. Laville (Eds.), *The third sector in Europe* (pp. 169-87). Cheltenham, UK: Edward Elgar.

Mariñez Navarro, F. (Ed.). (2007). *Ciudadanos, decisiones públicas y calidad de la democracia*. Mexico City: Limusa Noriega Editores.

Means, R., & Smith, R. (Eds.). (1994). *Community care: Policy and practice*. London: Macmillan.

Ministère de la santé et des services sociaux (MSSS) and Société d'habitation du Québec (SHQ). (2007). *Cadre de référence sur le soutien communautaire en logement social: Une intervention intersectorielle des réseaux de la santé et des services sociaux et de l'éducation.* Québec City: MSSS and SHQ.

Morin, P. (2007). Les pratiques d'action communautaire en milieu HLM: Un patrimoine d'expériences et de compétences. *Nouvelles Pratiques Sociales, 19*(2), 144–58.

Morin, P., Aubry, F., & Vaillancourt, Y. (2007). *Les pratiques d'action communautaire en milieu HLM: Inventaire analytique.* Research report drafted by LAREPPS/UQAM for the Société d'habitation du Québec. Québec: Government of Québec.

Munck, R. (2006). Global civil society: Royal road or slippery path. *Voluntas: International Journal of Voluntary and Nonprofit Organizations, 17*(4), 324–32. Accessed 30 April 2012. http://dx.doi.org/10.1007/s11266-006-9019-z

Ndiaye, S. (2005). La coproduction de services collectifs urbains en Afrique de l'Ouest. *Comparaisons Internationales series* 22. Canada Research Chair in Community Development, Université du Québec en Outaouais, Gatineau.

Olvera, A.J. (Ed.). (1999). *La sociedad civil: De la teoría a la realidad.* Mexico City: El Colegio de México.

Oszlak, O. (2007). El Estado democrático en América Latina: Hacia el desarrollo de líneas de investigación. *Nueva Sociedad* (210), 42–63.

Pestoff, V. (2006). Citizens and co-production of welfare services. *Public Management Review, 8*(4), 503–19. Accessed 30 April 2012. http://dx.doi.org/10.1080/14719030601022882

Pestoff, V., Osborne, S.P., & Brandsen, T. (2006). Patterns of co-production in public services: Some concluding thoughts. *Public Management Review, 8*(4), 591–95. http://dx.doi.org/10.1080/14719030601022999

Pierre, J., & Peters, B.G. (2000). *Governance, politics and the state.* New York: MacMillan Press Ltd and St. Martin's Press.

Pierre, J. (2005). ¿"Poder para"... o "poder sobre"? Repensando la fuerza del Estado. *Reforma y Democracia* (32).

Proulx, J., Bourque, D., & Savard, S. (2007). The government-Third Sector interface in Québec. *Voluntas: International Journal of Voluntary and Nonprofit Organizations, 18*(3), 293–307.

Proulx, J., Dumais, L., Caillouette, J., and Vaillancourt, Y. (2006). Les services aux personnes ayant des incapacités au Québec: Rôle des acteurs et dynamiques régionales. *Cahiers du LAREPPS, 6*–12.

Réseau québécois des OSBL d'habitation (RQOH). (2004). *Pour un programme de financement du soutien communautaire en OSBL d'habitation.* Montréal: RQOH.

Réseau québécois des OSBL d'habitation (RQOH). (2007). *Parce que l'avenir nous habite*. Les actes du colloque, 9 November 2006. Montréal: RQOH.

Rich, R.C. (1981). Interaction of the voluntary and governmental sectors: Toward an understanding of the coproduction of municipal services. *Administration & Society*, *13*(1), 59–76. Accessed 30 April 2012. http://dx.doi.org/10.1177/009539978101300104

Rouillard, C. (2006). Les partenariats public-privé et la reconfiguration de la gouvernance: Réflexion sur la construction d'un État entropique. *Les Cahiers du 27 juin*, *3*(1): 33–7.

Rouillard, C., Montpetit, É., Fortier, I., & Gagnon, A.G. (2004). *La réingénierie de l'État: Vers un appauvrissement de la gouvernance québécoise*. Québec: Les Presses de l'Université Laval.

Roy, F. (2007). Pour une reconduction du Programme AccèsLogis. *Le Devoir*, 23 May 2007, p. A7.

Salam Fall, A., Favreau, L., & Larose, G. (Eds.). (2004). *Le Sud… et le Nord dans la mondialisation: Quelles alternatives? Le renouvellement des modèles de développement*. Québec: Presses de l'Université du Québec and Karthala.

Thériault, J.-Y. (2003). L'avenir de la social-démocratie au Québec. In M. Venne (Ed.), *L'annuaire du Québec 2004* (pp. 631–40). Montréal: Fides,.

Thériault, L., Jetté, C., Mathieu, R., & Vaillancourt, Y. (1997). Qualité de vie et logement social avec 'support communautaire' à Montréal. *Canadian Social Work Review/Revue canadienne de service social*, *14*(1): 55–81.

Thériault, L., Jetté, C., Mathieu, R., & Vaillancourt, Y. (2001). *Social housing with community support: A study of the FOHM experience*. Ottawa: Caledon Institute of Social Policy. Accessed 10 July 2011. http://www.caledoninst.org/Publications/PDF/fohm.pdf

Tremblay, M., Tremblay, P.-A., & Tremblay, S. (Eds.) (2006). *Le développement social: Un enjeu pour l'économie sociale*. Québec: Presses de l'Université du Québec, Collection Pratiques et politiques sociales et économiques.

Ulysse, P.-J., & Lesemann, F. (2007). *Lutte contre la pauvreté, territorialité et développement social intégré: Le cas de Trois-Rivières*. Québec: Presses de l'Université du Québec, Collection Problèmes sociaux et interventions sociales.

Vaillancourt, Y. (2003). The Québec model in social policy and its interface with Canada's Social Union. In S. Fortin, A. Noël, & F. St-Hilaire (Eds.), *Forging the Canadian Social Union: SUFA and beyond* (pp. 156–95). Montréal: Institute for Research on Public Policy.

Vaillancourt, Y. (2006). Le tiers secteur au Canada, un lieu de rencontre entre la tradition américaine et la tradition européenne. *Canadian Review of Social Policy/Revue canadienne de politique sociale*, *56*, 23–39.

Vaillancourt, Y. (2007a). Le cadre national sur le soutien communautaire en logement social: Un test pour la réforme Couillard. In RQOH, *Parce que l'avenir nous habite* (pp. 35–40). Les actes du colloque, 9 November 2006, Montréal: RQOH.

Vaillancourt, Y., Aubry, F., & Jetté, C. (Eds.). (2003). *L'économie sociale dans les services à domicile.* Québec: Presses de l'Université du Québec.

Vaillancourt, Y., Aubry, F., Kearney, M., Thériault, L., & Tremblay, L. (2004). The contribution of the social economy towards healthy social policy reforms in Canada: A Québec viewpoint. In R. Dennis (Ed.), *Social determinants of health: Canadian perspectives* (pp. 311–29). Toronto: Canadian Scholars' Press. See Cahiers du LAREPPS 04–04.

Vaillancourt, Y., & Charpentier, M. (Eds.). (2005). *Les passerelles entre l'État, le marché et l'économie sociale dans les services de logement social et d'hébergement pour les personnes âgées.* Montréal: LAREPPS.

Vaillancourt, Y., & Ducharme, M.-N., with the collaboration of R. Cohen, C. Roy, & C. Jetté. (2001). *Social housing – A key component of social policies in transformation: The Québec Experience.* Ottawa: The Caledon Institute of Social Policy. Accessed 10 July 2011. www.caledoninst.org

Vaillancourt, Y., & Laville, J.-L. (1998). Les rapports entre associations et État: Un enjeu politique. *Revue du MAUSS semestrielle, 11*(1): 119–35.

Vaillancourt, Y., in collaboration with P. Leclerc. (2007b). Vers un État stratège, partenaire de la société civile. *Cahiers du LAREPPS, 07–10.* Montréal: Jointly published with Les Cahiers du CRISES and Les Cahiers de l'ARUC-ISDC.

Vaillancourt, Y., in collaboration with P. Leclerc. (2008). Note de recherche sur l'apport de l'économie sociale dans la coproduction et la coconstruction des politiques publiques. *Cahiers du LAREPPS, 08–01.* Montréal: Jointly published with Les Cahiers du CRISES and Les Cahiers de l'ARUC-ISDC.

Vitale, D. (2005). Reforma del Estado y democratización de la gestión pública: La experiencia brasileña del Presupuesto Participativo. *Reforma y Democracía, 33* (October 2005).

5 The Uncertain Evolution of Association Law in Québec: The Achilles' Heel of the Social Economy?

LOUIS JOLIN

Introduction

Historically, the main forms of organization in the social economy were associations, cooperatives, and mutual organizations (Desroches, 1983; Demoustier, 2001). To use these terms is to define the social economy from the standpoint of the legal status of its actors, although it is also possible to define it in other ways – for example, by defining its actors according to their primary task or sector.

Over the last 20 years, cooperatives in Québec have faced significant legislative changes. In the 1990s, there were changes to existing laws, both at the federal and Québec levels, mostly to facilitate the inflow of capital and the creation of a new type of cooperative in Québec, the solidarity cooperative.[1] There were also changes to mutual companies that were active in insurance, several of which initiated and gave concrete expression to a demutualization movement in order to improve their access to capital.[2]

Despite several declarations of intent, discussion papers, and federal bills (the last, Bill C-4, was finally adopted, but the others died on the Order Paper),[3] the legal status of associations in Québec has hardly changed to date. The exceptions are the Civil Code of Québec's formal recognition of partnership agreements, in force as of January 1, 1994,[4] and the obligation of incorporated partnerships to comply with the provisions of the Act Respecting the Legal Publicity of Enterprises.

This chapter deals specifically with associations that enjoy legal person status, commonly referred to in Québec as *organisme sans but lucratif*

(OSBL) or *organisme à but non lucratif* (OBNL; non-profit organizations [NPOs] or non-profit-making organizations [NPMOs]).

Under Québec law, these organizations may also be considered enterprises – a fortiori social economy enterprises – but they are also beset by difficulties for which the recent intentions of the Québec government may provide some solutions, as confirmed in a discussion paper. After briefly discussing the questions that are currently being raised in France and Belgium on the appropriateness of the associative status and the operation of a business, we will look at the compatibility between the associative status and the operation of a social economy enterprise under Québec law. We will then discuss the principal legal problems affecting incorporated associations in Québec. The third section of the chapter is devoted to a discussion on the possible adoption of a Québec law on associations. This discussion reveals divergent positions on the significance of the association and its in the third sector and in society as a whole. Lastly, we will suggest approaches that could resolve these issues and unify the various points of view.

Beyond Québec: Association Status in Belgium and France

There has been a debate in France and Belgium over the last few years about the legal status of associations. In 2001, France celebrated the centenary of the French Law of 1901 on association agreements.[6] The anniversary was highlighted with lectures, symposia, and publications, discussing, among other things, the relevance and topicality of this law for the twenty-first century. While the law is still considered highly valid, some observers, such as Gérard Sousi (2001, pp. 21–4), have asked whether the time has come to formally incorporate the freedom of association established by the law into the French Constitution itself. Still others have questioned the relevance of proposing a new category of non-profit enterprises with a social mission for groups that form part of the market sector and perform commercial operations on a regular basis. A report by Alain Lipietz (2000) on the opportunity afforded by a new type of company with a social mission takes this hypothesis seriously but suggests instead parent legislation to develop the social and solidarity economy. "As our investigation-negotiation progressed, it did not really seem appropriate to create 'a new type of legal entity' – as a component of the third sector in the social and solidarity economy – to represent enterprises with a social mission and mixed financing, at least not in the form of a legal structure that would be distinct from current forms found in the social economy" (Lipietz, 2000, p. 75; TT).

The idea of introducing a different status that would be better adapted than the associative status of the 1901 law is not new: in 1975, the Comité d'étude pour la réforme de l'entreprise (Research Committee on Enterprise Reform), chaired by Pierre Sudreau, proposed "filling the gap that exists in the array of legal forms of organization adopted by non-profit activities" (Sudreau, 1975, p. 121; TT). It suggested a new status: namely, that of the non-profit-oriented enterprise; however, it was not followed up. About 10 years later, the Conseil national de la vie associative (CNVA, National Council on Associations) suggested that some of the attributes associated with the merchant status be assigned to associations conducting commercial activities on a regular basis, but that the association not be compelled to change its status: "Thus, an association that, to achieve its social mission, was convinced it should carry out commercial activities on a regular basis, would be subject to the rules of commercial law in performing these activities, while accepting furthermore that it would come under civil law – but without being placed in the same category as a merchant" (CNVA, 1988, p. 81; TT).

In Belgium, the 2002 law on not-for-profit associations, international not-for-profit associations, and foundations should be viewed as an update of a previous law.[7] In parallel with the NPO status, a new status emerged in 1999, that of the *société à finalité sociale* (company with a social purpose).[8] In reality, Belgian law did not create a new type of company but, rather, a form that could be introduced into the statutes of any firm with a corporate status. To be considered as having a social purpose, a company must ensure that its statutes include specific conditions (e.g., associates are not allowed to make profits or, if at all, only to a limited degree; a precise definition of the social mandate is written into the statutes; the number of votes that can be held by an associate at the general assembly is limited to one-tenth of the total votes, or to one-twentieth if the associate is a company employee). Sections 668 and 669 of the Code des sociétés (Company Code) also make provision for a not-for-profit association to be transformed into a company with a social purpose.

What justifies adopting one status over another? The domestic law of each country includes measures that facilitate or impede economic or commercial practices on the part of associations. Thus, is creating a new status advisable? Would it not be better to consider legally modifying the conditions required for operating the business without necessarily resorting to a new status? This was the approach favoured by France (Jolin, 1995).[9]

Association Status under Québec Law: Relevant, but with Little Room for Improvement

Under Québec law, is the association status appropriate for operating a business or even a social economy enterprise? We examine this question below.

The Association: A Legal Status for Operating an Enterprise

The definition of a partnership agreement in Section 2186 of the Civil Code of Québec[10] is extremely permissive: "A partnership agreement is a contract by which the parties agree to pursue a common goal other than the making of pecuniary profits to be shared between the members of the association" (TT). Thus, the not-for-profit nature is intended only for the association's members, who may not share the profits among themselves. There is nothing to stop an unincorporated association (i.e., one without juridical personality or corporate status) from carrying on an economic or commercial activity.

There are certain nuances, however, in the case of incorporated associations. If we refer to Section 218 of the Companies Act[11] or Section 154 of the Canada Corporations Act,[12] the association's goal can be national, patriotic, religious, philanthropic, charitable, scientific, artistic, social, professional, sports-related, or something similar. If the economic or commercial objective predominates, it may come up against the limited capacity of the incorporated partnership under current Québec law. This would not occur if the economic or commercial objective was secondary to the principal goal, which for its part must accord with what is indicated in the act of incorporation. Are the official objectives broad enough to give incorporated associations adequate room to manoeuvre, however? For all that, can they be considered enterprises?

Section 1525 of the Civil Code of Québec gives no definition of the term "enterprise." Instead, it clarifies what is meant by operating an enterprise, since it is not the enterprise that is a subject of law but rather various kinds of natural or legal persons (including incorporated associations) who, in certain cases, can be considered to be operating an enterprise. The Civil Code of Québec replaced the idea of merchant and that of the commercial act (contained in the Civil Code of Lower

Canada)[13] with the idea of operating an enterprise and gives special treatment not only to commercial activities but also to the entire domain of economic activity.

What does the third paragraph of Section 1525 say? "The carrying on by one or more persons of an organized economic activity, whether or not it is commercial in nature, consisting of producing, administering or alienating property, or providing a service, constitutes the carrying on of an enterprise" (TT). Under Québec law, can this carrying out of an organized economic activity constitute the predominant objective of an association? This would be difficult to accept if we take into account the limited capacity of incorporated partnerships; however, there is no problem if the operation of the enterprise permits the pursuit of objectives for which letters patent have been granted.

Canadian courts, including the Supreme Court, seemed to draw a distinction between association and enterprise. According to the work of Antoni Dandonneau (1978), however, this is primarily a problem of translation: The term "business," which sometimes connotes profit, has too often been translated into French as the term *entreprise*. According to Dandonneau, the terms to be juxtaposed are not *association* and *entreprise*, but rather "business corporation" (*société anonyme*) and "nonprofit organization" (*association*).

Lastly, an association that is registered as a charity for tax reasons may conduct supplementary commercial activity, provided that that activity remains linked and subordinate to the charitable purposes of the organization or is performed largely by unpaid volunteers. (Revenue Canada, 2003).

The Association: A Legal Status Appropriate for Pursuing a Disinterested Activity or an Activity in the Public Interest

The disinterestedness characterizing associations refers to the absence of profit for members. Inasmuch as making a profit is not the main objective of its activities, the association constitutes an appropriate framework for pursuing social, cultural, or environmental causes, defending the interests of consumers as well as those of producers from elsewhere, or performing a public service. While most would agree with this understanding of association, the notion that an association could be an appropriate framework for operating an enterprise does not enjoy the same consensus. Moreover, Section 258 of the Companies Act and Section 154 of the Canada Corporations Act are very clear in this matter.[14]

The disinterestedness of associations does not mean that they are not allowed to derive benefits, only that the benefits may not be pecuniary gain to be divided up among members. The gains are to be of a moral, social, cultural, or even economic nature, in the sense that they may lead to savings for their members or otherwise contribute to their economic health.

The distinctive features of an association (the bringing together of individuals, the pooling of goods and knowledge, the combining of activities, the non-profit-making character, the absence of share capital, the principle of equality among members – though not absolute – and its decision-making mechanisms) make it suitable for conducting activities of public interest, although associations may also be created to pursue a special interest agenda.

The Association: A Legal Status Appropriate to a Social Economy Organization or Enterprise

Even if advocacy organizations and trade associations (such as manufacturers' associations) are not affected by social economy problems, many of them play a leading role in the social economy. They incorporate two basic characteristics of the social and solidarity economy: (a) joint creation – by professionals and users – of the supply and demand for services; and (b) hybridization of non-monetary resources (voluntary work), non-market resources (redistribution by the state; subsidies), and market resources (self-financing through the sale of goods and services).

Notwithstanding the diversity of laws under which associations in both Québec and Canada can obtain corporate status – a diversity that impedes the recognition of a solid associative status – associations can create a flexible legal framework for entrepreneurship that is collective, innovative, and socially responsible. This flexibility, despite the formalistic organizational requirements found in current positive law (yet often not complied with), has resulted in a number of social economy enterprises choosing associative rather than cooperative status. This has generated considerable debate within the social economy movement. In addition, before the advent of the solidarity cooperative, cooperative status did not allow bringing together different types of partners (workers, consumers, producers, etc.), something that had always been possible in an association. Given that cooperatives are not always guided by the principle of non-profitability, governments have often insisted that certain types of projects obtain associative status before giving them subsidies.

The Main Legal Problems Affecting Incorporated Associations in Québec

There is a real compatibility in principle between the associative status on the one hand and the carrying out of a disinterested activity as a commercial and economic activity on the other. Despite this, several factors have prompted associations to question their status and to propose significant legislative changes. These factors include the conditions under which associations develop and carry out their activities, the fierce competition from profit-oriented enterprises, the difficulties they face in obtaining funding, and various legal irritants. We examine the main problems.

A Legal Tangle

The largest problem stems from the multiplicity of laws under which associations can obtain corporate status. Aside from Québec's Companies Act, Part III, and the Canada Corporations Act – still the most relevant laws in this regard – there are (a) about 15 general laws in the Revised Statutes of Québec; (b) over 80 mixed laws, playing a constituent or constitution-making role, for establishing associations; (c) laws that lay down a specific method for incorporation; and (d) over 1,500 specific laws that can create or change the structure of a given association.

Given this multiplicity of laws, we may conclude not only that they create a legal tangle, but also that the law on associations in Québec is incoherent and unstable. Several of the laws are outdated and hardly used (Labrecque, 2001, pp. 27–32; GTSJA, 2003, p. 12).[15]

Inappropriate Hard Laws

The laws – of which the Companies Act, Part III, is particularly representative in this respect – contain many hard laws on structures and functions that are not always needed, and several of which are derived from the law on share capital companies. Even if, fundamentally, association law in Québec constitutes a right of exemption from company law, companies have been subject to legislative changes not experienced by "companies without share capital," the first being the incorporating instrument.

A commercial share capital company can obtain corporate status by simply filing the articles of incorporation; however, an association must obtain its letters patent from the province of Québec, which may or may not grant them.[16] The fact that obtaining the status of corporate entity is still a privilege and not a right goes counter to the freedom of association.

Several provisions found in incorporating acts, and inspired by the working methods of companies, are mandatory for associations. The Companies Act expressly provides for the powers of boards of directors as well as those of general assemblies, the latter being very few in number.[17] The Act even specifies that only boards of directors can adopt and modify general by-laws, subject to ratification by the general assembly; it is thus illegal to have by-laws adopted or amended directly by the general assembly.[18] In this regard, however, the law on for-profit companies recognizes the unanimous shareholder agreement, for which there is no counterpart for incorporated associations.[19] The sovereign assembly is therefore more of a myth than a legal reality.

Even if certain measures in the Companies Act recognize that associations are free to regulate as they see fit, several other measures are mandatory, formalistic, or not based on membership rights, public interest, or public policy.

A Lack of Means

Lastly, there is a lack of legislation on the means by which associations may obtain better financing and greater capitalization. Associations may finance themselves through donations, gifts, or membership dues. They may also use the money they generate from their activities or obtain financing by borrowing, using their property as collateral; however, if their assets are meagre they may be unable to put up the required collateral, which can paralyse operations.

The Difficult Beginnings of New Legislation on Associations

All these irritants have prompted several stakeholders and groups to call for the adoption of new laws on associations at both the federal and Québec levels. In a report entitled *Osons la solidarité* ("Daring

Solidarity," Groupe de travail sur l'économie sociale, 1996), we find the following passage:

> The difficulties experienced by not-for-profit organizations, associations, and cooperatives in obtaining conventional financial services are due in part to their legal status. Currently, close to 20 laws concurrently apply in framing and defining an administrative structure and operational rules for the power of the various social economy organizations. There are grounds for simplifying the legal framework in a way that would allow organizations to take advantage of government programs, measures, and services and gain access to financial services while preserving their distinctive characteristics, which derive, in part, from their social mission and democratic process. (TT)

Given the importance of this question for all not-for-profit organizations, the Groupe de travail (working group) is asking the government to take action to ensure that its representatives will be involved in an eventual revision of Part III of the Companies Act.

A working group on the legal status of associations, set up in 2001 by CIRIEC-Canada, conducted several interviews with the heads of Québec's large umbrella associations. While the interviews brought out divergent views on some aspects of a future reform of association law, there was genuine consensus on the need, "given the importance of the association sector in our society, to have a separate law specifically for associations" (GTSAJ, 2003, p. 15; TT).

Over several years, studies have been conducted to revamp the laws on associations; these studies were formerly realized by officials from Québec's Inspecteur général des institutions financières (Inspecteur General of Financial Institutions) and, more recently, from the Registraire des entreprises du Québec (Enterprise Registrar). In the wake of these studies, an initial "private" consultation, which was held in 1996 with about 30 representatives of Québec associations, came up with no concrete results. By 2004, the Government of Québec authorized a second consultation based on a policy paper (Registraire des entreprises du Québec, 2004), which raised several controversies concerning proposed approaches despite the fact that here too there was agreement on the importance of providing Québec with a new law on associations. This second consultation, carried out on the fly, has not yet convinced the government to conduct a follow-up, be it via the tabling of a bill or by additional and more in-depth consultations. However, in the fall of

2008, the Québec Finance Ministry tabled a new consultation paper entitled *Droit des associations personnalisées* ("Legislation on incorporated associations," Finances Québec, 2008) and inviting those interested to share their comments before 31 March 2009.

In 2002, and in parallel with these studies, the federal government conducted similar consultations, with a view to reforming the Canada Corporations Act. These led to the tabling, in 2005, of Bill C-21, dead on the Order Paper with the calling of elections; it was replaced by Bill C-62 in 2008, also dead on the Order Paper for the same reason. Finally a new bill, Bill C-4, was adopted in June 2009.[20]

While this historical review is limited and all too brief, we may conclude that there has been a definite interest in resolving certain legal irritants through the adoption of new legislation on associations, at both the federal level and in Québec. There are also different views, however, on which approach should be adopted.

Different Approaches to New Legislation on Associations

Several differences were brought to light during debates relating to the orientation of new legislation on associations, mainly those retained in the discussion paper of the Registraire des entreprises du Québec. These differences were not limited to technical issues and reflected entrenched ideological positions.

Contract or Institution?

Although some associations represent those seeking civil liberties, they fall within the domain of private law. Essentially, associations are a contract between individuals who share knowledge and resources for any reason other than that of distributing financial profits among their members. Even when an association is granted corporate status by the state (possibly through the filing of articles rather than the granting of letters patent) the latter must limit its involvement to the greatest possible extent. Any new legislation on associations will have to limit its hard laws as much as possible to respect and encourage freedom of contract, which guarantees the freedom of association. The only admissible hard laws would be those aiming to protect third parties and public order. In that sense, the Registrar's 2004 policy paper proposed only one legally required administrative body, in contrast to current law, which requires that there be a board of directors and a general

assembly. That said, nothing would prevent an association from avail-
ing itself of more complex or innovative mechanisms if this was the will
of its members, who are party to the contract. However, the paper also
proposed highly complex accounting rules, among them the introduction of patrimonies by appropriation for associations receiving donations or grants.

For others, the incorporated association is, rather, an institution that
enjoys certain privileges, especially fiscal privileges, not only because
it is non-profit but also because it fosters democracy by giving voice
to citizen demands and initiatives; the association represents a public forum for debate and action. As such, associative governance must
be taken seriously, for it affects democracy itself. Associations require
hard laws to ensure respect not only for laws affecting third parties
and public order, but also – and especially – for those laws' underlying logic. This includes not only democratic governance through the
furtherance of bodies such as the general assembly and the board of
directors, but also the values and principles of the independent community-based movement, as called for, among others, by the report of
the Comité aviseur de l'action communautaire autonome (Independent
community action advisory committee, 2003). The new 2008 consultation paper by the Finance Ministry stipulates that: "the association continues to act through the intermediary of its bodies, namely, its board
of directors and its general assemblies of members" (Finances Québec,
2008, p. 10).

This division (contract vs. institution) is not a new occurrence in
this sphere. The works of historians such as Yvan Lamonde (2000) and
Jean-Marie Fecteau (1992) remind us that in the nineteenth century
there were not only middle-class cultural associations but also working-class associations, such as mutual benefit societies (Petitclerc, 2001).
Fecteau analysed the political aspects of the associative phenomenon,
especially conflictual relationships among associations, the state, and
liberal law. Thus, more than just a straightforward contract, the association became "a new institutional form in 19th century liberal society"
(Petitclerc, 2001, p. 13) to the point where there was real growth in asso-
ciationism within working-class circles:

> When the "mystique of the association" began to develop in the early
> 1840s, the question of incorporation was of concern to the political author-
> ities. At the height of the process of transitioning to liberal capitalism, the
> legislature was at odds concerning the incentives which the state had to

implement in order to encourage civil society to organize into associations. In fact, the state had an ambiguous attitude toward the system of special laws that were closely linked, as we have seen, to the privileges of the old order. However, nor could the state ignore the increasingly urgent demands for a framing of various associative forms to go beyond the basic protection provided by common law. One of the favoured solutions, which nevertheless encountered tremendous opposition, was the adoption of general legislation, following the example of England and the United States. (Petitclerc, 2001, p. 88; TT)

In 1850, a general law was adopted to provide mutual associations with legal protection. It did not yet constitute an incorporating act, however, with the result that several mutual benefit societies continued to avail themselves of laws on private incorporation to obtain full corporate status. A general law on incorporation did not emerge until the late nineteehtn century, which coincided with the commercialization of the "pure mutual benefit systems" that were active in insurance.

To preserve the dream of an independent worker community – a dream briefly made real in 1867 through the Grande association ouvrière (Grand Worker Association) project[21] – mutual benefit associations fought against control by elites right up to the end of the nineteenth century while seeking legal protection from the state. That said, does obtaining rights also open the door to control mechanisms? How does one preserve the spirit of mutual benefit societies, and ideas relating to concrete forms of interdependence and participatory democracy, while hoping for a framework law that would apply to the different types of associations found in liberal society? This question, which is far from new in light of the work of various historians, becomes highly topical in the context of revising Québec legislation on associations. As Léopold Beaulieu, president of CIRIEC-Canada, noted at the Séminaire international sur l'avenir des associations (International Seminar on the Future of Associations):

> We should not forget that the raison d'être of associations goes well beyond individuals endowing themselves with an association to meet personal objectives. Its raison d'être even goes well beyond the collective that creates it. To varying degrees, associations involve public interest. One way or another, it is the associations' social utility that not only justifies its fiscal privileges but also necessitates providing it with an established framework reflecting the characteristics of associationism. (CIRIEC-Canada, 2003, p. 9; TT)

The fundamental differences in approach pervade and cut across the content of debates regarding the conditions for running associations. In recent years, several social economy enterprises have requested improvements to the conditions for operating associations. These are tied to an improved ability to obtain funding and capital. The policy paper put forward for consultation by the Registraire des entreprises (REQ, 2004) suggests authorizing the issue of social capital, which could include various categories of associative shares, with or without face value. Profit sharing would be allowed, albeit in a limited form so as to comply with the objective of allocating an association's resources, including profits, primarily to the carrying out of its mission. This proposal had also been put forward by the Groupe de travail sur le statut juridique des associations (GTSJA [Working group on the legal status of associations], 2003, p. 29). It raised a controversy concerning the way associations were viewed. The 2008 consultation paper "invites the associations and organizations of the social economy sector to formulate precise proposals on how to settle this question" (Finances Québec, 2008, p. 8; TT).

Deciding Whether to Issue Social Capital

If associations come under private law, and are allowed to pursue any type of objective other than the sharing of profits among members, then why not allow them to issue shares with limited earnings, as do cooperatives? This could be done in a way that does not give them decision-making power over the association's overall mandate, which would remain in the hands of its members.

For the supporters of an institutional and democratic approach, allowing social capital rather than promoting donations is "a political, indeed, a philosophical, choice: the government encourages 'business' (read: the lure of gain) rather than social solidarity" (Comité aviseur de l'action communautaire autonome, 2005, p. 8; TT). From this point of view, there would be a real danger of a decline in public trust in associations and a decrease in public financing.

Within Québec's social economy, cooperatives have raised objections to this proposal. In its report, the Conseil de la coopération du Québec (Québec Cooperation Council, 2005, p. 5) deplored that economic rights would be granted to associations without any requirement that they have any collective responsibility or clear rules to ensure the continuity of the association or the protection of the collective interest. Should we read into this a desire on the part of cooperatives to maintain their advantage over associations in terms of access to capital or, rather, a plea for the introduction of precise and clear rules for running associations in terms of structure and governance (as there are for cooperatives) before allowing associations to issue shares? For its part, the Chantier de l'économie sociale (Social Economy Task Force) was pleased to find that the policy paper of the Registraire des entreprises contains proposals on social capital, which ought to be considered separately from the more general question of financing. However, the Chantier also finds that it "seems appropriate to ensure first that the democratic principles and values of associations are secure before contemplating forms of capital and taking steps to facilitate the issuing of shares" (Chantier de l'économie sociale, 2005, p. 10).

The Pro and Cons of a Classification System

The Conseil de la coopération du Québec, probably drawing its inspiration from the Cooperatives Act, which recognizes various categories of cooperatives, proposed in 2003 that "any reform of laws dealing with associations take into account certain categories based on their activities and needs. Thus, we need to distinguish between associations, non-profit organizations, foundations, and charitable organizations" (Conseil de la coopération du Québec, 2003, p. 13). Recognizing distinct categories and establishing a classification system for a law on associations would certainly reflect the diversity of associations and allow for the adoption of specific legislation for certain categories. Yet how should we classify the various associations? It is not clear that the functions or objectives of associations justify distinct categories or legal frameworks. Is it therefore possible to classify them on another basis? The working group on the legal status of associations did not support the introduction of a formal classification system for associations as part of a new law. Their reasoning took into account both the complexity of certain associations, which can pursue various objectives and conduct multiple activities, and the exclusionary effects inherent to every classification system. Instead, the working group recommended "a grading of responsibilities according to the type of activities conducted by the associations" (GTSJA, 2003, p. 26).

The question of the classification of associations takes us back to our initial dialectic alternative: Are associations more oriented towards contractual regulation or institutional regulation? If the association is primarily a private contract among its members, and between the latter and the legal entity that results from this contract, to facilitate the introduction of objectives into the contract and provide shareholders with a measure of protection, then it is pointless to contemplate any kind of classification. If, on the contrary, the association has a more institutional character, with principles and values that must be protected because it is a player on the political scene and within the plural economy, then perhaps we need to distinguish among associations, taking into account the rights and privileges that the state may grant. A brief study in comparative law revealed that most laws contain a classification system. This is the case with contractual systems, such as those found in France, in which several distinctions are made. It also applies above all to Canada's corporate systems, however, the institutional dimensions of which are more pronounced.[22]

Towards a Solution

A Law on Associations and Other Non-Profit Legal Entities

While Québec associations constitute a very important sociological reality, Quebeckers often hesitate to employ the term *association* per se. They prefer the expression *organisme sans but lucratif* (OSBL, or non-profit organization, NPO) or even *organisme à but non lucratif* (OBNL, or non-profit-making organization, NPMO). Why go to the trouble of using a generic term instead of the term already used in French? Is this simply a matter of an anglicism, given that Anglophone circles often use the term "non-profit organization"?

These are reasonable questions, unless the terms NPO or NPMO, which can refer to a wide range of organizations, aptly designate the entire legal hodgepodge pertaining to Québec in this matter, as well as the fact that the general laws on incorporation have provided special status to organizations without share capital while failing to specify the organizations to which they wish to refer, unlike what was done in the case of cooperatives.

When the Registraire des entreprises, seeking to create order in Québec's legal jumble, proposed to replace laws as diverse as the Companies Act (Part III), the Amusement Clubs Act, the Act representing *fabriques*, or the Roman Catholic Bishops Act with a general law on associations, it sought to advance the idea of a one-person association, a suggestion widely criticized during the 2005 public consultations.

The saying "grasp all, lose all" is appropriate here. One general law on associations is required to affirm freedom of association and to recognize, in a positive way, the legal status of organizations that emerge as the result of the desire of individuals (in the plural) to form an association. The objective of these individuals is to pool their knowledge and resources in the pursuit of any goal other than the sharing of profit among themselves. An example would be the operation of a social economy enterprise, as a cooperative status is not always appropriate for organizations with different goals and various types of members. Nonetheless, not all non-profit legal entities that come under private law can be considered associations. For example, in many instances a foundation may resemble a patrimony by appropriation, more so than a group of individuals.

Should we replace all the existing general and mixed laws with a single law dealing with associations? Would such a law not sow total confusion? I maintain, as does the Groupe de travail sur le statut légal des associations, that it is preferable to avoid a formal system for classifying associations. Instead, we should introduce a system for grading responsibilities based on the type of activities pursued by associations. That said, a new law on associations must acknowledge that there are other non-profit legal entities in private law that have the right to exist, although these have nothing in common with associations. Moreover, the new consultation paper of the Finance Ministry no longer suggests replacing the 15 general laws but only a certain number of them with a new law (Finances Québec, 2008, p. 14).

What approach should be taken by a future law dealing primarily with associations? Should it recognize the contractual dimension of associations? Such recognition would lead to proposing "full rights at law" for associations as well as flexible organizational and operational forms based on the goodwill of the membership, which would, in a way, guarantee freedom of the association itself. Or should the future law reaffirm the institutional character of the association as a sphere for deliberation and action, a school for democracy, so to speak, or an alternative way of collectively initiating an enterprise? It is clear that the institutional dimension of associations requires that they have a minimum number of clear, democratic rules of administration. The challenge of coming up with a new law on associations (and other non-profit legal entities) consists in reconciling these two approaches in a way that will respect both the diversity of associations and their role in the social economy and society as a whole.

A Framework Law for the Social Economy

Not all associations have the same social function, so should they all benefit from the same advantages or be subject to the same restrictions? This question can also be asked about cooperatives. To resolve the dilemma, we should perhaps consider adopting two new laws: (a) a general law on incorporated associations, that is, an open and relatively unrestrictive law dealing with status as such; and (b) a framework law on the social economy that would define the characteristics of a social economy enterprise, the conditions that must be met to qualify as this kind of enterprise, the advantages they may be granted, the requirements with which they must comply, and so forth. This solution of a framework law was inspired by the above-cited report by Alain Lipietz:

> It involves devising a sector delimited by a collective label, essentially within the field of the social economy as it now exists, but with a possible extension into the private sector, a sphere defined by a charter dealing simultaneously with social goals and internal structures. Enterprises differentiated primarily by their legal status could come under this label: associations, cooperatives, social economy unions, associations, cooperatives, social economy unions, private enterprises, individual workers, and local exchange systems. The sector could then be differentiated according to the enterprise's type of socially oriented activity understood in a broad sense (ecological, cultural). (2000, p. 75; TT)

This solution, taking cues from France and certainly meriting further study in the Québec context,[23] would allow us to distinguish matters of associative status per se from those that deal with the social aims, roles, and functions of certain associations.

We need to reopen the discussion on legislation for associations. Maintaining the status quo and the current legal hodgepodge while continuing to include associative status as part of the right-of-exemption framework does not help Québec's social economy in the long term. The uncertain evolution of our legislation on associations risks becoming the Achilles heel of the social economy in Québec. The current tensions characterizing relations among Québec's major social economy organizations (the Conseil Québécois de la coopération et de la mutualité[24] and the Chantier de l'économie sociale) possibly reflect the vagueness surrounding the status of associations.

During 2010, the ministère des Finances du Québec, which is responsible for everything concerning the status of private corporations, finally decided to follow up on the consultations held in 2008. Because the National Assembly enacted the new *Business Corporations Act* (S.Q., c. 52) in 2009, which had the effect of replacing the first parts of the *Companies Act* when it came into force in February 2011, it became necessary to revise the third part, "Legal Persons or Associations having no Share Capital." In fact, the federal government took the initiative and enacted its own legislation regarding not-for-profit organizations. It is within this context that the government of Québec is finally willing to table its own bill regarding not-for-profit associations or organizations. What will the content be?

NOTES

1   In Québec, see the Cooperatives Act, R.S.Q. c. C-67.2. It was amended in 1993, 1995, and 1997, and more recently in 2003 and 2005. The solidarity cooperative has existed as a category since 1997. See also An Act Respecting Financial Services Cooperatives, R.S.Q., c. C-67.3. At the federal level, the new Canada Cooperatives Act was sanctioned on March 31, 1998: S.C., 1998, c. 1.

2   The Insurance Companies Act, S.C., 1991, c. 47, constituted the beginning of demutualization in Canada. Changes made in 1999 allowed all mutuals with a federal charter to change their status (previously, under the 1993 regulation, demutualization applied only to mutuals valued at less than $7.5 billion [Gosselin, 2000, p. 19]). In Quebec, the Act Respecting Insurance, R.S.Q., c. A-32, was amended in 2002 to allow mutual insurance companies to be transformed into share capital companies (sections 200.0.04 to 200.0.13, which are no longer in force).

Mutuals were not always associated with the world of insurance. The shift towards insurance occurred in the twentieth century in parallel with the emergence of the lower and middle classes within the mutual benefit society movement. However, in the nineteenth century, mutual organizations were fraternal societies, the members of which were overwhelmingly working class. These societies were based on several principles: voluntary membership, democratic membership, and the absence of profit. According to Martin Petitclerc, who wrote a doctoral thesis on this form of working-class mutual aid: "[m]utual aid societies resembled cooperatives in that each member was simultaneously an owner of the society and a beneficiary of the services it provided." This is why he found it legitimate "to broach the subject of mutual aid societies within the context of Quebec's cooperative movement" (Petitclerc, 2005, p. 2). At the same time, the history of mutuals also allows us to better understand the development of the associative movement, since "by allowing us to penetrate the inner recesses of workers' associations, the study of mutual aid societies allows us to discover concretely what constitutes the working-class experience of the association in the nineteenth century" (Petitclerc, 2005, p. 4).

3   Bill C-21, the Act Respecting Not-For-Profit Corporations and Other Corporations without Share Capital, died on the Order Paper on 29 November 2005 following the dissolution of Parliament due to a general election. Another bill, namely, Bill C-62, An Act Respecting Not-For-Profit Corporations and Certain Other Corporations, was adopted upon first reading in 2008 but also died on the Order Paper on 7 September 2007 with the onset of the fall 2008 elections. Finally, Bill C-4, An Act Respecting Not-For-Profit Corporations and Certain Other Corporations, received royal assent in June 2009.

4   Civil Code of Quebec, S.Q., 1991, c. 64 (in force as of 1 January 1994), s. 2186.

5   An Act Respecting the Legal Publicity of Enterprises, R.S.Q., c. P-44.1.1.

6   Loi 1901 sur les associations. J.O., 2 July 1901 (amended many times).

7   The Loi du 2 mai 2002 relative aux associations sans but lucratif, aux associations internationales sans but lucratif et aux fondations, published on December 11, 2002 in the Moniteur Belge, modifies the law of 27 June 1921 (published on 1 July 1921 in the Moniteur Belge) without repealing it. The latter viewed NPOs and institutions of public interest as juridical personalities.

8   See Code des sociétés, 7 May 1999, Livre X: Sociétés à finalité sociale, in force since 6 February 2001.

9   However, since 2001 a new form of cooperative enterprise has emerged in French cooperative law. It is known as the *société coopérative d'intérêt collectif* (SCIC, or Cooperative Company of Collective Interest). The SCIC allows all types of actors to associate with the same project and produces all types of goods and services to meet the collective needs of a territory. In a way, this new form of cooperative is akin to Québec's solidarity cooperative. See Law No. 2001-624 of 17 July 2001, which amends Law No. 47-1775 of 10 September 1947.

10   Government of Québec. (2011). *Code civil du Québec: Édition critique 2011-2012*. Cowansville: Éditions Simon Blais.

11   Companies Act, R.S.Q., c. C-38.

12 Canada Corporations Act, R.S.C., 1985, c. C-32. This limitation disappears with the new federal law adopted in June 2009, S.C. 2009, c. 23.

13 Government of Québec (1865). *Code civil du Bas Canada*. Québec: G.E. Desbarats.

14 This list of objectives no longer exists in the new federal law (S.C. 2009. c. 23), which does not prevent non-profit organizations with corporate status under this Act from carrying out a disinterested activity.

15 GTSJA, Groupe de travail sur le statut juridique des associations (Working group on the legal status of associations), created by the Centre interdisciplinaire de recherche et d'information sur les entreprises collectives (CIRIEC-Canada).

16 Sections 123.1 and 218 of the Companies Act.

17 Sections 83 and 91 of the Companies Act.

18 Sections 91(2) and 91(3) of the Companies Act.

19 Sections 123.91 to 123.93 and 224 of the Companies Act and section 146 of the Canada Business Corporations Act, R.S.C., 1985, c. C-44. The new federal law (S.C. 2009, c. 23) on not-for-profit organizations recognizes the unanimous member agreement.

20 See note 3.

21 The Grande association pour la protection des ouvriers du Canada was an initiative of Médéric Lanctôt, a politician, and sought to unite the various trades. It formed quickly but waned just as quickly. The constitution of the Grande association was adopted in April 1867 by an assembly attended by 3 000 individuals at the Marché Bonsecours in Montréal (Jean Hamelin, "Médéric Lanctôt," *Dictionnaire biographique du Canada*, CD-ROM.)

22 As part of the work of the Groupe de travail sur le statut juridique des associations, Maître François Roch conducted a comparative law study in 2003. Covering Canadian laws (Saskatchewan, Alberta, Ontario), American laws (New York, California), and European laws (France, United Kingdom, Belgium, Germany), the study analysed in particular the classification systems of associations. Different classification systems generally emerge because of a desire to adapt laws to each type of association's special characteristics, as based on its objective. However, associations can have several objectives. In addition, other characteristics may be taken into account: for example, size, role, and social function of the association.

23 In the Québec setting, by making the requisite distinctions a framework law could deal simultaneously with both the social economy and community action. It must be kept in mind that an association can serve concurrently as both a social economy enterprise and an independent community group.

24 The Conseil de la coopération du Québec changed its name in 2006 from
    the Conseil québécois de la coopération et de la mutualité (Quebec Council
    of Cooperation and Mutuality).

REFERENCES

Chantier de l'économie sociale. (2005). *Raffermir le statut associatif et promouvoir
    les valeurs démocratiques*. Report presented to the Registraire des entreprises
    du Québec.
CIRIEC-Canada in collaboration with Aruc-És. (2003). *Proceedings of the inter-
    national seminar "Avenir des associations. De nouvelles loi?"* Cahier no. 2003–4.
    Montréal: CIRIEC-Canada.
Comité aviseur de l'action communautaire autonome. (2005). *Vers un cadre ju-
    ridique respectueux des valeurs et des principes du mouvement communautaire
    du Québec*. Montréal: Report presented to the Registraire des entreprises du
    Québec.
Conseil de la coopération du Québec (CCQ). (2005). *Le droit des associations:
    Pour une véritable gouvernance*. Lévis: Report presented to the Registraire des
    entreprises du Québec.
Conseil national de la vie associative. (1988). *Pour une vie associative mieux re-
    connue dans ses fonctions économiques et dans ses actions d'intérêt général*. State-
    ment given on 4 February 1988, and published in CNVA. Paris: Bilan de la
    vie associatives en 1986–1987, La documentation française.
Dandonneau, A. (1978). La francisation à l'aveuglette du droit des corpora-
    tions. *Revue juridique Thémis, 13*(1): 89–97.
Demoustier, D. (2001). *L'économie sociale et solidaire: S'associer pour entreprendre
    autrement*. Paris: Syros.
Desroches, H. (1983). *Pour un traité d'économie sociale*. Paris: CIEM.
Gosselin, Y. (2000). La démutualisation: Outil plutôt que solution. *Sécurité fi-
    nancière*. 19–21 April.
Groupe de travail sur l'économie sociale. (1996) *Osons la solidarité*. Québec:
    Governement of Quebec.
Groupe de travail sur le statut juridique des associations. (2003). *Vers un nou-
    veau droit associatif*. Report presented to the Board of Directors of CIRIEC-
    Canada. Montréal: CIRIEC-Canada.
Hamelin, J. (2001). Médéric Lanctôt. In John English (Ed.), *Dictionnaire bio-
    graphique du Canada*, CD, Toronto: University of Toronto Press; Québec: Les
    Presses de l'Université Laval.

Jolin, L. (1995). *Associations et activités touristiques en droit français et en droit québécois.* Doctoral dissertation, Université Jean Moulin–Lyon III.

Labrecque, M.-A. (2001). Principales carences du droit québécois des associations personnifiées et présentation d'hypothèses de solution. In L. Jolin and G. Lebel (Eds.), *L'association: du contrôle à la liberté?* (pp. 27–48). Montréal: Wilson & Lafleur and Martel.

Lamonde, Y. (2000). *Histoire sociale des idées au Québec.* St-Laurent: Fides.

Lipietz, A. (2000). *Rapport sur l'opportunité d'un nouveau type de société à vocation sociale, Volume 1.* Report presented to the French Minister of Employment and Solidarity. Paris: CEPREMAP.

Ministère des Finances du Québec. (2008). *Droit des associations personnalisées.* Québec: Document de consultation.

Petitclerc, M. (2005). Une forme d'entraide populaire: Histoire des sociétés québécoises de secours mutuels au 19e siècle. *Cahiers du CRISES*, collection Thèses et Mémoires (TM0503).

Registraire des entreprises du Québec. (2004). *Propositions pour un nouveau droit québécois des associations personnifiées.* Québec: Document de consultation, REQ.

Revenu Canada. (2003). *Qu'est-ce qu'une activité commerciale complémentaire?* Notice CPS-019. Ottawa: Government of Canada.

Revenu Québec. (2003). *Registraire des entreprises.* Accessed 18 June 2011. http://www.registreentreprises.gouv.qc.ca/fr/a_propos/

Roch, F. (L. Jolin, Ed.). (2003). *Statut juridique des associations personnifiées sans but lucratif: Analyse de droit comparé.* Working Paper 2003–2, CIRIEC-Canada.

Sousi, G. (2001). Pour la consécration constitutionnelle de la liberté d'association. In L. Jolin and G. Lebel (Eds.), *L'association: du contrôle à la liberté?* Montréal: Wilson & Lafleur and Martel.

Sudreau, P. (Ed.). (1975). *Rapport du Comité sur la réforme de l'entreprise.* Paris: La Documentation française.

6 Solidarity Finance: History of an Emerging Practice[1]

GILLES L. BOURQUE, MARGIE MENDELL,
AND RALPH ROUZIER

Introduction[2]

Financialization of the economy over the last 20 years has spurred new thinking about finance. Financialization is a notion that summarizes the following economic, social, and organizational phenomena. Deregulation, globalization, and advancements in communications technologies have increasingly delinked financial markets from the real economy. Mass savings generated by the baby-boom generation underlie the development of numerous short-term, speculative, and opaque financial instruments. Financialization is embedded in shareholder capitalism, a business model that has transferred power to financial leaders who prioritize shareholder value in strategic business decisions. It defines a global regulatory environment prescribing socially regressive policies – lowering taxes, cutting social programs – to satisfy rating agencies.

This chapter describes initiatives in socially responsible finance (SRF)[3] that have emerged in opposition to the process of financialization (see Table 6.1). SRF takes into account ethical, social, or environmental considerations as well as traditional financial objectives. In Québec, SRF includes a wide range of practices, which are divided into two broad categories: responsible indirect investment and responsible financing. Responsible indirect investing (placement responsable) involves financial institutions that use exclusionary and inclusive screening, ESG (environmental, social, and governance) analysis, and shareholder activism to promote socially responsible corporate practices within publicly traded companies. Responsible financing is a more direct intervention in which non-financial objectives such as job creation, local and

Table 6.1. Socially Responsible Finance

	Form	Activity	Actors
Responsible indirect investing (*placement responsable*)	Portfolio screening (exclusionary or inclusive)	Investments in financial markets using exclusion or inclusion filters based on environmental, social, and corporate governance (ESG) criteria	Ethical funds, foundations, religious communities
	Shareholder activism	Shareholders who use their power to influence corporate practices	Pension funds, religious communities, some ethical funds
Responsible investing (pro-active/direct)	Development capital	Venture capital set apart by socio-economic objectives, including job creation, local and regional development, and environmental concerns	Investment tools developed by associational actors (labour funds, cooperatives), CleanTech funds
	Solidarity finance (social finance)	Financing of community economic development and social enterprises	Micro-credit, financial cooperatives, hybrid innovative financial funds

regional development, and support of the social and solidarity economy are important factors in selecting investment opportunities. Taken independently, these approaches to investment appear marginal, even insignificant. However, from the point of view of those engaged in this activity, they represent concrete responses to financialization.

The focus of this chapter is on the social economy and innovations in finance and investment to meet its needs for capital, including development capital and solidarity finance, in particular. We will describe financial instruments now available to social economy enterprises (SEEs) and the innovations, issues, and challenges that have characterized their development.

Solidarity finance refers to direct investment in community economic development and social economy initiatives. Governed by actors, solidarity finance may take the form of secured or unsecured loans; it also involves the renewal of social capital in communities. Solidarity finance takes different forms in different parts of the world, including a diversity of ways to mobilize collective savings to respond to inequality and social injustice. Solidarity finance is distinguished from development capital by its clientele (collectively owned enterprises and marginalized communities), financial instruments, and its relationship to money, even if the overall socio-economic objectives are the same. It includes a wide range of instruments, from microcredit (or community funds) to patient capital. It also includes financial institutions that work with this clientele. Of course, the credit unions, cooperative banks and what are known more broadly as "social banks" have historically met the needs of collective enterprises and marginalized communities. In the United States, Britain, and, most recently, in Canada, the terms to used to describe this activity include impact investment, social finance, and community-based finance, to name a few. In continental Europe, the notion of "solidarity finance" is more common.

Responsible finance has changed dramatically in Québec. Today, it includes many new actors and a panoply of new financial instruments. In 1997, the Chantier de l'économie sociale, in partnership with the Québec government and the private sector, created the Réseau d'investissement social du Québec (RISQ), complementing the Caisse d'économie solidaire Desjardins (formerly the Caisse d'économie des travailleuses et des travailleurs), the Fonds de solidarité (FTQ), and the Fondation CSN, two worker investment funds created by the labour movement. The socio-economic objectives of these institutions providing solidarity finance and development capital distinguish them from traditional banks and venture capital. As noted above, some mainstream financial institutions do invest in the social economy – for example, in social housing – but their priority is profit.

Financing the Social Economy: Issues and Challenges

Access to capital is often cited as a major concern by social economy actors, despite the many responses to this need that exist today. Many financial institutions provide investment capital to SEEs. Despite this, the unmet needs for capital remain, largely due to the absence of a diversity of financial instruments or products that correspond with the life-cycle of SEEs. Until recently, financing SEEs was limited to debt finance. Although the possibility to purchase privileged shares in cooperatives exists, this seldom occurs. New instruments have been developed and, more importantly, technical and administrative assistance is offered by these financial institutions to support SEEs.

The most important innovation in this financial market in recent years has been the creation of the Fiducie du Chantier de l'économie sociale in 2007. Previously, available long-term loans required repayment of the principal in the first years of operation. SEEs needed "patient capital" with no repayment of principal in the short term. The Fiducie du Chantier de l'économie sociale designed such an instrument with no repayment of principal for 15 years. This new initiative is on a continuum of innovation in socially responsible finance in Québec. With Fondaction (CSN), Fonds de solidarité (FTQ), and the provincial and federal governments as investors in this new initiative, it demonstrates the significant economic role played by the labour movement and the social economy, and the importance of solidarity finance and development capital they have developed in Québec. Moreover, their increasing investment in the social economy confirms the viability of SEEs.

Government plays an instrumental role in this development, both as a partner and as a facilitator. In Québec, it is part of a process to re-embed finance into socio-economic development objectives in the province. The Québec model of development engages all stakeholders, public and private, in a collaborative development process. It not only mobilizes capital, but also expertise and social capital. A report published by the government of Québec in 2003, evaluating the role of venture capital in the economic development of Québec, concluded that insufficient social capital was one of the main obstacles to economic growth in Québec.[4] Not only did the Charest government reverse its decision to weaken workers' funds in favour of private venture capital, but it ultimately found itself obliged to participate in financing the Fiducie du Chantier de l'économie sociale.

The solidarity finance market is expanding, representing significant sums on the international financial market. Even so, access to capital remains a challenge, including the need for specialization within the financial world, which is still largely unfamiliar with these new financial instruments and their specificities. For example, accounting practices and regulations need to be reformed so that they can better evaluate the performance of collective enterprises and thus reflect their true value. Misconceptions about the risks associated with SEEs limit potential investment. These perceptions are often reinforced by legislation and regulations designed with corporate structures in mind and inflexibly applied to SEEs. The obstacles to investing in SEEs are more often structural or institutional. Although studies confirm the long-term viability of SEEs, thus dispelling the myth that investing in these enterprises is high risk, raising capital remains a challenge. A lower bankruptcy rate than private enterprise and secure returns on investment are insufficient to reduce these obstacles. In an earlier work, Mendell, Lévesque, and Rouzier[5] identified four obstacles, to which we would add a fifth:

1. For the most part, SEEs do not generate competitive returns on investment: This is not their main objective. Individual or institutional investors seeking high short-term returns thus tend to avoid them.
2. Financial institutions, especially banks, often consider transaction costs to be too high for small loans, especially for non-profits or cooperatives. Moreover, these institutions consider SEEs to be high-risk investments, largely due to misconceptions about their nature and long-term potential.
3. New social economy actors are unfamiliar faces in the corporate and finance communities.
4. The complex governance models that replace shareholder agreements in SEEs limit the participation of individual and/or institutional investors interested mainly in return on the investment.
5. Finally, there remains some reluctance on the part of SEEs to take advantage of the debt instruments offered by lending institutions, choosing instead to turn to government subsidies.

Small SEEs chronically lack liquidity. This is in part due to the desire for autonomy in management and administration, and to an aversion to long-term debt (despite the need for long-term capital). It is also due to misunderstandings about appropriate responsible financing practices, where investments should correspond to short-term (working capital) and long-term (capital assets) needs.

For social economy initiatives, financing has traditionally been linked to their socio-economic objectives, and includes donations, government subsidies, and program funding in exchange for services, loans as well as loan guarantees, and self-financing. These streams of financing are not always sufficient or available, however. As mentioned previously, new financial instruments have recently been created to meet the growing needs of small businesses operating within and outside the social economy. There are two types of these funds:

1. The first type involves institutions that rarely invest directly in the social economy, but use socially responsible criteria to select the companies they invest in; and
2. The second type are funds dedicated exclusively to SEEs, including nonprofit organizations and cooperatives.

In Québec, the two types are closely linked and share some characteristics, including:

- a strong commitment to partnerships, mainly with the public sector but with the private sector as well;
- an emphasis on long-term investment based on regional development priorities set by intermediaries;
- capital investments combined with technical assistance and follow-up; and
- small loans to help SEEs leverage more capital from financial institutions.

Solidarity Finance in Québec

In this section, we will briefly review some events in the history of the social economy that led to the creation of the financial instruments available today. This will be followed by a detailed discussion of the different financial instruments and institutions that invest in the social economy. Chapter 1 provides a more detailed account of the history of the social economy in Québec.

The history of the social economy in Québec begins in the nineteenth century with the establishment of mutual aid societies and insurance companies. In the twentieth century, small agricultural producers established cooperatives and then joined with small producers and merchants to establish credit unions. This paved the way for the creation of the Mouvement des caisses populaires et d'économie Desjardins. In the 1980s, a new movement emerged in response to the numerous crises facing Québec – the economic crisis, the crisis of the welfare state, and unemployment. The Fonds de solidarité (FTQ), a workers' fund created in 1983,[6] was committed to creating and maintaining jobs throughout Québec.[7] Its investment decisions combine social and economic objectives: For the Fonds to invest in a company, these objectives have to appear in the company's social audit. While the Fonds did not finance social economy enterprises specifically until recently, it can itself be considered part of the social economy given its dual mission of economic development and job creation.[8] The Régime d'investissement coopératif is another notable example: Created in 1985, it provides a 125 per cent tax credit on the purchase of shares by workers, members of cooperatives, and eligible federations.[9]

The social economy experienced rapid growth in the second half of the 1990s. In 1996, a second workers' fund – Fondaction, le Fonds de développement de la CSN[10] pour la coopération et l'emploi – was created to promote economic development in Québec and to invest in enterprises with participatory management, distributed control, and environmental stewardship.[11]

Prior to a "Summit on the Economy and Employment" convened by the government of Québec in October 1996, a social economy working group was established to propose how the social economy could contribute to job creation and economic development in Québec. The working group presented its report to the Summit and was invited to continue its work for another two years. Its mandate was to identify 20 social economy projects that would create 20,000 jobs in three years. In 1997, the working group was incorporated as the Chantier de l'économie sociale; in 1999, it became a permanent non-profit organization. In 1997, its first year, the Chantier created an investment fund for the social economy, the Réseau d'investissement social du Québec (RISQ), in partnership with the Québec government and a few private investors. RISQ invests exclusively in the social economy through loans and loan guarantees.

During this period, several measures and programs introduced by the government reflected, in part, its recognition of the potential of the social economy to contribute to economic development in Québec. A few examples include:

- The Fonds de développement des entreprises d'économie sociale (FDEES), created in 1998 to provide development funding for SEEs. The FDEES is one of the financial instruments managed by local development centres, the centres locaux de développement (CLD), established at the same time throughout Québec. These funds provide subsidies to SEEs and are governed by the CLDs.

- The fonds locaux d'investissement (FLIs), local investment funds, also managed by CLDs and launched in 1998 to promote business development throughout the province. The total budget for all CLDs was $130 million, or approximately $1 million for each CLD. This amount is not a subsidy; CLDs must repay these loans to the government of Québec, although repaid capital can, in theory, be reinvested. A large portion of these funds was already invested in the early years, between 1998 and 2002.[12] Although FLIs focus mainly on the private sector, SEEs are not excluded and may receive loans of up to $50,000.[13] In 2008, CLDs invested close to $28.3 million throughout the province.[14]

- In 2007, the Fiducie du Chantier de l'économie sociale was created to provide patient capital or "quasi-equity" to SEEs. A subsidy of $22.8 million by the federal government (through Economic Development Canada) leveraged the participation of large investors in this initiative, including the Fonds de solidarité (FTQ), Fondaction, and the Québec government, which invested $12 million, $8 million, and $10 million, respectively, in the Fiducie.[15] The Québec government is an investor in the Fiducie, confirming its commitment to the social economy and the recognition of its potential to contribute to job creation, enterprise development, and economic growth.

This brief overview of recent events in the history of the social economy provides the context for the financial innovations in development capital and solidarity finance in Québec. In the remainder of this chapter, we will identify the main actors in development capital and solidarity finance. These are ideal types; in fact, the boundaries between them are fluid, which allows for the creation of innovative hybrids involving different institutions.

Development Capital

Fonds de solidarité FTQ

The Fonds de solidarité FTQ was created in 1983 to create and maintain employment in Québec. The Fonds invests mainly in small and medium-sized enterprises (SMEs), but as of 2005, it can also invest in larger companies with assets of up to $100 million. By law, the Fonds is required to invest 60 per cent of its assets at the end of the previous year in Québec enterprises. The net assets of the Fonds, $7.3 billion on 31 May 2010, include the savings of 577,511 subscribers. Since 1983, the Fonds has invested $4.8 billion in Québec enterprises, and has created or maintained 150,133 jobs.[16]

As noted above, the Fonds invests directly in the social economy through the Fiducie du Chantier de l'économie sociale, but also through its Fonds immobilier de solidarité FTQ (created in 1991, then known as SOLIM), which specializes in real estate investment and development. While it is not specifically linked to the social economy, the Fonds immobilier invests in SEEs in construction or renovation. The local investment funds of the Fonds, the sociétés locales d'investissement pour le développement de l'emploi (SOLIDE), now also invest in the social economy (Fonds locaux de solidarité).

Fondaction CSN pour la coopération et l'emploi

Fondaction was created in 1995 and began its operations in 1996. Its mission is to help create or maintain employment, privileging those enterprises with participatory management, self-managed firms, or with a clear commitment to sustainable development. Like the Fonds de solidarité, it is subject to the 60 per cent rule. On 31 May 2010, its net assets were $699.4 million; there are 99,692 subscribers. Since it was established, Fondaction has invested $477.3 million in enterprises, which helped create or maintain 11,843 jobs.[17] While it invests primarily in SMEs, its Fonds de financement coopératif also invests from $100,000 to $250,000 in cooperatives and non-profit organizations. Fondaction is also the main financial partner of Société de développement Angus.[18] Because the investments undertaken by Fondaction in SMEs are generally between $2 million and $5 million (although it can invest as little as $500,000), it created Filaction, le Fonds pour l'investissement local et l'approvisionnement des fonds communautaires in 2001, to meet the need for smaller loans (between $50,000 and $500,000) and to invest in community funds.[19] Fondaction also invests in the Fiducie du Chantier de l'économie sociale, as previously mentioned. On its tenth anniversary, in 2006, Fondaction published its first sustainable development report.

Mouvement Desjardins (Including Capital régional et coopératif Desjardins)

The Mouvement Desjardins was established in the early 1900s. Although it has undergone significant changes over the years and competes with other financial institutions, its presence in every region and sector of the social economy demonstrates its commitment to an economy embedded in values of solidarity and collective well-being. The Mouvement is made up of several independent institutions, including Capital régional et coopératif Desjardins (development capital), and Caisse d'économie solidaire (solidarity finance). Capital régional et coopératif Desjardins was created in 2001. While it does not provide financing exclusively for SEEs, one of its priorities is to contribute to the capitalization of cooperatives and to develop resource regions in Québec.[20] This priority is now enforced by law. As of 2006, the share of Capital régional et coopératif Desjardins in eligible enterprises must be at least 60 per cent of its average net assets and at least 35 per cent of that percentage (60 per cent) will be invested in Québec cooperatives or enterprises located in resource regions in Québec.[21] Investors may purchase a maximum of $5,000 in shares annually, thereby qualifying for a 50 per cent provincial tax credit. Shares must be held for at least seven years. On 31 December 2009, Capital régional et coopératif Desjardins reported assets of $905.9 million. In total, $539.7 million was invested in 228 enterprises, creating or maintaining 32,000 jobs.[22] In 2009 alone, $94.5 million was invested in 69 cooperatives and enterprises throughout Québec.

Investissement Québec

Although Investissement Québec is not a social economy financial institution, its involvement in the social economy is written into the recent history of the movement. Founded in 1998, Investissement Québec is a public corporation that coordinates numerous programs to finance enterprises throughout Québec. It replaced the Société de développement industrielle (SDI), which was created in 1971. In January 2001, Investissement Québec became a new public corporation taking over the activities of the Société générale de financement, which was created in 1962 to provide development capital. In 2001, Investissement Québec launched a new subsidiary, La Financière du Québec. La Financière manages two programs that finance collective entrepreneurship: one that provides loan guarantees, and one that provides loans. Of the $100 million allocated for business financing under these two programs, $15 million is earmarked for non-profit organizations and cooperatives. In 2009–10, the first program, now known as Collective Entrepreneurship: Funding Social Economy Enterprises, invested $31 million in loans or loan guarantees in 99 projects, creating 165 jobs and maintaining 52 jobs over a three-year period. The second program, now known as Capitalization of Social Economy Enterprises, invested $4.3 million in 62 projects over the same period, creating 63 jobs and maintaining an additional 129 jobs.[23]

Fonds d'intervention économique régional

The Fonds d'intervention économique régional (FIER) is a development fund designed "to help companies obtain financing (equity or quasi-equity) for start-up, development, succession or turnaround stages. It also supports the creation of sectoral funds and the implementation of development projects, mainly in the regions."[24] It has three components: Fonds Soutien, FIER-Régions, and FIER-Partenaires. Cooperatives throughout the province are eligible for this funding, as are private enterprises. The capitalization of FIER includes public and private participation: $318 million from the Québec government, $50 million from the Fonds de solidarité, $25 million from Capital régional et coopératif Desjardins, and $15 million from Fondaction.[25] As of 31 December 2009, $176.1 million had been invested in Québec enterprises through FIER-Regions and FIER Soutien. As of 31 March 2010, FIER-Partenaires had invested $137 million in 10 sectoral funds.[26]

Solidarity Finance

Caisse d'économie solidaire Desjardins

Created in 1971, the Caisse d'économie solidaire Desjardins (formerly the Caisse d'économie Desjardins des travailleurs et travailleuses) provides guaranteed loans to SEEs. Its mission is to contribute to social justice and solidarity by supporting collective and social enterprises and the cooperative movement.[27] On 31 December 2009, the Caisse reported assets of $545.2 million, of which $331.6 million (65 per cent) was allocated to collective enterprises. The Caisse invests primarily in cooperatives and NPOs, including social and community housing. In order to achieve its mission, the Caisse mobilizes savings ($489.4 million) of its 12,537 members, including 9,801 individuals and 2,736 collective enterprises.[28] The Caisse has also created the Fonds de soutien à l'action collective solidaire, in which depositers forego their interest in order to benefit collective initiatives.[29] These solidarity savings reinforce the mission of the Caisse.

Réseau québécois du crédit communautaire (RQCC)

The Réseau québécois du crédit communautaire (RQCC) was created in 2000 to form a network of community funds, many of which had been active since the 1990s. The first community fund in Canada was the Montréal Community Loan Association, established in 1990. In 2010, the RQCC had 23 members, including 12 community loan funds and 11 loan circles. Its mission is to promote the development of community credit in Québec to ensure a better quality of life for individuals and communities and to eliminate poverty. The RQCC provides its members with alternative access to capital and technical assistance for economic development in local communities. In 2009–10, the RQCC reported assets nearing $3.5 million. Since 2000, members have been loaned $7.8 million, with a 91 per cent repayment rate. These investments have contributed to the creation of 3,688 jobs.[30] The network is recognized by the Québec government, which facilitates access to more funds, in particular to cover operating costs. Community credit is a significant partner in financing SEEs.

Réseau d'investissement social du Québec (RISQ)

Created in 1997, the Réseau d'investissement social du Québec (RISQ) is a risk capital fund with assets of $7.8 million in 2009, to which $5 million was recently allocated by the ministère des Affaires municipales, des Régions et de l'Occupation du territoire in its 2009–10 budget for pre-start-up loans (up to $100,000) for SEEs.[31] RISQ is dedicated exclusively to SEEs; one of its main objectives is to create and maintain jobs in these enterprises. RISQ provides capitalization of up to $50,000 to SEEs and, if necessary, $5,000 in technical assistance prior to obtaining a loan. RISQ provides loans, loan guarantees, or participating loans. As of 2009, RISQ had invested $13 million: $11.7 million in capital and $1.3 million in technical assistance. These investments have leveraged almost $152 million of additional investment. The 577 financed projects, including 292 capitalization loans and 285 receiving technical assistance, helped create or maintain 7,803 jobs (4,733 through capitalization and 3,070 through technical assistance).[32] RISQ investors include the Québec government, Cirque du Soleil, Conseil québécois du loisir, Alcan Aluminum Ltd., Bank of Montréal, National Bank of Canada, Royal Bank of Canada, the Jean Coutu Group (PJC), Imasco Inc., and the Mouvement Desjardins. Whether it is to ensure its continued survival, to attract new investors, or to encourage current investors to continue to support its activities, the projects financed by RISQ must be viable, but the repayment terms for capitalization loans are flexible. In the case of technical assistance, the loans are interest-free if the project is carried out, but the enterprise must contribute 10 per cent of the project cost.[33]

Filaction

Filaction, le Fonds pour l'investissement local et l'approvisionnement des fonds communautaires, was created in 2001 by Fondaction to meet the demand for small loans ($50,000 to $500,000) and to help capitalize community funds[34] through participating loans or loan guarantees. Filaction mainly provides financing to small businesses that encourage participatory management, SEEs, and projects that promote individual and community self-reliance.[35] The initial capital of $7 million was provided by Fondaction. Repayment terms are based on the ability to repay within three to seven years for businesses, or five to seven years for funds. As of 31 December 2009, Filaction had invested $23 million in 124 organizations; it helped create or maintain 3,764 jobs.[36]

An innovative partnership between Filaction, the Réseau québécois du crédit communautaire, and the Réseau des fonds d'investissement des femmes entrepreneures supports a network of start-up funds for cooperatives provided by the Coopératives de développement régional (CDR, regional associations supporting the development of cooperatives) and the Groupes de ressources techniques (GRT, technical assistance for cooperative housing). Recently, Filaction became a major partner in a $1-million fund, Capital Equitable; its mission is to promote the fair trade sector in Québec.[37] Filaction also manages the Fonds de financement coopératif, created by Fondaction and RISQ. This $6-million fund offers loans from $100,000 to $250,000 to collective enterprises – non-profit organizations and cooperatives.[38] Fondaction and RISQ contributed $4.8 million and $1.2 million, respectively. This can be also complemented by a loan from Filaction of up to $400,000. This collaboration is an important example of how partnerships between solidarity finance institutions are better able to respond to the needs of SEEs.

Fiducie du Chantier de l'économie sociale

Despite the availability of development capital in Québec, the need for patient capital by SEEs, whether in the form of equity or quasi-equity, was not met. The Fiducie du Chantier de l'économie sociale was created in 2007 to respond to this need. It offers patient capital for SEEs with a 15-year moratorium on repayment of the principal. The Fiducie's investments range from $50,000 to $1.5 million, not exceeding 35 per cent of the project's cost. The interest rate is fixed when the loan is approved and remains the same for the duration of the investment. Fees include 3 per cent of the investment to mitigate risk and a 1 per cent annual management fee payable with each monthly interest payment.

Products offered by the Fiducie give SEEs greater flexibility to expand or deal with contingencies. Because of the 15-year moratorium on repayment of the principal, patient capital offered by the Fiducie can be leveraged to obtain more financing.[39] Fiducie financing is available for start-up or expansion as well as for the development and improvement of the enterprise and the adaptation of its products and services. It does not finance business recovery, refinancing, or those initiatives in which there is a transfer of jobs or responsibilities from the public sector.[40]

In April 2009, the Fiducie du Chantier de l'économie sociale had invested a total of $9.9 million in 29 social enterprises (11 in 2007, 14 in 2008, and 4 in 2009), for an average investment of $340,458 per project. Projects vary according to the type of organization (NPOs and cooperatives), development stage (mainly start-up and expansion, but also consolidation), and sector and region (urban or rural).[41] As of 2010, $17.2 million had been invested in 55 SSEs in different sectors and regions of Québec. The Fiducie has projected that these investments will generate $144.2 million and maintain over 1,510 jobs.[42] Clients are satisfied with the services and the availability of long-term capital provided by the Fiducie.[43]

Evolution of Investments in SEEs, 1996–2005

Prior to the "Summit on the Social and Solidarity Economy," organized by the Chantier de l'économie sociale in 2006, a working group composed of researchers and practitioners associated with ARUC-ÉS

Figure 6.1. Evolution of Investments in the Québec Social Economy since 1996

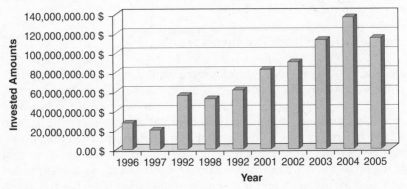

(Community-University Research Alliance on the Social Economy) conducted a survey of solidarity finance institutions to determine their level of engagement in the social economy over the previous decade. Data were collected from the majority of actors in capital development and solidarity finance and intermediaries with financial tools, such as the CLDs. The data for CLDs were gathered directly from annual reports from 1998 to 2004 (a study sponsored by the ministère du Développement économique, de l'Innovation et de l'Exportation [MDEIE]). While a great deal of activity has occurred since 2006, this study remains significant.

Over $755 million was invested in SSEs by the institutions surveyed from 1996 to 2005. There is a definite upward trend (see Figure 6.1): investment grew almost 600 per cent, from a total of $20 million, in 1997, to $136 million in 2004. Growth was relatively stable during this period, with a peak in 1998. Unfortunately, while 2005 data are incomplete (data from CLDs were not available at the time of the survey), the decline in 2005 is most likely a consequence of the economic policies adopted by the Québec government at the time.

If we limit our observations to the investments made by CLDs, there is still an upward trend, but the curve shifts up and down (see Figure 6.2). The first peak, of $12 million, was reached in 2000, followed by a marked decline in 2001. The next peak, of $16 million, was reached in

Figure 6.2. Total Investments in the Social Economy for all Québec CLDs, 1998–2004

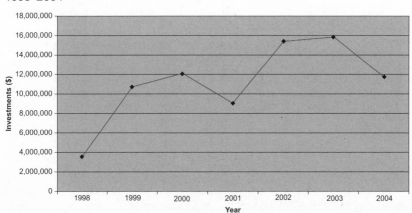

2003. In 2004, however, the last year for which we could obtain data, CLD investments in the social economy again dropped below $12 million. The number of financed projects increased from 111 in 1998 to 715 in 2002. In 2004, 602 social economy projects were financed by CLDs.

Future Challenges

The history of development capital and solidarity finance in Québec is one of ongoing innovation, invention, creativity, audacity, and commitment. In order to meet the investment needs of SEEs, solidarity finance has developed a diversity of products, including debt instruments, quasi-equity, and patient capital. These are essential for a more coherent and structured financial market with regulations that reflect the specificities of the social economy. Many challenges remain, including how to develop financial tools to enable the growth and consolidation of SSEs while ensuring an acceptable rate of return to attract investors. What new institutional forms and structures are required to achieve these goals? What financial innovations can improve access to capital for SEEs? And how can portfolios be diversified to include debt and equity products that are crucial to the development of the social economy?

These are the challenges for solidarity finance today: how to develop new products, but also how to use existing instruments effectively to achieve social objectives and meet the needs of the social economy; how to adapt tools and processes from mainstream financial markets is also being explored. Secondary markets and securitization are among the possible ways to increase the volume of capital available for investment in the social economy. Experience elsewhere provides important lessons. For example, securitization (bundling loans into securities) was adopted in the United States by some community development financial institutions (CDFIs), including the innovative New Hampshire CDFI. This creates incentives for investors, who are often reluctant to invest because of the perceived risks and lack of performance of community development initiatives in the United States. This is but one example of the need to explore initiatives in other countries. Knowledge about impact investing in the United States, social finance in Great Britain, and solidarity finance in Europe will increase the capacity to build a solidarity financial market adapted to the specificities of the social economy in Québec.

One important challenge identified by solidarity finance actors, which is also related to access to capital, is the importance of raising awareness about the performance of SEEs within institutional funds (such as pension and insurance funds). This remains a large source of untapped capital. Efforts to attract potential investors in Québec and elsewhere are producing results. For example, in British Columbia, Concert Properties, a consortium of 27 pension funds totalling $800 million in assets, is investing in affordable housing. In Québec, the profitability and competitiveness of investments in social housing is well known, and institutional funds are increasingly adopting responsible investment policies.

The large sums managed by institutional investors, which include private pension funds and the Caisse de dépôt et placement du Québec, present an excellent opportunity to increase the supply of capital for SSEs, but requires innovative intermediaries. More enabling public policy measures are also required. For example, in the United States, the government adopted the Community Reinvestment Act in 1977, which requires banks to reinvest in communities in which they operate, including low-income communities. Since its adoption, the Act has generated investments of $1.7 billion USD. Furthermore, the New Markets Tax Credit Program, passed in 2000, was designed to generate $15 billion USD in equity investments for low-income communities. More recently, the CDFI network launched a campaign to promote the allocation of 1 per cent to community investment.

In Canada, working with both provincial and federal governments is essential if we are to design public policies that address the needs of the social economy. The public sector has always played a key role in the evolution of the social economy, a role that it must continue to play in this process of innovation. Legislation adopted in Québec and Canada to create the Fonds de solidarité (FTQ) in the early 1980s can serve as a model for the rest of Canada and abroad. This legislation recognized the important role of workers' funds in job creation and socio-economic development in many regions. In 2006, proposals were made to revise outdated legislation (such as the acts governing trusts and pension funds) to encourage investment in the social economy, and to promote the development of solidarity finance. This remains a work in progress.

How important are networks to promote the development of solidarity finance? What kind of networks can be developed in Québec and abroad to promote solidarity finance? What progress has already been made, and what future developments can we anticipate? These were questions that were raised by researchers and practitioners prior to the 2006 Summit in Québec. In France, the Finansol network brings together members who work to develop solidarity savings tools, to pool these savings and to invest them in socially oriented projects. One of Finansol's missions is to strengthen the solidarity finance sector while raising government and public awareness.[44] Another network, the European Federation of Ethical and Alternative Banks (FEBEA), created in 2001, includes institutions that provide financing for social and solidarity initiatives. With capital assets reaching 324 million euros, its objective is "to create a refinancing bank for ethical and alternative financial institutions on a European scale."[45]

A Canadian Task Force on Social Finance was created in the late 2000s to help build this emerging market, in which capital investment meets social and economic objectives. The objective of the task force was to connect private investors with SEEs, charities, or social entrepreneurs who link economic growth to the needs of communities through, for example, job creation.[46] Québec is represented on this task force by the president of the Chantier de l'économie sociale. This group plays a important political role: Its report, which it submitted to the federal government, includes numerous recommendations for enabling public policies to help social finance actors achieve their objectives, one of which is the creation of a national fund with private, philanthropic, and institutional partners.

In Québec, developing a secondary market for solidarity finance is a priority. Experiences in other parts of the world, including Brazil's Bovespa and the South African Social Investment Exchange (SASIX), are inspiring a growing interest in developing a social capital market at the international level. Québec is participating in these international discussions.

While these initiatives demonstrate a willingness to build an economy embedded in communities and individuals, the reality of the social economy in Québec confirms the important role of social capital, partnerships, and networks in achieving these objectives. An informal yet very active network based on trust and common values has existed for many years, bringing together actors in development capital and solidarity finance sector. The goal of formalizing this network was realized at the end of 2010. Formalizing the informal network of solidarity finance institutions was a priority announced at the "Summit on the Social and Solidarity" in 2006 . The founding members of CAP Finance, a responsible and solidarity finance network created in 2010, include the Fonds de solidarité (FTQ), Fondaction, Filaction, RISQ, Réseau québécois du crédit communautaire, Fiducie du Chantier de l'économie sociale, and the Caisse d'économie solidaire Desjardins. CAP Finance gives greater visibility to solidarity finance and development capital institutions in Québec.

This chapter has focused on the different actors engaged in solidarity investment in Québec, on the supply side of investment. Clearly, there are important issues linked to demand; that is, to the ability of financial institutions to meet the need for capital in the social economy in Québec. We distributed a short survey to gather the views of some directors of social economy networks; the preliminary findings show that many do not use existing instruments.[47] A number of factors could explain this, including questions of eligibility and the availability of products, which often take the form of loans. It is important to note that funds must manage risk and that some have difficulties covering their operating costs, especially small community funds, thus reducing their capacity to finance initiatives.

Conclusion

In this chapter, we have described the context in which solidarity finance has developed in Québec and elsewhere. The financialization of the economy is forcing new thinking in the world of finance. Growing concerns about the impact of economic activities on the environment and socio-economic inequalities in rich and poor countries are turning attention to financial institutions that invest more responsibly. It is not surprising that responsible investors are more visible today, given their commitment to a model that creates wealth while respecting the social and physical environment.

Today, the social economy in Québec and elsewhere represents a different vision, an economy that is profitable and embedded in values emphasizing societal well-being and respect for the environment. The SSEs that represent another new way of doing business, however, require new financial instruments, a need that solidarity finance and development capital institutions are working to meet.

This chapter provides a synthesis of the development of solidarity finance and its ongoing challenges. As these alternative financial institutions, which are committed to societal goals while contributing to wealth creation, emerge in Québec, Canada, and abroad, governments are compelled to design enabling policy measures and to collaborate with actors to increase the capacity of their institutions to meet their goals. In Québec, international experiences are inspirational. As well, the Québec experience has become an inspiration for other regions and countries. Actors in solidarity finance are the architects of a new financial market who can compete effectively with financial institutions driven by profit. Today, it is no longer necessary to argue for the need for financial institutions to be more socially responsible. In contrast to mainstream financial institutions, solidarity finance contributes to an alternative vision of finance, in which profitability is measured by the capacity to respond to critical societal issues.

NOTES

1   This chapter was written before the subprime crisis. We have updated the quantitative data, without, however, revising our critical analysis to account for the ongoing situation. We believe that our views on the financialization of the economy and the need to rethink finance are more relevant than ever. The actual and long-term impact of the financial crisis remains to be analysed. It appears clear, however, that the values in practice in social economy organizations and their partners helped minimize the impact of the crisis. Several analysts predict that the principles of responsible finance – solidarity finance in particular – will influence the reconstruction of the financial sector. More research on this topic is needed.

2   This chapter was translated from the French by Susan Mott and Valérie Bourdeau.

3   See Bourque G.L., & Gendron, C. (2003), La finance responsable: La nouvelle dynamique d'une finance plurielle? *Économie et Solidarités, 34*(1) 21–36.

4   Ministère du Développement économique et régional (2003), *Rapport du Groupe de travail sur le rôle de l'État québécois dans le capital de risque.* Québec: Government of Québec.

5   Mendell, M., Lévesque, B., & Rouzier, R. (2003), New Forms of Financing Social Economy Enterprises and Organisations in Québec. In *The Non-profit Sector in a Changing Economy.* Paris: OECD, pp. 139–68.

6   Solidarity Fund (FTQ) since 2001.

7   Lévesque, B., et al. (2000), *Un cas exemplaire de nouvelle gouvernance : Fonds de solidarité FTQ.* Montréal: CRISES and Fonds de solidarité FTQ.

8   Mendell, M., Lévesque, B., & Rouzier, R. (2003).

9   In 2009, $33.3 million was invested in 147 cooperatives eligible for the tax credit. Source: Ministère du Développement économique, de l'Innovation et de l'Exportation (2010), *Le Régime d'investissement coopératif. Résultats 2009,* Québec: Direction des coopératives.

10 CSN, the Confédération des syndicats nationaux (now called the Fondaction).

11 Note also that the creation of the Comité d'orientation et de concertation sur l'économie sociale (COCES) in 1995 led to the creation of the comités régionaux d'économie sociale (CRES) in the 16 administrative regions of Québec. COCES included representatives from Marche des femmes, regional women's groups, and government departments and agencies that believed in the capacity of the third sector to promote employment. The CRES were created in 1995 to integrate the concerns of the social economy in regional strategic planning while facilitating cooperation between social economy actors at the local and regional level. See: D'Amours, M. (1999), Procès d'institutionnalisation de l'économie sociale au Québec, *Cahiers du LAREPPS,* 99-05; Belley, T. (1997), L'économie sociale, saveur régionale. *Relation, 635* (November), pp. 273–4.

12 Lévesque, B., et al. (2002), *Analyse de la gestion des fonds et portefeuille des Centres locaux de développement du Québec.* Report presented to the Association des CLD du Québec. Montréal: CRISES-IRECUS-GRCR.

13 Note that the Québec government had allocated $90 million in the 2007–08 budget to promote entrepreneurship in the regions, a sum that was to be managed by CLDs over a five-year period. Source: Ministère des Finances (2007), *Stratégie pour le développement de toutes les régions. Budget 2007–2008.*

Gouvernement du Québec. In 2009–10, $53.5 million was provided to municipalities to fund CLDs. Source: Ministère du Développement économique de l'Innovation et de l'Exportation (2010), *Étude des crédits 2010–2011. Demande de renseignements particuliers de l'opposition.* CLDs will begin to repay the sums provided by the Québec government for FLIs in 2011–2012. Initially, repayment was to begin in 2005–2006, and was postponed to 2009–2010. Source: Ministère des Finances (2009), *Renseignements additionnels sur les mesures du budget 2009–2010.* Gouvernement du Québec, ss. A to C.

14 Ministère du Développement économique de l'Innovation et de l'Exportation (2010), op. cit.

15 For more information, visit http://www.chantier.qc.ca.

16 Fonds de solidarité FTQ (2010), *Rapport annuel et de développement durable 2010.*

17 For more information, see http://www.fondaction.com/?cat=32.

18 "Fondaction CSN pour la coopération et l'emploi is our development partner. Established in February 2004, the Fondaction–Angus partnership is the first association between a venture capital fund and a social economy business. Both partners contribute equal shares into each new project and share the same vision of sustainable development, combining economic, social and environmental performance objectives." Source: http://www.technopoleangus.com/an/angus/.

19 For more information, see http://www.fondaction.com/?cat=17.

20 For more information, see http://www.capitalregional.com/Fr/societe/mission.html. Resource regions are Abitibi-Témiscamingue, Bas-Saint-Laurent, Côte-Nord, Gaspésie–Îles-de-la-Madeleine, Mauricie, Nord-du-Québec, and Saguenay–Lac-Saint-Jean.

21 For more information, see http://www.capitalregional.com/fr/societe/repartition.html.

22 For more information, see http://www.capitalregional.com/Fr/gestion/message_president_conseil.html.

23 Investissement Québec (2010), *Rapport annuel 2009–2010.*

24 For more information, see http://www.investquebec.com/en/index.aspx?page=1771.

25 Ibid.

26 For more information, see http://www.investquebec.com/documents/fr/publications/RAIQ_2009-2010_fr.pdf.

27 For more information, see http://www.caissesolidaire.coop/savoir-etre/economie_solidaire/.

28 For more information, see http://www.caissesolidaire.coop/bilan/2009/rapport/caisse.html.

29 Caisse d'économie solidaire Desjardins (2009), *Rapport écosolidaire 2009.*

30 For more information, see http://www.rqcc.qc.ca/images/rqcc/publications/statistiques_rqcc_2009-2010.pdf.
31 RISQ (2009), *Rapport annuel 2009*.
32 Ibid.
33 For more information, see http://www.fonds-risq.qc.ca/francais/retombeeseconomiques.htm and the 2003 Annual Report.
34 Fondaction (2010), *3ᵉ rapport de développement durable: Faits saillants*.
35 For more information, see http://www.fondaction.com/pdf/Dev_durable/RDD_Faits%20saillants_abrege.pdf.
36 Fondaction (2010).
37 For more information, see http://www.filaction.qc.ca/fond-financement-exemple.php.
38 Fondaction (2003), *Rapport annuel 2002–2003*.
39 Fiducie du Chantier de l'économie de l'économie sociale (2008), *La Fiducie du Chantier de l'économie de l'économie sociale: Un produit unique pour le développement des entreprises d'économie sociale*.
40 Revised Fiducie Agreement adopted on November 15, 2006.
41 For more information, see http://fiducieduchantier.qc.ca.
42 For more information, see http://fiducieduchantier.qc.ca/?module=document&uid=316.
43 Canada Economic Development (2008), *Formative evaluation of the Funding Component of the Social Economy Support Initiative for Quebec – Final Report* (http://www.dec-ced.gc.ca/eng/publications/agency/evaluation/82/page-3.html).
44 For more information, see http://www.finansol.org.
45 For more information, see http://www.fébea.org.
46 Canadian Task Force on Social Finance (2010), *Mobilizing Private Capital for Public Good*.
·47 This was an informal survey conducted by ARUC-CAP Finance that served as the basis for a better understanding of the demand side. It confirmed the need to conduct a more formal survey as well as our conclusion that the supply of capital was not necessarily greater than demand, as some suggested, but rather that the disequilibrium reflected a mismatch of available instruments and needs.

REFERENCES

Belley, T. (1997). L'économie sociale, saveur régionale. *Relation* (635): 273–4.
Bourque G.L., & Gendron, C. (2003). La finance responsable: La nouvelle dynamique d'une finance plurielle? *Économie et Solidarites*, 34(1), 21–36.

Caisse d'économie solidaire Desjardins. (2009). *Rapport écosolidaire 2009*. Accessed 19 June 2011. http://www.caissesolidaire.coop/bilan/2009/rapport/caisse.html

Caisse d'économie solidaire Desjardins. (2011). *Qui nous sommes*. Accessed 19 June 2011. http://www.caissesolidaire.coop/savoir-etre/economie_solidaire

Canadian Task Force on Social Finance. (2010). *Mobilizing private capital for public good*.

C.A.P. Finance. (2011). *Répondre aux besoins et penser autrement la finance*. Accessed 19 June 2011. http://capfinance.ca/page_accueuil.php

Chantier de l'économie sociale. (2006a). *Investir solidairement: Bilan et perspectives*. Accessed 19 June 2011. http://www.chantier.qc.ca/userImgs/documents/root/documents_gen/rapport-investir-solidairement.pdf

Chantier de l'économie sociale. (2006b). *Investir solidairement: Bilan et perspectives*. Accessed 19 June 2011. http://www.chantier.qc.ca/userImgs/documents/root/documents_gen/rapport-investir-solidairement.pdf

Chantier de l'économie sociale. (2009). *Chantier de l'économie sociale*. Accessed 19 June 2011. http://www.chantier.qc.ca

Commission des syndicats nationaux. (2011a). *Fondaction CSN pour la coopération et l'emploi: Statistiques*. Accessed 19 June 2011. http://www.fondaction.com/?cat=32

Commission des syndicats nationaux. (2011b). *Fondaction CSN pour la coopération et l'emploi: Conditions generals*. Accessed 19 June 2011. http://www.fondaction.com/?cat=17

D'Amours, M. (1999). Procès d'institutionnalisation de l'économie sociale au Québec. *Cahiers du LAREPPS* (99–05), 50.

Desjardins. (2011). *La société: La mission*. Accessed 19 June 2011. http://www.capitalregional.com/Fr/societe/mission.html

Desjardins. (2011a). *La gestion: Message du président du conseil et directeur général*. Accessed 19 June 2011. http://www.capitalregional.com/Fr/gestion/message_president_conseil.html

Desjardins. (2011b). *La société: La répartition de l'actif*. Accessed 19 June 2011. http://www.capitalregional.com/fr/societe/repartition.html

Développement économique Canada. (2008). *Évaluation formative du volet financement de l'initiative d'appui à l'économie sociale au Québec: Rapport final*. Accessed 19 June 2011. http://www.dec-ced.gc.ca/fra/publications/agence/evaluation/82/page-2.html

Fédération européenne de finances et banques éthiques et alternatives. (2009). *FEBEA: Objet du réseau*. Accessed 19 June 2011. http://www.febea.org/objet_reseau.php

Fiducie du Chantier de l'économie de l'économie sociale. (2008a). *La Fiducie du Chantier de l'économie de l'économie sociale: Un produit unique pour le développement des entreprises d'économie sociale.* Accessed 19 June 2011. http://fiducieduchantier.qc.ca/

Fiducie du Chantier de l'économie sociale. (2008b). *Projets financés.* Accessed 19 June 2011. http://fiducieduchantier.qc.ca/?module=document&uid=316

Filaction. (2009). *Fonds de financement dédiés.* Accessed 19 June 2011. http://www.filaction.qc.ca/fond-financement-exemple.php

Finansol. (2011). *L'association Finansol: Présentation générale.* Accessed 19 June 2011. http://www.finansol.org/UPLOAD/rubrique/pages/60/60_rubrique.php

Fondation. (2003). *Rapport annuel 2002–2003.* Accessed 11 July 2011. http://www.fondaction.com/pdf/rapport_annuel/RapportFondaction2003F.pdf

Fondation. (2010). *3e rapport de développement durable: Faits saillants.* Accessed 19 June 2011. http://www.fondaction.com/pdf/Dev_durable/RDD_Faits%20saillants_abrege.pdf

Fonds de solidarité FTQ. (2010). *Rapport annuel et de développement durable 2010.* Montréal.

Investissement Québec. (2010). *Rapport annuel 2009–2010.* Accessed 19 June 2011. http://www.investquebec.com/documents/fr/publications/RAIQ_2009-2010_fr.pdf

Investissement Québec. (2007). *Fonds d'intervention économique régional (FIER).* Accessed 19 June 2011. http://www.investquebec.com/fr/index.aspx?page=1771

Lévesque, B., et al. (2000). *Un cas exemplaire de nouvelle gouvernance: Fonds de solidarité FTQ.* Montréal: CRISES et Fonds de solidarité FTQ.

Lévesque, B., et al. (2002). *Analyse de la gestion des fonds et portefeuille des centres locaux de développement du Québec.* Report presented to the Association des CLD du Québec. Montréal: CRISES-IRECUS-GRCR.

Mendell, M., Lévesque, B., & Rouzier, R. (2003). New forms of financing social economy enterprises and organisations in Québec. In *The non-profit sector in a changing economy* (pp. 139–68). Paris: OECD.

Ministère du Développement économique de l'Innovation et de l'Exportation. (2010a). *Étude des crédits 2010–2011: Demande de renseignements particuliers de l'opposition.* Québec: Government of Québec.

Ministère du Développement économique, de l'Innovation et de l'Exportation. (2010b). *Le Régime d'investissement coopératif: Résultats 2009.* Québec: Government of Québec.

Ministère du Développement économique et régional. (2003). *Rapport du groupe de travail sur le rôle de l'État québécois dans le capital de risque.* Québec: Government of Québec.

Ministère des Finances. (2007). *Stratégie pour le développement de toutes les régions: Budget 2007–2008*. Québec: Governement of Québec.

Ministère des Finances. (2009). *Renseignements additionnels sur les mesures du budget 2009–2010*, Québec: Government of Québec, ss. A to C.

Réseau québécois du crédit communautaire. (2010). *Statistiques 2009–2010*. Accessed 19 June 2011. http://www.rqcc.qc.ca/images/rqcc/publications/statistiques_rqcc_2009-2010.pdf

RISQ. (2003). *Rapport annuel 2003*. Montréal: Réseau d'investissement social du Québec.

RISQ. (2009). *Rapport annuel 2009*. Montréal: Réseau d'investissement social du Québec.

Technopôle Angus. (2007). *Choisir Angus*. Accessed 19 June 2011. http://www.technopoleangus.com/fr/angus

Vienney, C. (1994). *L'économie sociale*. Paris: Éditions La Découverte.

7 The Social Economy, the Environment, and Sustainable Development: From Specialized Sector to Renewed Social Vision[1]

CORINNE GENDRON AND MARIE-FRANCE TURCOTTE

Introduction

The aim of this chapter is to explain the relationship between the social economy and sustainable development. It is the environmental dimension of sustainable development that attracts the attention of most researchers, while its social dimension remains poorly studied. Thus, a pressing need exists for the social economy to better grasp, define, and implement sustainable development, not only in practice, on the ground, but also within a theoretical and conceptual analysis. Conversely, sustainable development issues are part of the fundamental questioning raised by the social economy movement and reform of practices. It is thus all the more interesting to examine how social economy actors have appropriated sustainable development initiatives, as well as their participation therein.

Social economy definitions continue to elicit lively debate. As shown by Lévesque and Mendell (1999), controversies surrounding the definition of the social economy may be due to the fact that the concept simultaneously covers a multitude of empirical, theoretical, and normative realities. The social economy is at times described as an economic sector and at other times as a movement, and its innovative potential is often invoked.

Although the social economy "project" has acquired varied forms over time and with various state configurations, as demonstrated in this work by Lévesque but also Dancause and Morin, conceptualizations of social economy have always oscillated between the idea of a complementary sector integrated into the capitalist economy, and an outright alternative social vision (e.g., Charles Gide's "cooperative republic"). We may, therefore, view the social economy as a social movement that advances a social vision focused on social, environmental, and economic concerns.[2] Moreover, the social economy movement is driven both by needs and by aspirations.[3] It is founded in specifically designated organizations, which dispense services that respond to the real needs of groups and individuals. Yet, following the ideas of Polanyi (1983), it is also the manifestation of aspirations to redefine the economy and embed it firmly within the social sphere.

For Bernard Eme and Jean-Louis Laville, the economy they term "solidary" is akin to a true project of political action, as it expresses solidarity between social groups, including the most disadvantaged. To identify social economy as a social movement is not trivial. Indeed, it is the acknowledgement of a new mode of social action, that is, social mobilization expressed not only in the institutional and social domains (such as formal workers' unions or civil rights movements), but also in previously uncharted economic territory (through solidarity-based economy and fair trade, for example). It is in this perspective that the social economy's innovative potential comes into its own. Social economy actors participate in the generation of social movements that aim to co-opt the economy, steering it towards social concerns.

We begin by briefly describing the concept of sustainable development and its relationship to the concept of development itself. Subsequently, we outline the convergences and linkages between the social economy and sustainable development, in their theoretical dimensions and in practice. Finally, we outline practical junctures between the social economy and sustainable development on each of three bases: sector, movement, and innovation.

The Environment, Development, and Sustainable Development

As is the case with the social economy, sustainable development is at the heart of ongoing debates. As pointed out by Gendron and Revéret (2000), what is most striking is that the notion of sustainable development has propagated largely without reference to the already abundant existing literature on development itself. Sustainable development, as will be seen below, has been subject to a wide variety of interpretations, but the same can also be said of development, which has stimulated hard-fought theoretical debates among social actors, including many researchers who have attempted to explain the causes of Third World underdevelopment and its development conditions (Gendron, 2001).

Development

The concept of development first took shape as a geopolitical vision in the years following World War Two. In a speech delivered in 1949, American President Harry Truman first put forward the idea of a program that was to see the United States sharing its scientific and industrial knowledge and capabilities with the underdeveloped regions of the world. Subsequently, national agencies, international organizations (such as the World Bank's IBRD, the International Bank for Reconstruction and Development), and regional development banks were set up in order to produce "development," with the aim of integrating these regions into the global economy (Gendron & Revérêt, 2000).

Ever since, development has been at the core of numerous debates between North and South. Northern actors justified their interventions by invoking modernization theory and, as per Rostow's (1970) stages of economic growth, emphasizing the importance of capital, infrastructures, and urbanization, and treating cultural and socio-political factors as obstacles to the transition towards a consumerist-industrial society, seen in this perspective to be the ultimate stage of economic development. Southern voices denounced this "modern," neo-liberal vision, seeing in it neocolonialist designs, and demanded autonomy invoking the dependency theory postulated by the Economic Commission for Latin America and the Caribbean (ECLAC).[4]

The convictions of modernists and the analyses of dependency theorists both were shaken by the oil crisis and subsequent economic crash of 1973. From that moment on, the North, reeling, could no longer claim to be an exemplary model, while in the South there emerged three increasingly distinct blocks: oil countries, newly industrialized countries, and underdeveloped countries. The great multinational companies developed international market strategies and, thereby, contributed to the creation of a global economic sphere, ushering in the era of globalization. Globalization, as well as the preceding economic crisis and the demise of the Soviet block, all ushered in a great shift in the thinking and theorization of development, which previously had been based on the liberalization of markets, privatization, and deregulation policies. At the same time, the North imposed structural adjustment programs on the South, which have since widely been decried for the devastating consequences they have had on the populations of developing countries.

A Multidimensional and Polysemous Concept

It is generally accepted that, as a multidimensional concept, sustainable development calls for the reconciliation of the ecological, social, and economic dimensions of development while seeking equity,[5] and implies that cultural and spatial dimensions must be taken into account (Sachs, 1997). In the ecological dimension, it redefines nature as a foundational substratum, inferring that the preservation of nature is a necessary condition for the creation of wealth. In the social dimension, it casts serious doubt on "percolation of wealth" arguments, which state that all generated wealth will eventually reach the poorest populations and that there is no need to oversee its redistribution. Last, in the economic dimension, sustainable development aims to instrumentalize the economy to make it subservient to social needs, and strives to rethink and adapt it in accordance with ecological factors. This should not be taken to mean, however, that ecological concerns ought to become dictates: indeed, the recognition of these concerns can only result from a social compromise among all actors as to the various dimensions of sustainable development.

The concept of sustainable development is also polysemous: that is, subject to multiple, varied, and even contradictory interpretations by the various actors involved in the process. The origin of this polysemy may be located in the condition of sustainable development as a space of negotiation between actors; this is also true of connected concepts, such as corporate social responsibility (B.-Turcotte, 2005) or the precautionary principle (Maguire & Hardy, 2006). All the actors seek sustainable development, social responsibility, and precaution, but each actor has a different definition or vision of what those terms should mean in practice. Thus, it is the polysemous property of sustainable development that accounts for its simultaneous status both as a developing "legitimating principle" (Gendron & Revéret, 2000) and as a controversial domain whose ideals, definitions, and means of implementation are not subject to consensus.

It has been widely acknowledged that sustainable development emerged from distinct events and organizational publications, such as the World Conservation Strategy (1980), the Brundtland Report (1987), and the Rio Declaration on Environment and Development (1992), although its origins can be traced to earlier works, such as those of the Hammarskjöld Foundation and of Ignacy Sachs on the notion of ecodevelopment.[6] These homogenous origins have not resulted in a uniform body of literature. Rather, they have given way to an ambiguation of the basic definitions of reference, be it the one proffered by the International Union for the Preservation of Nature and Natural Resources or the one given in the Brundtland Report. Although this may seem paradoxical, it is the outcome of the collective authorship processes leading up to these publications, which involved people from a variety of backgrounds, geographic origins, and ideological inclinations. Indeed, the Brundtland definition is so wide as to include almost any interpretation. Daly (1990) argues that, in fact, this ambiguation cannot be dissociated from the popularity of the concept.[7] Indeed, sustainable development was quickly taken up by social movements, leaders of government, and the corporate arena (Sachs, 1997).

Gendron and Revérêt (2000) distinguish among three approaches that social actors adopt towards sustainable development: sustained growth, economy-environment harmonization, and the "tri-polar conceptualization." The first approach follows a direct line set by the traditional vision of development, with the distinction that it includes the environment as an additional variable in management decisions related to economic growth. The second approach aims to harmonize the economy and the environment, recognizing that the economic system has lost touch with ecosystems and the processes of natural regulation, notwithstanding its proponents' claims that it is the system best able to regulate "rare resources." The third approach takes its inspiration from the definition provided by the International Union for the Preservation of Nature and Natural Resources, which has since been adopted by various public authorities. Notably, the Québec government has opted for the tri-polar conceptualization of sustainable development, in which the social domain is recognized as a fundamental element of development, on an equal footing with the environment and the economy.

Gagnon (1995a), for her part, has identified four sustainable development approaches: ecological, economic, humanist, and planned. As we will see, each of these approaches focuses on either processes or results. The ecological and economic approaches do not take the social dimension into account. The ecological approach adopts an ecosystemic conception of the world to explain human interactions with the biosphere, but often ignores the socially constructed dimension of environmental issues and the existence of actors capable of transforming the social domain. (It must be noted, however, that many environmental groups and ecologists do integrate social and political questions into their analysis.) The economic approach to sustainable development, according to Gagnon, has its roots in environmental economics, from which it takes its methodology of monetization (founded on the principle of externality) and environmental management (linked to the ecological modernization of production processes), although it does not question over-consumption or the ecological unsustainability of the dominant development model. This approach implicitly accepts that the environment, as well as "human resources," is subordinate to, and at the service of, the economy and its priorities. In an increasingly globalized economy, profits are international and privatized while social costs are localized and collectively incurred. Not only does this approach ignore the social domain, but, more importantly, it is based on an exceedingly narrow conception of the environment and its ecosystems.

The Social Dimensions of Sustainable Development

The two other approaches (humanist and planned) identified by Gagnon (1995a) acknowledge, each in its own way, the social dimension of sustainable development. The planned approach emphasizes the decision-making process of resource management and the importance of democratic participation. This approach thus situates itself at the operational level and addresses sustainable development as a procedure and, indeed, as a decision-making process. The humanist approach can be situated in both the conceptual and the operational realms. Its perspective is conditioned by development research, and places most emphasis on actors, human beings, and the universal improvement of life conditions and living standards. It places a high importance on environmental justice as a way to tackle the increasingly evident linkages between poverty and environmental degradation, in the North as well as in the South.

Various studies and reports, the most famous being *Our Common Future* (also known as the Brundtland Report), published in 1987 by the World Commission on Environment and Development, have shown that poverty, understood as a measure of the social and demographic conditions of subsistence, is closely linked with environmental degradation. This link has been the subject of a particular focus by Third Worldists and the environmental justice movement (in the United States). In comparisons with wealthy communities and neighbourhoods, it has been demonstrated that Black and ethnic minority communities (whose lower-than-average income and adverse life conditions are widely acknowledged), are far more likely to be affected by urban constructions that are detrimental to their physical and living environments, such as highways or sanitary landfills. Such constructions, termed "developments," only accentuate the cleavages that maintain these communities' socially and environmentally detrimental conditions. Correlatively, the degradation of their physical environment is a prime accelerator of their pauperization.

In Rio de Janeiro (1992) and in Johannesburg (2002) there were forceful negotiations that took place between North and South, in the course of which the poor nations protested against the demands of their Northern counterparts, who sought the suspension of mass extractions of natural resources, as this would have deprived them of foreign currency earnings. The stance from developing countries amounted to a refusal of draconian measures, on the grounds that the North must also adapt by modifying consumption patterns and proposing alternative solutions. However, because the majority of developing countries' resources are consumed by Western countries, this may well be a false argument. It is well worth asking: What are the real costs of these resources, which generally fuel the Western and global economies, leaving local and regional populations to cope with the social end environmental costs? Developing countries are faced with rising poverty levels. This, in turn, causes increased environmental degradation, be it in the course of efforts to ensure subsistence (cutting wood for domestic use, tropical forest agricultural deforestation, and urban sprawl, among others), or because of resource exploitation methods employed by foreign concerns that cater to the needs of the North (mono-cropping, including the use of pesticides, and non-environmental mineral extraction).

Both the humanist and the planned approaches argue that sustainable development should result from participatory decision-making processes, thus linking sustainable development with social mediation and collective learning, where the social externalities of economic decisions are taken into account. The humanist approach employs an impact-evaluation process to identify those who stand to benefit and those who are likely to be adversely affected by a given development project. In this way, the actors of a community or territory can question the justification of a "development" project and factor its social costs into the impact evaluation, as well as implement corrective measures to avoid, diminish, or compensate for social costs.

In this context of local sustainable development, the social domain dominates sustainable development, providing a new development paradigm that offers alternative visions of objectives, decision-making processes, and citizen participation in the choice of development projects. The humanist approach certainly takes environmental limits into account in the maintenance of productive activity, but the real contribution of this approach is, above all, the inclusion of a social dimension of value notions, social change, ethics, and local communities. All these elements constitute a dimension of sustainable development that had long been neglected, but which now has come to be recognized as inextricable from sustainable development. Indeed, equitable sustainable development and viable local development are not possible unless social equity (if not an outright redistribution of power and wealth skewed in favour of the poorer sectors of society) is not recast as a central consideration of decision-making and policy formulation, both locally and globally.

On the conceptual and practical levels, the inclusion of the social dimension and the integration of environmental concerns (as well as the ways of managing that integration), constitute the distinguishing characteristics that set sustainable development apart from traditionally dominant conceptualizations of development and confirm it as a thoroughly revolutionary paradigmatic shift.

The Social Economy and Sustainable Development: The Potential for Exceptionally Promising Integration

Although originating from different currents within social movements, organizations, and institutions, the two notions of social economy and sustainable development are amenable to fusion in several aspects: (1) they rest on similar principles: that is, autonomy, development as a means to address human needs, and democracy; (2) they offer alternative means to satisfy social needs; and (3) they promote a fundamental re-examination of the definitions of the common good, of collective social welfare and, more generally, of the public interest. Despite offering diverging analyses of human activity, particularly in its social and economic dimensions, it is in the melding with the public interest that the social economy and sustainable development can find common linking points.

As well, reflections on sustainable development and the social economy have highlighted the various insufficiencies and biases among

social actors that traditionally have been justified by economic rationality. Such reflections call for an awareness of the human, as well as
social, consequences and impacts of economic actions and their implementation. This awareness of social externalities raises the question of
who profits from a given decision, and who is left to suffer its costs.

To say that social economy and sustainable development are both
carriers of the same societal objective (to rethink and reform the implementation of development), implies that each contains the dimension
of a social movement. Let us take as an example the citizen groups that
have formed in order to voice collective claims in the face of rising concerns over the protection of the environment. Both movements – social
economy and sustainable development – highlight the gap between economic and social approaches to development through referring to the
notion of externality, and by calling for these externalities to be taken
into account in decisional processes. Both movements also propose new
practices and methods that traditional capitalist enterprises may integrate into their modernization, with a view to sustainable development.
Social economy networks repeatedly have lent support to ecological
movements. This has been the case of the Chantier de l'économie sociale
du Québec (Québec Social Economy Project, CÉS), which has supported
ecological groups' applications for financial support (CÉS, 2001).

In a brief submitted to the Québec Ministry of Sustainable Development, Environment and Parks, within the scope of public consultations on the Ministry's Plan de développement durable (Sustainable
Development Plan), the Chantier positioned itself at the core of the
movement towards sustainable development in Québec. The Chantier
described its own contribution to sustainable development in the following terms:

> The concepts of social economy and sustainable development are founded
> on common principles, such as:
>
> - the acknowledgement of human and social consequences and impacts
>   of economic actions and their implementation (henceforth, and nec-
>   essarily, we must weigh the social externalities created by economic
>   activity);
> - the integration of social and economic considerations into decisional
>   processes (to terminate all indiscriminate development or growth of
>   companies and their profits);

- the primacy of the quality of life and human dignity, for individuals and groups (rethink and reform the implementation of development). (CÉS, 2005, p. 4)

In addition to these common principles, the Chantier also identifies concerns shared by social economy and sustainable development, including:

- the importance of democratic decision-making;
- the importance of citizen involvement;
- the importance of redistributing profits into the community;
- the acknowledgement of a social dimension;
- a concern for the public interest; and
- an alternative vision of development channelling social objectives. (CÉS, 2005, p. 4)

Beyond these discourses of some of its actors, the social economy displays a myriad of experiences and emerging practices that combine social and ecological aspirations within a common project. We can cite, for example, fair trade, community-supported agriculture, organic food distribution, "buy local" programs, the slow food movement, and car-pooling.[8] The following sections will first examine the connections and linking points between the social economy and sustainable development on theoretical and conceptual grounds, and then analyse interactions between the two domains in practice. The social economy can play a primary role by, on the one hand, participating in the exercise of rethinking economic and social development with a view to ecological imperatives, but also, on the other hand, by making explicit the true social impacts of ecological crises and the means to remedy those impacts.

Theoretical Interconnections

The link between social economy and sustainable development can be formalized, but its nature depends on the definition assigned to each term. Keeping in mind our discussion leading up to this point, we can identify four linking modes: (1) the environment and sustainable development exposing the socially constructed aspects of the economy, (2) the social economy and sustainable development sharing social interfacing, (3) the social economy as an operationalization of sustainable development, and (4) the social economy and sustainable development as mutual contributors.

REVEALING THE SOCIALLY CONSTRUCTED DIMENSION OF THE ECONOMY

Environmental problems reveal the dysfunctionalities and inadequacies of the economic system vis-à-vis sustainable development concerns. Social economy enterprises called "resourceries" in Québec argue that material waste is an indicator of all that is wrong with the economy. In order to transform waste, production and consumption modes must be rethought. In other words, environmental issues call the autonomization of the economic sphere into question, since the successful resolution of environmental issues necessitates the participation of social actors. Henceforth, these issues must be approached, simultaneously, from economic, social, political, and scientific angles; indeed, they must be viewed as social constructs. This implies, on the one hand, the acknowledgement of social controversies inherent to ecological polemics – water management, factory waste, modes of waste management – and, on the other hand, the involvement of representatives of industry, politicians, health workers, and scientists, as well as social groups and environmentalists. In addition, it infers the need for innovation so that the social and environmental dimensions may reintegrate the various measurements and calculations. We will see this in more detail in another section.

THE SUSTAINABLE DEVELOPMENT/SOCIAL ECONOMY INTERFACE

Environmental problems force the adoption of a social perspective on the economy, as demonstrated by the perspective of social economy. It is precisely this social dimension that corresponds to the central point of the second conjunction between the social economy and sustainable development, which is formalized by the concept of interface.

In this case, sustainable development and the social economy are somewhat incongruent. Sustainable development is the goal of the actions of a varied ensemble of actors, as well as a process of change. The social dimension of the social economy corresponds to the social dimension of sustainable development, but sustainable development includes other dimensions, too – the environment and the economy – that are not necessarily integrated into the social economy. For its part, the social economy consists, as well, of dimensions that are alien to sustainable development. The challenge, therefore, is to understand the interface between the two.

THE SOCIAL ECONOMY AS A MEANS TOWARDS ATTAINING SUSTAINABLE DEVELOPMENT

The third link situates the social economy as a means towards attaining sustainable development. Sustainable development is seen as an ideal aim: the objective and result of actions (requiring the participation of multiple sectors, notably the social economy) carried out through distinct (perhaps alternative) methods taken on voluntarily and collectively. Here, social economy is about the implementation of sustainable development. Thus, the contribution of the social economy reaches a higher level – that of an ideal of development. Under such conditions, the social economy takes on a major role and a privileged position, notably because of its values, which are aimed at a process of socio-economic transformation, while the concept of sustainable development represents, rather, an alternative expression of the common good.

MUTUAL CONTRIBUTIONS

The fourth linking point is to be found in the mutual contributions between the social economy and sustainable development, although, as mentioned previously, sustainable development contains dimensions that are not necessarily integrated by the social economy. The social economy is neither a necessary nor a sufficient condition for sustainable development, and vice versa. As well, the social economy in itself does not necessarily imply sustainable development. However, the social economy represents an opportunity because, at least in principle, social economy enterprises exhibit characteristics that branch out to connect with sustainable development principles, such as democratic decision-making, insistence on citizen involvement, the consideration of internalizing environmental issues, and the redistribution of wealth into the community. Moreover, we may advance the hypothesis that social economy enterprises already operate and are evaluated in a context of multiple objectives (multiple bottom lines) in which a hierarchy of objectives works in favour of the public interest (or, at the very least, members' collective interest), which is an essential building block of sustainable development.

These conceptual linking points may resonate differently when observed in practice. Before moving into the practical dimension, however, it is interesting to note that sustainable development and the social economy do not rest on the same empirical bases. We might say that in the social economy, practice precedes research or theoretical reflection (in the present current of work, at least), while in sustainable development, theoretical reflection tends to precede practice and, even, to exhort sustainable innovation and institutional, as well as organizational, modernization. We can go so far as to say that studies and reflections on sustainable development readily provide guiding principles, but are seldom based in empirical research.

Linkages, in Practice

In many cases, social economy organizations (non-profit, cooperative, mutualist sectors) are actors that are essential to sustainable development because they are instigators of change, be it through institutional, social, or economic mobilization. As we noted at the beginning of this chapter, the social economy is sometimes described as an economic sector and sometimes as a movement, and its potential for innovation is often invoked. The following section explores the linkages between the social economy and sustainable development in practice, from the perspective of three conceptualizations: sector, movement, and innovation.

THE SOCIAL ECONOMY AND THE SUSTAINABLE DEVELOPMENT SECTOR

In 2004, the Conseil québécois de la coopération et de la mutualité (CQCM, Québec Council of Cooperation and Mutuality) created a five-year plan, the principal objective of which was to reinforce the impact of cooperatives in rural communities affected by demographic decline. In 2009, the five-year plan laid out three objectives: demographic change, sustainable development, and occupation of territory. These objectives included the goal that federations would create a sustainable development policy by 2012; that, by 2014, 50 per cent of cooperatives and mutual associations would also have implemented such a policy; and that the movement would produce an initial social responsibility and cooperative report in 2014. The main theme that has been directly promoted by the CQCM is that of renewable energies.[9]

The Chantier de l'économie sociale du Québec promulgates the predominance of social concerns in its perspective on the economy, and insists on the synergy between this perspective and the concept of sustainable development. Thus, the social economy implies sustainable development by the very fact of its social specificity in terms of governance and social impacts. This statement may not be erroneous, but it does need to be qualified. On the one hand, the social dimension of sustainable development includes, to be sure, certain elements of governance, but also the idea of welfare – in other words, public interest. Since this is the subject of reflection inside the social economy movement, the social economy is called upon to base itself more on solidarity, implying that it has not yet done so. On the other hand, the collective interest of the members of a social economy organization does not always accord with social public interest. Thus, the social dimension of sustainable development cannot be assumed to be automatically fulfilled by the very fact of an organization's claim to being part of the social economy.

Moreover, if environmental concerns are a condition of sustainable development, social economy enterprises must examine the ecological impacts of their activities, which is a prerequisite of their adherence to a sustainable development perspective. The Chantier ties the social economy to the ecological dimension of sustainable development by supporting applications for financial aid made by ecological groups and by promoting the distinct sector of resourceries.

The social economy must, in fact, be recognized for the environmentally friendly goods and services that it offers. In the waste-management domain, a multitude of environmental groups have put forth innovative methods to reduce, reuse, and recycle waste. Residual materials' treatment concepts and procedures have been adapted by public and private enterprises (Lounsbury, 2003), while certain social economy organizations, such as the Réseau des ressourceries (Resourcery Network), extend these operations beyond the search for innovative alternatives.

The synchronization of social economy organizations with environmental action is even postulated in certain government policies, although this is subject to change according to changes in government. In 1999, citing the social economy, the Québec Ministry of Environment (as it was then known) implemented a five-year plan that saw $17 million directed into investments in resourceries. These investments served to strengthen communities' capacity for action, reduce waste (or residual materials) generated on their territories (environmental objective), and create sustainable employment (socio-economic objective).

The program is set up so that only non-profit organizations (NPOs) and cooperatives have access to the funds, and the jobs created under its aegis must be permanent positions.[10] These criteria suggest that in the eyes of civil authorities, in order to be legitimate, environmental objectives must be coupled with socio-economic objectives and must be backed by organizations typical of the social economy. More cynically, this may also suggest that civil authorities consider it legitimate to attribute the less profitable segments of this sector of activity to social economy initiatives.

CONTRIBUTION OF THE SOCIAL ECONOMY TO THE SUSTAINABLE DEVELOPMENT MOVEMENT

Social economy networks have supported the ecological movement on various occasions. This has been the case with the Chantier de l'économie sociale du Québec, which has backed ecological groups' applications for financial support (CES, 2001). As well, various social economy enterprises have added missions resembling those of pressure groups to their mandates.

A study into the social utility of Québec's leisure associations conducted by the Alliance de recherche universités-communautés en économie sociale (ARUC-ÉS)[11] showed that these associations tended to contribute to the general movement towards sustainable development, notwithstanding the fact that this was not explicit in their mission. For example, we may look at the Fédération québécoise du canot et du kayak (FQCK, Québec Canoe and Kayak Federation) which, through its mandate to develop and promote canoeing and kayaking activities, also contributes to the preservation of Québec's rivers and lakes, as well as to the protection of the environment by integrating sustainable development principles into its code of conduct (Allard & Turcotte, 2009). Other organizations, such as 4-H Clubs, contribute to environmental protection through the organization of "environmentally friendly educational leisure activities" by promoting "clean-up chores." Others still integrate "green" values and behaviours into their activities and sensitize their clientele to various issues, such as pollution, recycling, and respect for the natural habitat (Lessard, Shields, & Allard, 2009).

THE INNOVATIVE FORCE OF THE SOCIAL ECONOMY AND SUSTAINABLE DEVELOPMENT

This movement is an innovative force. Numerous social economy initiatives and emerging practices illustrate, with much imagination, how economic activity may be rethought in the light of sustainable development. They aim to show that alternatives are possible, either through the creation of a new sector, agents of change in existing sectors or, simply, the adoption of responsible business practices by existing enterprises.

Resourceries (Loursbury, 2003), organic food distribution (Jones, 2000), fair trade, community-supported agriculture, and the slow food movement are all examples of the creation of new markets and sectors of activity. From a strategic standpoint, we may say that social economy enterprises innovate by creating new market shares, and we may expect that this will generate innovation and reform in other segments of industry. In an ecosystemic analysis, the innovativeness of these enterprises creates new ecological niches that transform the industrial field and render it more efficient by avoiding externalities, such as pollution, and by generating social benefits, such as job creation. From the perspective of social critique, these organizations demonstrate viable alternatives to models that they consider to be non-functional from social and environmental standpoints. For example, fair trade may be practised as a commercial venture, but through alternative networks and with the goal of supporting marginalized producers. This calls all other modes of commerce into question, since the implication is that they are "unfair." In doing so, these social economy enterprises, as service providers, can indirectly become industry change agents.

Other social economy organizations, by their positioning at the boundary of the economic and social spheres, have been entrusted with the mandate of leading the innovation process. Consider the case of the Sorel-Tracy-Contrecoeur region in Québec, once known for the dynamism of its metallurgical sector, but which, by consequence, housed industries that were counted among Québec's major polluters. Following the decline of the metallurgical sector, the region's political decision-makers sought out new directions and, enticed by subsidy programs, hoped to steer the region towards sustainable development through a policy of industrial ecology. In the end, it was social economy organizations that assumed the leadership of the movement to "go green" (Pouliot, 2006) and to implement industrial ecology structures and markets. "Industrial ecology aims to optimize systems of production and consumption through the reduced flow of materials and energies, reduced waste, and the valorization of residual materials by turning the residues of given production processes into raw materials for others" (Cournoyer, 2006, p. 7).

In order to achieve this last objective, markets must be created for these residues and exchange networks among industries must be established. If the neoclassical economic perspective tells us that the implementation of these markets is self-evident and should come off fairly easily, the institutionalist perspective, however, has a good deal more to tell us about the considerable challenges that this implementation poses. Some of these challenges result from the limits on actors' rationality, which quickly become evident since a priori it is far from evident who can use these residues, and to what ends. Efforts at innovation must, therefore, be expended to identify these variables, which implies a measure of risk and incertitude.

Moreover, the production system optimization objective aims at obtaining a collective good and is, therefore, subject to the "logic of collective action" (Olsen, 1967): that is, to the paradox that, within a perspective of rational and individual calculation, even if all the involved actors agree on the objective, there is a strong possibility that that no action will be taken in the absence of an organized effort. As things stand today, it is the mandate of some collective enterprises to assume the costs of organizing efforts to attain collective objectives. In the case of the implementation of industrial ecology in the Sorel-Tracy-Contrecoeur corridor, it is collective enterprises – including research groups, technology transfer centres, training centres, and a Community Future Development Corporation (CFDC) – that have taken on this role in leading the industrial ecology project, creating connections between various enterprises, and setting up technology innovation projects (Cournoyer, 2006).

The goods and services offered by many social economy enterprises are notable for their distinct commitment to one or another dimension of sustainable development. One example of the demonstrated leadership of a social economy enterprise in sustainable development, particularly its environmental dimension, is to be found in the tourist industry. Indeed, Hostelling International, which counts 4,200 youth hostels across 60 countries and has over 3 million members, has, since 1994, adopted an environmental charter to which all its hostels must adhere (de Bellefeuille, 2004). This charter comprises energy conservation, recycling, pollution and consumption reduction, and the promotion of public transport, as well as ecological education and respect for nature. The charter also includes recommendations for the use of nontoxic cleaning and gardening materials.

In the distribution domain, Mountain Equipment Co-op (MEC), a Canadian social economy enterprise, which has 2 million members and 1,200 employees, has adopted a policy of social responsibility that touches on questions of working conditions and the environment. This policy leads the company to monitor working conditions throughout its supply chain and to request that its suppliers be accredited by the Fair Labor Association (Allaire, 2006), which conducts independent verifications of factories. MEC has implemented various programs with a view to the environment, including a "green building" program; a program that guarantees 100 per cent organically grown cotton in MEC-brand clothing; an equipment rental and exchange program (to reduce consumption); a waste reduction program (including, for example, encouraging customers not to use plastic bags), and on-site recycling; and an environmental fund that turns over 0.5 per cent of sales receipts to environmental groups (Allaire, 2006).

Among numerous other examples in Québec, we may also point to the Technopôle Angus Urban Business Park and the Granby Zoo. Within the social dimension, the approaches of these social economy organizations may be considered unusual from the standpoint of private enterprise but, conversely, may be said to be typical of those in the social economy. The Technopôle Angus Urban Business Park was created in the wake of a study of social needs, rather than a market study (Yaccarini, 2006). The Granby Zoo opened in 1953 as a not-for-profit organization with the notable objective of contributing to the economic and cultural development of the region. Following a wave of criticism and disinterest towards traditional zoos during the 1970s, the Granby Zoo widened its social mission during the 1980s, focusing on global species conservation (Hodge, 2006), and progressively committed to a renewal of its methods and a rethinking of its relationship with animals. More recently, the zoo attempted to establish an explicit link between species conservation and environment protection by proceeding with an "environmental modernization" (Drolet, 2006), which consists in finding diverse ways to move towards greater eco-efficiency. Both the Granby Zoo and Technopôle Angus have erected structures that stand as models of "green" building.

These examples, by virtue of their legal status and because of their aims, fit the definition of a social economy organization well. They are illustrative examples of the innovative, common potential of the social economy and sustainable development. It should be noted, however, that such examples of commitment to sustainable development can also be cited from among private enterprises. Our goal was to present examples of organizations that stand out because of their commitment to social and environmental responsibility, but such commitment is not a matter of fact for all social economy enterprises, nor is it their exclusive purview. Nevertheless, we advance the hypothesis that the commitment of a social economy enterprise stands a better chance of perduring because it is institutionalized in a system of governance that, de facto, includes social and economic objectives and is controlled by at least one of the organization's stakeholders, while the logic of profit that is inherent to capitalist enterprise is focused solely on a microeconomic objective. By adopting socially responsible policies and practices, social economy organizations participate according to their means and on a voluntary basis in a movement of social and ecological modernization of enterprises and of the economy as a whole, establishing them firmly on a path towards sustainable development.

Conclusion

The social economy can play a leading role by participating in the exercise of rethinking economic and social development according to ecological imperatives, and also by bringing to the fore the social impacts of the ecological crisis and the best means by which to remedy the situation. Despite the convergences, it is clear that the social economy does not necessarily translate into sustainable development practices, or vice versa. Indeed, the acknowledgement of social dimensions does not make sustainable development inevitable. By the same token, all social economy enterprises do not necessarily behave in ways that are favourable to the environment.

In short, the social economy is perhaps the shortest path towards sustainable development (CÉS, p. 17), but this notion should not obscure the fact that there is a path to be trod. The social economy is fertile ground for new practices aimed squarely at social and ecological concerns, provided its actors take the full measure of the role that they can play towards sustainable development. In its social movement dimension, the social economy could constitute distinctively promising alliances driven by alternative social visions. In this regard, the social economy can contribute much to reflections on sustainable development through its experience with democratic governance and the focus on the public interest evident in some of its organizations.

NOTES

1   This study is the continuation and expansion of a working paper issued

from the work of the CAP Développement durable de l'ARUC en Économie sociale. Gendron, C., et al. (2004). Développement durable et économie sociale: Convergences et articulations. *Cahier de l'ARUC*, collection Recherche, no. 17-2004.

2 The term "social movement" can be problematic. It cannot be reduced solely to the actors on the ground, or to their discourses. As researchers, we must instead demonstrate the ways in which observable collective actions, emerging from a social structure (social issues) and expressed in various practices (actors), are consonant with "social movement." The questions are many: Does this movement aim to change capitalist modes of production? Does it aim to reform capitalism? What position does it accord to the environment (sustainable development)?

3 The idea of the social economy as having a dual dimension (responding to needs and channelling social aspirations) was formulated by Lévesque (2002).

4 Dependency theories analyse geopolitics within the framework of a "world system," in which the "core" exploits the "periphery" by, among other means, maintaining inequitable trade relations, as delineated in the concept of "unequal exchange."

5 The Centre québécois de développement durable du Saguenay-Lac Saint-Jean (CQDD), for example, quotes these guiding principles of sustainable development. See www.cqdd.qc.ca.

6 One of the principles of sustainable development, once known as ecodevelopment, is to address the fundamental needs of individuals and communities, with a view to equity, according to an intergenerational temporality (Gagnon, 1994).

7 "The Brundtland Commission Report has made a great contribution by emphasizing the importance of SD and in effect forcing it to the top of the agenda of the United Nations and the multilateral development banks. To achieve this remarkable consensus, the Commission had to be less than rigorous in avoiding self contradiction" (Daly, 1990, p. 1).

8 A connection with the questioning of overconsumption and the "simple living" movement.

9 CQCM, *Développement durable*, http://www.coopquebec.coop/fr/accueil. aspx, 14 December 2009.

10 By fall 2002, "resourceries" had transformed 45,000 tonnes of waste (residual materials) into resources, while creating, or maintaining, 526 employment positions (Séguin, 2003).

11 Community-University Research Alliance on the Social Economy.

REFERENCES

Allaire, M.-È. (2006). La coordination pour la responsabilité sociale et environnementale. In *Conférence publique: Changement et continuité vers le développement durable: Les enjeux stratégiques et de gestion dans les entreprises collectives*. Montréal: Université du Québec à Montréal, 21 April.

Allard, M.-C. & Turcotte, M.-F. (2009). *Utilité sociale du milieu associatif au Québec: Le cas de la Fédération québécoise du canot et du kayak*. Montréal: ARUC en économie sociale, no. C-07-2009.

Bélanger, P.R., & Lévesque, B. (1991). La théorie de la régulation, du rapport salarial au rapport de consommation: Un point de vue sociologique. *Cahiers de recherche sociologique* (17), 17–51.

B.-Turcotte, M.-F. (2005). Conclusion. In M.-F. B.-Turcotte & A. Salmon (Eds), *Responsabilité sociale et environnementale de l'entreprise*. Québec: Presses de l'Université du Québec.

Brundtland, H. (1987). *Notre avenir à tous*. Genève: Rapport de la Commission Mondiale sur l'environnement et le développement de l'ONU.

Chantier de l'économie sociale. (2001). *Définition de l'économie sociale*. Accessed 16 July 2011. http://www.chantier.qc.ca

Chantier de l'économie sociale. (2005). *L'économie sociale: Au cœur du développement durable*. Accessed 18 June 2011. http://www.chantier.qc.ca/userImgs/documents/CLevesque/memoirecoeurdevdurable2005.pdf

Commission mondiale sur l'environnement et le développement (Rapport Brundtland). (1988). *Notre avenir à tous*. Montréal: Éditions du Fleuve.

Cournoyer, J. (2006). *La jonction du volet technique et du volet social dans la mise en oeuvre de l'écologie industrielle: Le cas du corridor Sorel-Tracy-Contrecoeur*. Mémoire de maîtrise. Montréal: Université du Québec à Montréal.

Daly, H.-G. (1990). Sustainable growth: An impossibility theorem. *Development, 3*(4).

De Bellefeuille, A. (2004). Les auberges de Jeunesse Hostelling International: Un réseau conscient de son environnement. In *Conférence publique*. Montréal: Chaire de responsabilité sociale et de développement durable de l'UQAM, 13 May.

Drolet, S. (2006). Dynamique d'une modernisation environnementale. In *Conférence publique: Changement et continuité vers le développement durable: les enjeux stratégiques et de gestion dans les entreprises collectives*. Montréal: Université de Québec à Montréal, 21 April.

Gagnon, C. (1994). *La recomposition des territoires. Développement local viable: Récits et pratiques d'acteurs sociaux en région périphérique*. Paris: Harmattan.

Gagnon, C. (1995). Développement local viable: Approches, stratégies et défis pour les communautés. *Coopératives et Développement*, 26(2), 61–82.

Gendron, C. (2001a). Émergence de nouveaux mouvements sociaux économiques. *Revue Pour* (172), 175–81.

Gendron, C. (2001b). *Éthique et développement: Le discours des dirigeants sur l'environnement*. Doctoral thesis, Department of Sociology. Montréal: Université du Québec à Montréal.

Gendron, C., & Gagnon, C. (2004). *Développement durable et économie sociale: Convergences et articulations*. Cahier de l'ARUC, Research collection, No. 17–2004.

Gendron, C., & Revérêt, J.-P. (2000). Le développement durable. *Coll. Économies et sociétés*, Série F (37), 111–24.

Gendron, C., & Turcotte, M.-F. (2006). Les nouveaux mouvements sociaux économiques au cœur d'une nouvelle gouvernance. *Organisations et territoires*, 16(1), 23–32.

Hoffman, A. (1999). Institutional evolution and change: Environmentalism and the U.S. chemical industry. *Academy of Management Journal*, 42(4), 351–71. http://dx.doi.org/10.2307/257008

Hodge, A. (2006). Evolving corporate social responsibility in zoos. *Oeconomia Humana*, 4(12), 37–9.

Jones, D.R. (2000). Leadership strategies for sustainable development: A case study of Suma Wholefoods. *Business Strategy and the Environment*, 9(6), 378–89. http://dx.doi.org/10.1002/1099-0836(200011/12)9:6<378::AID-BSE260>3.0.CO;2-F

Laville, J.-L. (2001). Les promesses de l'économie solidaire: Un projet d'intégration sociale et culturelle. *Le Monde Diplomatique: Supplément économie solidaire (octobre)*, 1–2.

Lessard, M., Shields, G., & Allard, M.-C. (2009). *L'utilité sociale du milieu associatif du loisir du Conseil québécois du loisir: Une réalité méconnue, mais un impact majeur*. Research report under the direction of J.-M. Lafortune and S. Vaillancourt.

Lévesque, B., & Mendell M. (1999). L'économie sociale au Québec: Éléments théoriques et empiriques pour le débat et la recherche. *Lien social et politique* (41), 105–18.

Lévesque, B. (2002). *Pour repenser l'économie en vue d'un développement durable, un aperçu de la nouvelle sociologie économique*. Montréal: UQAM, cahier de l'ARUC-ÉS, Collection Intervention, No. I-04-2002.

Lounsbury, M., Ventresca, M., & Hirsch, P.M. (2003). Social movements, field frames and industry emergence: A cultural-political perspective on US recycling. *Socio-economic Review*, 1(1), 71–104. http://dx.doi.org/10.1093/soceco/1.1.71

Maguire, S., & Hardy, C. (2006). The emergence of new global institutions: A discursive perspective. *Organization Studies*, 27(1), 7–29. http://dx.doi.org/10.1177/0170840606061807

Melluci, A. (1983). Mouvements sociaux, mouvements post-politiques. *Revue internationale d'action communautaire*, 10(50), 13–50.

Olson, M. (1967). *The logic of collective action*. Cambridge, Mass: Harvard University Press.

Polanyi, K. (1983). *La grande transformation*. Paris: Gallimard.

Pouliot, S. (2006). Tendre vers l'écologie industrielle à Sorel-Tracy, In *Conférence publique: Changement et continuité vers le développement durable: les enjeux stratégiques et de gestion dans les entreprises collectives*. Montréal: Université de Québec à Montréal, 21 April.

Rostow, W.W. (1970). *Les étapes de la croissance économique*. Paris: Éditions du Seuil.

Sachs, I. (1997). *L'écodéveloppement, Stratégie pour le XXIe siècle*. Paris: Éditions la Découverte et Syros.

Séguin, M. (Ed.). (2003). L'économie sociale en environnement: Premier bilan international des ressources: Actes de colloque, 5 September 2002. Montréal: UQAM, *Cahiers de l'ARUC-ÉS*, No. T-04-2003.

Touraine, A. (1980). *La prophétie anti-nucléaire*. Paris: Éd. Du Seuil.

Vaillancourt, J. (1998). *Évolution conceptuelle et historique du développement durable*. Research report. Québec: Regroupement national des Conseils régionaux de l'environnement du Québec (RNCREQ).

Yaccarini, C. (2006). Le développement durable et la rhétorique à l'épreuve des faits. In *Conférence publique. Changement et continuité vers le développement durable: Les enjeux stratégiques et de gestion dans les entreprises collectives*. Montréal: Université de Québec à Montréal, 21 April.

8 The Social Economy: A Springboard for Local Development Projects?

JUAN-LUIS KLEIN AND PIERRE-ANDRÉ TREMBLAY

Introduction

The aim of this chapter is to examine the contribution of the social economy to local development. Globalization has transformed territorial dynamics and hierarchies, which provide the context for our analysis. Through globalization, territories develop new configurations. In conjunction with new forms of social inequality in national and local territories, global networks present new challenges for actors at the local-community level. The devitalization of communities may result in a loss of benefits and assets for businesses, services, and the population. This may result in job losses and negative growth at the local level, inasmuch as economic wealth and dynamism may start to become concentrated in so-called winning regions (Benko & Lipietz, 1992). Ultimately, these developments have an effect on social cohesion and relations of solidarity, which may disintegrate in many localities.

The above scenario presents new opportunities for the social economy, however, either by creating bridges between the rich and poor living together in winning regions, or by taking actions to counter the drift towards exclusion that may take hold in "losing regions" (Côté, Klein, & Proulx, 1995). In both cases, public authorities having generally supported the "new economy," and competitiveness and principal private investors having sought sectors that guarantee the best return on their investment, local social forces must grapple with the problems of distressed communities, which often react by demanding the right to develop their local milieus (Tremblay, Tremblay, & Tremblay, 2006). Our analysis deals with the capacity of the social economy to provide a foundation for these actors in their efforts to halt the drift towards the collapse of their communities, and perhaps even initiate specific local-development projects.

We will deal with the problem in four sections. First, we will briefly situate local development within the context of socio-territorial restructuring and the establishment of a glocalized society.[1] Then, based on a survey of the literature dealing with both theoretical and empirical analysis, and carried out in Québec and elsewhere, we will briefly examine the contribution of the social economy to the development of local communities and the inherent dangers of relying exclusively on its contribution. Following that, we will take three examples of Québec local initiatives – selected from three different milieus – that were incubated in social economy organizations and that mobilized social economy resources. To conclude, we will identify the winning conditions that allow the social economy to serve as a platform for local development and, consequently, as a component in sustainable and solidarity-based development.

The Local Development Framework: Conceptual and Theoretical Clarifications

As the aim of this chapter is to examine the contribution of the social economy to local development, we need first to conceptually clarify these two terms. Since other chapters have provided definitions and theoretical clarifications of the social economy, we will place less emphasis on the social economy as an identifiable and complex sphere of the global economy, and more on the enterprises and organizations that are associated with it and act locally. All of the activities of collective enterprises and community organizations producing goods or services, whether or not they give rise to monetary exchange, may be considered part of the social economy.[2] The second concept – local development – requires more conceptual analysis, however.

Local development is not an approach, and even less a doctrine (Joyal, 2002). It is, rather, an area of community development in which several approaches and perspectives may coexist while generating strategies that do not necessarily converge (Klein, 2006a). What these strategies have in common, however, is that they operate at a local level, be it a rural community or an urban area, although they may have different views on the concept of development and of what in fact constitutes the "local" level, as well on procedure and methods.[3]

As concerns their views on development, while some strategies associate development with personal enrichment and aim only to generate private investment, others pursue collective well-being and create or strengthen local systems of actors or local networks to stimulate local communities. Our analysis is conceptually closer to the latter view, inasmuch as these strategies foster democracy at the local scale and create a more sustainable social dynamic, where local-initiative promoters may become genuine social entrepreneurs.[4]

These strategies also more closely convey what we mean by "local." In our view, the term local does not have a strictly spatial connotation, nor does it refer to a phenomenon that has been localized. It refers, rather, to a level at which socio-economic systems are structured – the grassroots level, closest to the ordinary citizen – where identities and territorial belonging take on meaning and establish systems in which geographical proximity influences the resolution of social contradictions and informs social relationships. At this level, the meanings conveyed by the relationships, actions, and interactions (their "valence") overlap and merge – which does not mean, however, that they necessarily form a harmonious whole. Thus, in our view, local development does not mean enriching certain actors in a particular place, but, rather, refers to strategies implemented by local actors, who mobilize resources to strengthen local communities as social settings, as opposed to weakening or destroying them (Arocena, 2001; Klein, 2006a).

As noted in the introduction, the social economy contributes to local development, especially in those areas affected by major economic problems (Fontan, Klein, & Lévesque, 2003; Moulaert & Nussbaumer, 2005). These problems can be caused by several factors that often work in combination (production-related, social, political), can be either endogenous and exogenous in origin, and resist private and public investment. The factors operate in a complex context in which different stakeholders intervene at different territorial levels (local, regional, national, international). The context is that of a "glocalized world space."[5] This is the result of interaction among (i) world forces operating at a level in which there is a globalization of financial, production, technological, and informational networks; and (ii) local nodes in which networks of local actors of "Marshallian" inspiration become the territorial attachments of the global networks (Amin & Thrift, 1992).

The globalized world space is, of course, what Viard (1994) characterized as the "archipelago society," or that Veltz (1996) referred to as an "archipelago economy," in which spheres of wealth organized into networks exist alongside poor people, but without supporting them, and in which flexible and mobile capital seeking high levels of profitability dominates. The glocalized world space, however, also refers to a world in which, paradoxically, the specific characteristics of places and territories may constitute an advantage that certain communities will seek to protect through various forms of labellization (Pecqueur, 2006). The social construction of these specific characteristics is one of the foundations of the collective strategies driving local development. Many communities try to use these specific characteristics as a springboard to link up with global networks. To this end, they set up (a) enterprise clusters – that is, networks of enterprises and intermediate organizations within a specific sector of production; (b) local production systems, which involve close collaboration between networks of enterprises and networks of social and political actors; or (c) systems of innovation – that is, three-way relationships between research institutions, enterprises, and public authorities.

The structuring of the glocalized world space is taking place against a background of (i) crisis in the state-centred, territorial form of governance typifying the Westphalian nation-state,[6] and (ii) the questioning of the public mechanisms and programs – inspired by Keynesian policy – that were intended to directly support developing areas in difficulty. Thus, whereas government authorities dealt with territorial development objectives exposed to market forces and reacted to market indicators concerning return on private investments, local communities – neglected by both private and public investments – became "orphans" (Fontan, Klein, & Lévesque, 2003): that is, increasingly cut off from the networks distributing wealth. The challenge local communities and other actors assisting in their development therefore face consists in linking them up with global networks (Castells, 2004; Fontan, Klein, & Tremblay, 2005), which means that they must first unite and engage in joint action (Drewe, Klein, & Hulsbergen, 2009).

The Role of the Social Economy: Positive Impacts and Potential Dangers

With the exception of certain organizations whose purpose is explicitly territorial,[7] local development is never the primary or sole objective of social economy enterprises and organizations. Since social economy enterprises and organizations emerge from communities – that is, they carry out the wishes of the members and the populations

they serve – they have a certain legitimacy as actors in local development, since they are part of this milieu (Klein et al., 2005). In situations
where local communities in difficulty must select the most appropriate strategies for reorienting glocalization, the social economy may
develop an interest or become directly involved in local development.
In such situations, local communities sometimes insert themselves
completely (in the form of systemic nexuses) into global networks;
however, there may also be situations where they are delinked from
these networks and thus cannot benefit from them (Demoustier, 2004;
Favreau, 2004; Van Kemenade, 2000). These, then, are the kinds of situations that provide the basis for our analysis of the social economy's
role in providing assistance for or even serving as a component of
local development.

To begin, we need to propose general guidelines concerning the local
impacts of the social economy. To this end, we have conducted a survey of the literature. From this survey, it emerges that the impact of the
social economy on community-based development may be considered
major to the extent that the latter strengthens local markets, builds local
skills, establishes participatory bodies, and fosters experimentation in
new ways of responding to social problems, especially in the area of
services. However, the literature might also lead us to conclude that the
role of the social economy is negative when introduced into a political
context that polarizes society or when it causes widespread poverty.
Viewed in this way, the social economy would constitute a trap. Let us
examine these two dimensions in detail.

Positive Impacts: Economic and Social Reinforcement

Our objective in identifying the contribution of the social economy to
community-based development is not to assess its importance but to
present the trends that the consulted works themselves identify and
acknowledge. Some contributions are noted more often than others,
however, especially when empirical works of the evaluative type are
involved. For example, in the works consulted, nearly all of the authors
mentioned job creation and the integration of marginalized individuals into the labour market (Tremblay et al., 2002; Van Kemenade, 2000;
Delvetere, 1998; OCDE, 2003; Lipietz, 2001; Lukkarinen, 2005). These
were particularly pressing economic issues in the 1980s and 1990s,
which saw the revival of the social economy. The jobs created through
such initiatives allowed disadvantaged groups to become active on the

labour market (women, youth, and immigrants) (Amin, 2002, pp. 1 and 18; Comeau, 2003, p. 125). In addition, the jobs were created in sectors neglected by the market economy and governmental authorities. By creating jobs, social economy enterprises and organizations compensated for the low local disposable incomes in weak local markets. They also had much broader impacts, however, including the acquisition of skills and expertise and changes in the way communities perceived their identity.

It is accepted that a community's sense of belonging – its identity – can play an important role in the emergence of development initiatives. Now, the rediscovery of a community's identity is associated with the creation of a "territorial consciousness" (Klein, 2006a), which is accentuated by the social economy due to the characteristics of its actors and activities. Thus, the stronger community members' sense of belonging, the stronger their desire for involvement in community life. The social economy mobilizes local actors by calling up memories and symbolic experiences, thereby allowing actors to discover their collective identities and fostering citizen involvement in development.

A major contribution of the social economy at the local level involves building the local community itself. Social economy initiatives have a positive impact on forging social bonds and improving people's living environment and cultural development. This is what Lipietz (2001, p. 74) calls the "halo" effect in a community. The halo in question increases socialization and a sense of belonging, and thus has a formative influence on the local community (Seyfang, 2004, p. 67). If even limited projects are economically successful, they can help reverse actors' negative perceptions of the milieus to which they belong, transforming them into positive identities that will encourage them to get involved in other economic projects. This is what certain authors refer to as building social capacity,[8] which includes, on the one hand, networking among social economy actors, and, on the other hand, the networking activities of the latter with other community actors – namely, actors in the private and public spheres of the economy. In this way, there emerge what we call "development coalitions": that is, solidarity-based options, which contrast with "growth coalitions" (Stone, 2005) that the elites of major metropolises form to ensure their input into global networks. The former involve coalitions of *all* actors, thereby favouring the introduction of democratic forms of governance (Hula, 1997, p. 460).

From this analysis, we can also see the importance of the social economy's role in establishing organizations that further democracy and citizen involvement. The social economy strengthens democracy and encourages social debate by creating forums for discussion on common problems. It thus fosters personal involvement, including citizen involvement in collective projects, and forges local identity (Bardos-Féltoronyi, 2004, p. 50; Markey, 2005, p. 369). This aspect is reinforced by the fact that once they have concluded agreements with governmental bodies, social economy organizations such as the Community Economic Development Corporations (CDEC) in Montréal[9] become managers of public funds, thereby giving them a role in mediating and liaising between governmental and civil society organizations (Opula, 2007). These intermediary structures thus adopt strategic positions that help them to emerge as partners in local governance (Stone, 2005, p. 329; Hula, 1997, p. 480).

The social economy may therefore generate a culture of self-development and of taking responsibility for oneself (Bardos-Féltoronyi, 2004, p. 50; Markey, 2005, p. 369). Most of the authors surveyed claim that this type of citizen involvement has a beneficial effect on the social economy itself, since it promotes its development. Learning how to participate is intrinsic to social economy organizations, and is expressed in all areas of community activity; the social economy is a driving force of participation, but in turn also benefits from it. Social economy organizations are incubators for initiatives that become collective (Arocena, 2001; Klein, 2006). Since it provides a forum for debate and induces citizens to look for solutions to development problems, the social economy may be viewed as a medium for the cultivation of innovative projects resulting in social change (Klein & Harrisson, 2007). This also requires the mobilization of local and external resources and the establishment of alternative networks, however.

Traps: Between State Manipulation and the Economy of Poverty

While the works consulted point out the social economy's potential contribution to local development, they also show certain reservations regarding the social economy. These have less to do with the social economy itself than with its environment, which, they contend, influences the way the social economy is used – namely, working against the best interests of local communities rather than supporting them (De Mattos, 1999; Amin, 2005). Essentially, these authors are issuing a series of warnings, the most common being that, by itself, the social economy is unable to deal with the structural conditions faced by marginalized

– especially severely marginalized – communities. While the social economy may help to revitalize the local economy or offset a lack of local private entrepreneurs, the authors claim that, by itself, it is unable to reverse the general trends affecting territories in a state of devitalization. Social economy enterprises and organizations create jobs and consume locally. With a few exceptions, however, they are unable to compete with private or government institutions when it comes to investment or salaries.[10] Their expenditures and salaries do not generate sufficient economic dynamism at the local level to have an effect on globalization, even if they are crucial to the survival of some communities. Thus, the argument goes, the social economy could be considered an ancillary, secondary, or dominated form of economic activity.

There is also a danger that the social economy could become party to the creation of an extremely unequal society. The problem resides in the fact that, in certain cases, expanding the social economy in devitalized local communities constitutes a reaction to governmental re-engineering or even a re-engineering-oriented strategy. Governments sometimes withdraw from the field of local development when they eliminate action plans; alternatively, they may modify these plans by adapting program requirements to those of the competitive capabilities of capitalist enterprises (Lévesque, 2004). This has the effect of excluding developers that cannot rely on either the finance capital or social capital needed to carry out their development projects. Thus, the strengthening of social economy-based local development could turn out to be a burden for the local community (Amin, 2005).

In addition to income and local-market impacts, it could also have an effect on social cohesion. For example, this could arise when social economy enterprises and organizations, which have lower salaries and less expensive services, must deal with social groups that defend local communities' acquired benefits and rights, especially salaries and services provides by public institutions. In such cases, growth in the social economy could, while partially offsetting the effects of abandonment by the state, end up actually encouraging this abandonment – but without necessarily attracting private capital instead. This would result in lower incomes, a lower quality of life for citizens, and the institutionalization of an unsound social economy, which would limit these communities to a fragile economy. In this scenario, growth in the social economy would correspond to a modified neo-liberal model, thereby making it an accomplice of this model and its pernicious effects, which strengthen social dualism and exclusion (Vaillancourt & Favreau, 2000, p. 5).

Harmonizing the Economy's Various Spheres

Based on the works consulted, it is clear that the social economy can strengthen and stimulate local civil society by building networks and mobilizing resources. It is just as clear, however, that it must go beyond local networks and resources. This is certainly true of a variety of concrete situations discussed in these works, in which social economy enterprises and organizations do not operate in a vacuum but collaborate amongst themselves – and sometimes with public, para-public, and private actors. In this way, they establish horizontal and vertical networks whose main objectives are dialogue, information sharing, and the implementation of development projects in concert with various actors.

Thus, it is because it is capable of setting up a nexus connected to global networks that the social economy can participate in a form of local development that is solidarity oriented but not limited to a "minor development" role with a purely palliative function. This will be demonstrated in the cases of Technopôle Angus (in Montréal), Saint-Camille (in the Eastern Townships), and Sacré-Cœur (in the Upper North Shore region). A brief description of these cases will allow us to observe how the social economy participates in local initiatives that mobilize endogenous and exogenous resources. These resources increase the density of the local community by creating networks that are centrally located and linked to global networks.

Local Initiatives

Technopôle Angus: The Economic Impact of a Community-Based Actor[11]

The first case is that of Technopôle Angus, a project stemming from a community-based initiative with its roots in the Rosemont district, one of Montréal's oldest industrial districts. Devised by the Rosemont-Petite-Patrie CDEC, this project reveals the mobilization capabilities of local social forces with roots in the social economy (in this instance, a CDEC) confronted with the closing of a large firm that had shaped a district and its development. It also illustrates the commitment of the community and its associations to economic development.

In 1992, Canadian Pacific, one of the most important Canadian holding companies, closed the Montréal division of its industrial manufacturing activities, which had been carried out at Ateliers Angus (better known as the Angus Shops). This facility played a major role in Montréal's industrial history. An important industrial complex for manufacturing and repairing railroad equipment, railway cars, and engines, it employed between 5,000 and 12,000 workers, depending on the period. However, beginning in the 1970s, there was a drop in production and employment. When the facility closed completely in 1992, there were only about a thousand employees and a tiny proportion of the facilities that the complex had occupied in better times. A 500,000-square-metre plot of land located in the heart of Montréal was left derelict and needed to be re-developed. Two contenders of unequal size – Canadian Pacific, owner of the land; and the Rosemont-Petite-Patrie Community Economic Development Corporation (CDEC), representing the local community – fought over the type of re-development required. On the one hand, Canadian Pacific wanted to develop a vast residential project consisting of 1,200 housing units. On the other hand, CDEC put forward an economic recovery project that focused on developing a new industrial employment pool. CDEC formed the Angus Committee, which in 1995 would become the Société de développement Angus (SDA). This organization developed an industrial conversion project, whose goal was to create employment and revitalize the district.

The disagreement between the company that owned the property and the CDEC and SDA set in motion a conflict of epic proportions. In this conflict, the local actor mobilized the entire community of Rosemont to defend the local job-creation project. The battle ended in 1994, when it was decided to divide the land. Half of it was given to residential development; on the other half, SDA became the operator of an industrial-development project inspired by the technopolitan model and the innovative-environments approach. This approach involved setting up an industrial park where high-technology firms and the social economy were supposed to converge in a way that would give new life to the district. The implementation of the project proved difficult, however, and required significant SDA mobilization to obtain the support needed to carry it out. The total cost of the work was estimated to be $250 million.

The first phase consisted of decontaminating the land. The second phase involved converting the only building that was still standing[12] into an industrial mall – the first time this kind of reuse had occurred in Canada.[13] In the third phase, which is still going on, several buildings were erected. The construction went ahead partly as the result of a cost-sharing partnership with FondAction, the venture capital fund of the Confédération des syndicats nationaux, the CSN (Confederation of National Trade Unions, or CNTU).[14]

In February 2000, there were five buildings on the site. These buildings housed about 30 enterprises employing 700 people. The final objective was to create 2,000 jobs. The enterprises already in place included several manufacturers and services, and represented both private enterprise and the social economy. A vast network of public, political, and private participants enabled SDA to mobilize significant financial and organizational resources – primarily endogenous in the beginning, but mainly exogenous later on – to ensure completion of the successive projects that gave Technopôle Angus its structure.

The social economy figured prominently in the implementation period, first during the incubation period at CDEC, later because of the dynamic nature of certain social economy enterprise projects and vocational integration projects, and finally because of the financial partnership with FondAction. However, it gained stature primarily as an approach based on economic development with a social purpose. The Angus case is a good example of several roles noted earlier in this text: significant job creation in a Montréal district that needed it; positive economic diversification; the safeguarding of local commerce; the revival of territorial awareness and pride; the strengthening of the local organizational fabric; and, lastly, the drive and enthusiasm, which had a ripple effect. To implement this project, the local actors mobilized a variety of resources in the private, public, and social spheres of the economy, resulting in a coalition of enterprises and institutions in which the capitalist economy, the public economy, and the social economy coexisted.

Of course, while this was clearly a positive result, other project objectives proved harder to attain. For example, not all of the jobs created were filled by local district residents; starting up certain social economy enterprises proved more difficult than expected; and participation by local actors in managing the Technopôle was weaker than anticipated. Nonetheless, what was then known as "the Angus Project" became a reality. It was pitted against the tide of global market forces, which were incapable of creating an industrial-development experiment in Rosemont even had they tried to adapt to circumstances.

Saint-Camille[15]

The second example of a local-development project that was embedded in the social economy is that of the village of Saint-Camille. Located in the Nicolet River Basin, about 30 kilometres east of Sherbrooke in the "municipalité régionale de comté" (regional county municipality) Des sources, this rural municipality has slightly less than 500 inhabitants. In August 2006, the French newspaper *Le Monde diplomatique* awarded this municipality the title of World Village (Cassen, 2006). This recognition, combined with several others, has turned Saint-Camille into Québec's leading symbol of local development in a rural environment in the 2000s, in the same way that JAL[16] symbolized this type of development in the 1970s. The mobilization of this village goes back to the 1980s, when its citizens, who were becoming aware of its demographic decline and the threat this represented to its very sustainability, decided to form a cooperative. Since then, the cooperative has spawned almost 25 organizations, which implement projects and ensure participatory governance in the village (Lemay & Venne, 2006). The upshot is that Saint-Camille has become one of the most dynamic villages in Québec.

The project implemented by the village mobilized several resources. First, the cooperative acquired several of the main abandoned buildings in the village (including the general store and the church rectory). This in turn facilitated the implementation of projects that would shape local identity and strengthen ties among project participants. The old general store was transformed into a cultural centre that staged artistic activities (music, theatre) and portrayals of the village, which its founders presented through their recollections and historical reference. Named *P'tit Bonheur* in honour of Félix Leclerc, a legendary Québécois poet, songwriter, and political activist, this venue became both the symbol and headquarters for collective action in the village, providing leaders with a springboard for developing and setting up several other projects: the Popote roulante (Meals on Wheels), a mobile catering service for the elderly and school children; *La Corvée,* a housing cooperative for elders; *La clé des champs,* a market gardening cooperative; and a local paper circulated over the Internet. In addition, there were university courses given by the University of Sherbrooke and projects designed to link up the school and village citizens to the Internet. All of these projects created employment and allowed many residents to become involved in developing the village. However, the most important characteristic of the village was the aggressiveness with which its leaders decided to confront a demographic problem. A community meeting held in the 1990s revealed the depth of this problem. The village needed to reverse the population drain, which meant, on the one hand, stopping migration, and, on the other hand, attracting new residents. To this end, they initiated two residential development projects that facilitated the purchase – by non-village families – of small farmhouses with one or two acres of land.

These two projects did not simply involve land transactions, since farmhouses had to be acquired and infrastructure and equipment set up. It was a collective project, which justified using a cooperative formula. New residents were recruited in several places, particularly Sherbrooke and Montréal. Since the objective was to attract young families that were planning to occupy the plot of land they purchased, rather than urban dwellers looking for a second home, these small farmhouses were offered to population groups that were likely to give a boost to the village and embrace the local development project that had been set up. The operation was a success. By February 2007, all the plots had been reserved and the implementation of the two projects began.

Saint-Camille is a success story because it mobilized local resources based on projects that were social economy enterprises, or that had received their impetus from social economy organizations. In addition, its leaders were also able to mobilize exogenous socio-territorial resources, such as regional groups close to the city of Sherbrooke and the University of Sherbrooke. Its success was also due to support obtained from Solidarité rurale du Québec, an organization representing and acting as a pressure group on behalf of rural Québec, and to the use of financial resources from the Pacte rural (Rural Pact), a program that the Government of Québec set up in 2001 following its Politique nationale de la ruralité (National Policy on Rurality).

Saint-Camille demonstrates that the social economy is important for local development. It provides actors with the social capital they need to mobilize a variety of financial and human resources, endogenous as well as exogenous. However, it only succeeds when the actors are able to link the local project with broader networks, which in this case resulted in its winning recognition as a World Village. There can be no doubt that this was the most successful aspect of the Saint-Camille saga, and could be attributed to the quality of the local leadership, which seized the opportunity to organize the initiative and thereby acquired a wealth of invaluable experience. These linkages are a good illustration of building social capacity and "building a local environment." On the other hand, excessive reliance on leaders can make success stories short-lived. We must also take into account that Saint-Camille took advantage of the closeness of the city of Sherbrooke, its population, and its organizations; obviously, not all Québec villages enjoy this advantage. In this respect, the success of Saint-Camille demonstrates (i) that spatial hierarchies change; (ii) that social economy actors in a rural environment must innovate on a socio-territorial level by re-engineering the links between the local, regional and national levels; and (iii) that rural–urban links must be used to their advantage.

Sacré-Cœur[17]

The third example is that of the municipality of Sacré-Cœur-sur-le-Fjord-du-Saguenay, located at the mouth of the Saguenay River, in the Upper North Shore, 15 kilometres northwest of Tadoussac. (Its cultural environment is more closely linked with that of the Bas-Saguenay, however.) The municipality is located far from any urban centre. Like many other remote rural municipalities, the workforce is employed primarily in the logging industry. In the case of Sacré-Cœur, the population relied for its subsistence on a sawmill that had financial difficulties in the 1970s. In the early 1980s, following a series of changes in its name and ownership, the company closed once again, laying off many workers and jeopardizing the survival of the village. In 1983, as a response to the closing, a company called the Société d'exploitation de Sacré-Cœur was created; it mobilized former workers, and its mandate was to create jobs.

The company decided to acquire the sawmill, from that point on called Boisaco. Three different local groups formed a partnership to take possession of the mill: Investra, Cofor, and Unisaco. Investra is a Société de placement en entreprise québécoise (SPEQ, or Québec investment corporation),[18] to which a large part of the local population belonged through purchasing shares, and which enabled them to raise the capital needed to purchase the mill. Cofor and Unisaco are worker cooperatives that brought together, respectively, the mill employees and workers linked more directly to forestry activities.

Slightly less than 20 years later, the Boisaco industrial complex, which includes a sawmill and a planing mill, two dry kilns, and a timber yard with several storage areas, had 747 employees. This is a considerable accomplishment given that the population of the municipality barely surpassed 2,000. While the finances of the complex suffered the same woes as the forestry industry, there were many indications that the cooperative initiative muddled through better than other types of enterprises: The complex had three plants, a fourth would soon be built, and yet another would be bought erected in a neighbouring village, using the same financing methods as those that met with success at Sacré-Cœur.

At the same time, the Société d'exploitation, which in 1998 became the Société de développement de Sacré-Cœur inc., busied itself with diversifying the local economy by developing (i) recreational tourism and (ii) "inhabited forest" projects with multiple, integrated, and environmentally sustainable applications, especially in the area of development. In forming a partnership with the Ministère de l'Environnement et de la Faune, the development corporation attempted to capitalize on the impact of new public investment in the tourism industry (particularly in Parc Saguenay).

The opening of a day-care centre (with 13 jobs) is surely a sign of vitality, since it shows that efforts to revitalize the local economy have borne fruit for the municipality's demography. Although it did not generate real demographic growth, the new economic dynamism did stabilize the population. Between 1996 and 2006, the municipality's population declined from 2,115 to 2,076 inhabitants (–1.84 per cent). This slight decline may be considered a success, however, because the population declined to a much greater degree in surrounding municipalities.

As in Saint-Camille, demographic issues were fundamental to the community, though their economic foundations were even more visible in Sacré-Cœur. In essence, these foundations were continental in scope and relied on international mechanisms; both of these factors increased the vulnerability of rural areas located far from major centres. Sacré-Cœur's outlying location, which prevented it from relying on a major urban centre, meant that the question of social innovation in the area of development was, in this case, even more critical.

Given the existing and foreseeable difficulties of the logging industry, one might maintain that there is an even greater need for economic diversification here than elsewhere. In the 1970s, a high degree of diversification constituted an objective of Québec's first rural development movements, which advocated an integrated resource strategy (Dionne et al., 1983). By definition, this cannot be accomplished by a single actor or cooperative. It involves input from all social forces and the mobilization of both endogenous and exogenous networks. Thus, local actors put forward a strategy that was diversified both on the sector and entrepreneurial levels, and obtained capital from both the social economy and private enterprise. The Société de développement de Sacré-Cœur provided it with local governance based on principles of solidarity that drew their inspiration from the social economy.

A summary of the points discussed above (see Table 8.1) reveals that the social economy and local development can converge – even if the social economy cannot be reduced to local development, or local development to the social economy. On the one hand, local development as understood here refers to a process, an approach, or a mobilization of actors in a given territory; on the other hand, the social economy, too, as a specific form of production of goods and services, is territorially based. The territorial dimension refers to where populations live, problems arise, mobilization occurs, and solidarities emerge. Thus, social economy organizations are closely linked to territorial revitalization. Even when the social economy alone is unable to reverse general market trends or save all the jobs in a community in decline, it can help revitalize the local community by promoting the joint action and partnerships required to mobilize and pool resources – endogenous as well as exogenous, private as well as public. By virtue of its activities in associations, networks, and partnerships, the social economy has shown that it is capable of coordinating economic activity and establishing a plural economy that goes beyond the local level.

Conclusion: The Challenges Facing an Emancipatory Social Economy

It is clear that the actions and actors associated with the social economy can help revitalize and develop local communities that, due to market dynamics, have been abandoned by private capital and, due to the strategic decisions of governments, do not constitute a priority for public investment. The social economy is concerned with communities abandoned by "dominant" forms of development. This is why it is often viewed as an economy of poverty.

However, since the social economy is a hybrid of the market economy and the public economy, it opens up another sphere: that of civil society (stated differently, one cannot reduce local territory to the administrative delimitations of municipalities or local agencies). In so doing, the social economy incorporates the concept of use-value into the strategic decisions of the actors involved, while introducing it to other actors. From this standpoint, it is social not because it is more ethical or moral than the "other" economy, but because it is more global. It creates networks that are accessible to actors lacking access to business networks or to the share capital that is at the disposal of leading private investors. It redeploys marginalized individuals and develops marginalized localities, whereas liberal economies and markets place an emphasis on regions that are already performing well economically.

Table 8.1. Summary of the Social Economy's Role in The Three Cases Examined

Projects	Social and Geographic Circumstances	Type and Objectives	Social Economy	
			Actors	Role
Technopôle Angus, Montréal	• Former industrial district located close to the centre of the city, affected by the relocation of manufacturing activity in the metropolitan core	• Conversion of an abandoned industrial zone to create local employment and revitalize the district's economy • Establishment of an industrial park based on the concept of local-production systems • Combined different types of enterprises	• SDA • CDEC • FondAction of the CSN • Vocational integration enterprises	• Started with the incubation of the project • Management and development of the site • Mobilization of a broad network of entrepreneurs, public bodies and various institutions • Financial partnership to develop the site • Social integration and employability development for the marginalized
Village of Saint-Camille	• Rural village near Sherbrooke that was affected by the deterioration of agricultural activity and experiencing demographic decline	• Various rural-environment revitalization projects based on an intergenerational perspective • Cultural stimulation and identity reinforcement • Land-development projects from an ecological perspective	• Solidarity cooperative • Housing cooperative • Socio-economic development corporation • Various non-profit organizations and community organizations	• Mobilization of volunteers • Market gardening projects supported by the community • Establishing cultural and educational projects • Links with rural solidarity movements • Local governance
Municipality of Sacré-Cœur	• Forest village located at the mouth of the Saguenay River in outer region far removed from the main urban centres, affected by sawmill closures	• Reactivation of the forest economy • Diversification of the economy through the development of recreational tourism	• Worker cooperatives • Development corporation	• Management and acquisition of a forest-dependent business • Raising local finance capital • Business development • Economic diversification • Local governance

It helps redefine identity – that is, self-representations that serve as a basis for action. By stressing the importance of participation, it seeks to break the vicious circle of dependence that often ensues from the methods employed by the bureaucratic welfare state.

The social economy faces several challenges, however. The first challenge is directly linked to the role of social economy organizations, which apply a universalistic approach in their struggle to meet the vital needs of the poorest citizens. The social economy must create ways to meet the needs of the most needy while preserving their dignity. This means negotiating a new compromise with public authorities, in areas where the latter can play an active but not oppressive role (O'Boyle, 2005).

The second challenge lies in creating a financial framework to support the social economy, one in which its enterprises and organizations would not be limited solely to pursuing profitability, which would compromise their social objectives. Rather, the framework should allow them to keep their autonomy, so that in pursuing these objectives they will not be obliged to become subcontractors or even accomplices of the neo-liberal state (Bardos-Féltoronyi, 2004).

The third challenge has to do with the need to develop a normative, though flexible, institutional framework to attend to conflictual relationships with public and private actors at the local level, and facilitate communication among the various categories of actors. Local governance must be interlinked with national regulation to reduce the negative impact of inter-territorial competition.

At a more global level, if national governance is to be effective and inclusive, it must provide stronger and more stable institutional support and maximize the synergy with other initiatives. This would increase the overall spin-offs from local initiatives (Seyfang, 2004; Moulaert & Ailenei, 2005). In fact, given that there are many types of action models in the social economy, such cohesion is needed if the initiatives are to produce socially effective and lasting results.

Thus, social economy-based initiatives must keep a flexible relationship with institutions, mobilizing them without being completely institutionalized. Here, there is less emphasis on organization than on emergence, less on structuring than on mobilizing. It is true that part of the potential of the social economy resides in giving voice to new social needs arising from social conditions that are themselves new. The social economy cannot realize this potential, however, unless it links up with emerging social practices. The challenge, therefore, is to become more transversal, while the danger lies in turning the social economy into a "sector" like any other. The cases analysed in this chapter reveal a need to mobilize a variety of resources and activate hybridization strategies, combining local and supra-local networks, and endogenous and exogenous actors.

Establishing links among different fields of action is of course the specialty of social movements, whose methods include redefining initiatives and thus opening up new and innovative horizons (Benford & Snow, 2000). This explains why identity factors are so critical in developing social economy initiatives. An appealing aspect of social economy initiatives resides in their territorial embeddedness, which may promote a sense of identity. This clearly differentiates them from classic economic initiatives, which are mobile and fluid since they must obtain the maximum return on investment. To really appreciate the embeddedness of social economy initiatives, however – to appreciate it as socio-territorial capital rather than as something stagnant – requires a huge effort, including contextual analysis and a description of its essential features and proposed solutions. This may seem daunting and, furthermore, can only be achieved through a total rupture with the dominant approaches.

Mutatis mutandis, this is also what is at stake in "local development," which must consider these issues unless it wishes to follow the "regional development" path. There was a time when the latter was a dynamic field, since it went well with Keynesianism, a view of society that was innovative for its time. It facilitated the rise of social demands employing novel approaches, such as access to consumption, and an attitude that was more outward looking and rewarding than that of the more insular concept of "community." With time, it became a method of territorial intervention by the state, a "verticalized" sector cut off from its dynamic sociomatrix, which seldom innovated any more (Stöhr, 2003). If local development wishes to preserve its potential, it will have to maintain its ability to superimpose "interaction valences" (interactive capabilities). These permit transversality (in space) and simultaneity (in time), and thus facilitate innovation. The social economy already performs this role on behalf of local development. Thus, social economy and local development initiatives face the same needs and dangers. While the two approaches are linked, the linkage derives not so much from a relationship of cause and effect as from a confluence of the logic of necessity and the logic of desire, in which each can be fertilized through contact with the other.

NOTES

1   For a discussion on glocalized society, see Swyngedouw (1997).
2   For a discussion on this view of the social economy, see Klein et al. (2004). See also Lévesque, Bourque, and Forges (2001).
3   For a discussion about different definitions and conceptions of the local level, see Klein et al. (2003).
4   This is not the only possibility, since individualist models are very difficult to change and to keep present in the practices and consciousness of the actors (Tremblay, Dubé, and Émond, 2006).
5   The world-space (espace-monde) concept was advanced by Durand, Lévy, and Retaillé (1992), and was taken up and documented by Klein and Lasserre (2006).
6   On the crisis in the nation-state as a unified territorial system for regulating society, see Badie (1995), Urry (2001), and Klein (2006b).
7   In Québec, these include community economic development corporations (CDECs) and community development corporations (CDCs) (Tardif, 2007), these being locally based organizations of community groups.
8   On this point, see Tardif's thesis (2007) on the impact of CDCs on the "institutional capacity" of social actors at the local level.
9   Beginning in the 1980s, especially in Montréal, Québec's social movements changed their attitude towards economic development, one result of which was the creation of CDECs; see Fontan (2001).
10 Noteworthy among the exceptions was Mondragon in Spain. Based on social economy values and approaches, it became an important economic group with a presence in several countries. See Grellier, Larrasquet, Lopez Perez, and Ugarte (2007). The other classic example is, of course, the Mouvement Desjardins, a large financial institution.
11 For a complete examination of the Technopôle Angus, see Fontan, Klein, and Tremblay, 2004 and 2005. For an analysis on the direction taken by this project, see Lévesque, Fontan, and Klein, 1996.
12 This was Locoshop, a building where locomotives and railway cars were assembled. Following the initial agreement, SDA purchased a part of Locoshop from Canadian Pacific in order to transform it into an industrial mall.
13 Public Works Canada awarded the mall the title of first ecological industrial building in the country.
14 Since the 1980s, Québec's unions have been creating pension funds designed to create jobs in Québec and offset the impact of the crisis in Fordism and industrial relocation. The first fund, the Fonds de solidarité, was

created in 1883 by the Fédération des travailleurs du Québec. The second fund was the CSN's Fondaction, which had the specific target of supporting social economy enterprises.

15 For this case, see Cassen (2006). See also Lemay and Venne (2006).

16 Cooperative development located in the Lower St. Lawrence hinterland; the acronym JAL stood for the three municipalities from which it was formed: Saint-Juste, Auclair, and Lejeune. For this case, see Dionne et al. (1983).

17 In presenting this example, we drew inspiration from the case study carried out by Tremblay, Perron, and Germain (2002). We also used an unpublished work written in 2006 by Martin Belzile as part of a Master's seminar in the Department of Geography at the Université du Québec à Montréal.

18 A Société de placement en entreprise québécoise (SPEQ) is a private company that collects funds from individuals (tax deductible). Its activities consist primarily of acquiring and holding the common stock share capital of small and medium-sized companies. The Government of Québec created the program in 1985.

REFERENCES

Amin, A. (2005). Local community on trial. *Economy and Society, 34*(4), 612–33. http://dx.doi.org/10.1080/03085140500277211

Amin, A., Cameron, A., & Hudson, R. (2002). *Placing the social economy*. London: Routledge.

Amin, A., & Thrift, N. (1992). Neo-Marshallian nodes in global networks. *International Journal of Urban and Regional Research, 16*(4), 571–87. http://dx.doi.org/10.1111/j.1468-2427.1992.tb00197.x

Arocena, J. (2001). *El desarrollo local: Un desafío contemporáneo*. Taurus: Universidad Católica, Uruguay.

Badie, B. (1995). *La fin des territoires: Essai sur le désordre international et sur l'utilité sociale du respect*. Paris: Fayard, L'espace politique.

Bardos-Féltoronyi, N. (2004). *Comprendre l'économie sociale et solidaire*. Lyon: Chronique sociale, Brussels.

Beaudry, R., & Saucier, C. (2006). La richesse sociale: Le point de vue d'acteurs de l'économie sociale. *Economie et Solidarites, 36*(1), 27–42.

Benford, R.D., & Snow, D.A. (2000). Framing processes and social movements: An overview and assessment. *Annual Review of Sociology, 26*(1), 611–39. http://dx.doi.org/10.1146/annurev.soc.26.1.611

Benko, G., & Lipietz, A. (1998). From the regulation of space to the space of regulation. *GeoJournal, 44*(4), 275–81. http://dx.doi.org/10.1023/A:1006817514094

Benko, G., & Lipietz, A. (Eds.). (1992). *Les régions qui gagnent, districts et réseaux: Les nouveaux paradigmes de la géographie économique.* Paris: PUF.

Benko, G., & Lipietz, A. (Eds.). (2000). *La richesse des régions.* Paris: Presses universitaires de France.

Bouchard, M. (2004). Un exemple de service collectif innovant: Le logement communautaire au Québec. In D. Demoustier (Ed.), *Économie sociale et développement local* (pp. 103–8). Paris: L'Harmattan.

Bryant, C. & Cofsky, S. (2004). *Politiques publiques en développement économique local.* Ottawa: Economic Development Canada.

Cassen, B. (2006). Un village-monde au Québec: Longue vie à Saint-Camille. *Le monde diplomatique* (August), 11.

Castells, M. (2004). *The network society.* London: Edward Elgar.

Comeau, Y. (2003). *Le communautaire, la nouvelle économie sociale et leurs retombées en région.* L'Islet: Terres fauves.

Côté, S., Klein, J.-L., & Proulx, M.-U. (Eds.). (1995). *Et les régions qui perdent?* Rimouski: GRIDEQ.

DeMattos, C. (1999). Teorías del desarrollo endógeno. *Estudios avançados, 13* (36), 183–207.

Demoustier, D. (2004). *Économie sociale et développement local.* Paris: L'Harmattan.

Develtère, P. (1998). *Économie sociale et développement.* Paris: De Boeck.

Dionne, H. (Ed.). (1983). *Aménagement intégré des ressources et luttes en milieu rural.* Rimouski: GRIDEQ, No. 11.

Drewe, P., Klein, J.-L., & Hulsbergen, E. (Eds.) (2008). *The challenge of social innovation in urban revitalization.* Amsterdam: Techne Press.

Durand, M.-F., Lévy, J., & Retaillé, D. (1992). *Le monde: Espaces et systèmes.* Paris: Dalloz et Presses de la Fondation nationale des sciences politiques.

Favreau, L. (2004). Quand l'économie sociale participe au développement des territoires. *Revue organisations & territoires, 13*(1), 9–19.

Fontan, J.-M. (1991). *Les corporations de développement économique communautaire montréalaises: Du développement économique communautaire au développement local de l'économie.* Doctoral thesis in sociology, Université de Montréal.

Fontan, J.-M., & Klein, J.-L. (2005). Le territoire québécois. In L. Bherer et al. (Eds.), *Jeux d'échelle et transformation de l'État* (pp. 499–514). Sainte-Foy: Les Presses de l'Université Laval.

Fontan, J.-M., Klein, J.-L., & Lévesque, B. (2003). *Reconversion économique et développement territorial: Le rôle de la société civile.* Québec: Presses de l'Université du Québec.

Fontan, J.-M., Klein, J.-L., & Tremblay, D.-G. (2004). Collective action in local development. *Canadian Journal of Urban Research, 13*(2), 317–36.

Fontan, J.-M., Klein, J-L., & Tremblay, D.-G. (2005). *Innovation sociotérritoriale et reconversion économique.* Paris, l'Harmattan.

Grellier, H., Larrasquet, J.-M., Lopez Perez, S., & Ugarte, L. (2008). Thinking about transfer from the Mondragón experience. In P. Drewe, J.-L. Klein, & E. Hulsbergen (Eds.), *The Challenge of Social Innovation in Urban Revitalization* (pp. 235–50). Amsterdam: Techne Press.

Guillaume, R. (2005). *Les systèmes productifs au Québec et dans le Sud-Ouest français.* Paris: L'Harmattan.

Hula, R.C., Jackson, C.Y., & Orr, M. (1997). Urban politics, governing nonprofits and community revitalization. *Urban Affairs Review, 32*(4), 459–89. http://dx.doi.org/10.1177/107808749703200402

Joyal, A. (2002). *Le développement local: Comment stimuler l'économie des régions en difficulté.* Sainte-Foy: Les Presses de l'Université Laval, Éditions de l'IQRC.

Kirk, P., & Shutte, A.-M. (2004). Community leadership development. *Community Development Journal, 39*(3), 234–51. http://dx.doi.org/10.1093/cdj/bsh019

Klein, J.-L. (2006a). De l'initiative locale au développement territorial: Une perspective synthétique. In M. Simard, D. Lafontaine, S. Savard, M. Tremblay, & P.-A. Tremblay (Eds.), *Inégalités, démocraties et développement* (pp. 143–64). Rimouski: GRIDEQ.

Klein, J.-L. (2006b). La mondialisation: De l'État-nation à l'espace-monde. In J.-L. Klein & F. Lasserre (Eds.), *Le monde dans tous ses États: Une perspective géographique* (pp. 47–70). Sainte-Foy: Presses de l'Université du Québec, Collection Géographie contemporaine.

Klein, J.-L., & Harrisson, D. (Eds.). (2007). *L'innovation sociale.* Sainte-Foy: Presses de l'Université du Québec.

Klein, J.-L., & Lasserre, F. (2006). *Le monde dans tous ses États:* Sainte-Foy: Presses de l'Université du Québec.

Klein, J.-L., & Tardif, C. (Eds.). (2006). *Entre réseaux et systèmes: Les nouveaux espaces régionaux.* Rimouski: GRIDEQ.

Klein, J.-L., Tardif, C., Tremblay, M., & Tremblay, P.-A. (2004). La place du communautaire. *Cahier de l'ARUC*, No. R-07-2004.

Lachapelle, R. (1995). Les CDEC comme espace d'économie sociale. *Nouvelles Pratiques Sociales, 8*(1), 81–95.

Lemay, A.-M., & Venne, M. (2006). Cultiver l'avenir: Saint-Camille, village modèle. In M. Venne (Ed.), *L'Annuaire du Québec* (pp. 530–7). Montréal: Institut du nouveau monde.

Lévesque, B. (2004). Le modèle québécois et le développement régional et local: Vers le néolibéralisme et la fin du modèle québécois. Montréal: Cahiers du CRISES, collection Études théoriques, No. ET0405.

Lévesque, B., Bourque, G., & Forgues, É. (2001). *La nouvelle sociologie économique*. Paris: Desclée de Brouwer.

Lévesque, B., Fontan, J.-M., & Klein, J.-L. (1996), *Les systèmes locaux de production: Conditions de mise en place et stratégie d'implantation pour le développement du projet Angus*. Montreal: UQAM, Report prepared by the Société de développement Angus.

Lipietz, A. (2001). *Rapport sur l'économie sociale et solidaire*. Paris: Report submitted to the Prime Minister.

Lukkarinen, M. (2005). Community, development, local economic development and the social economy. *Community Development Journal, 40*(4), 419–24. http://dx.doi.org/10.1093/cdj/bsi086

Markey, S. (2005). Building local development institutions in the hinterland: A regulationist perspective from British Columbia, Canada. *International Journal of Urban and Regional Research, 29*(2), 358–74. http://dx.doi.org/10.1111/j.1468-2427.2005.00589.x

Moulaert, F., & Ailenei, O. (2005). Social economy, Third Sector and the solidarity relations: A conceptual synthesis from history to present. *Urban Studies, 42*(11), 2037–54. http://dx.doi.org/10.1080/00420980500279794

Moulaert, F., & Nussbaumer, J. (2005). Defining the social economy and its governance at the neighbourhood level. *Urban Studies, 42*(11), 2071–88. http://dx.doi.org/10.1080/420980500279752

O'Boyle, E.J. (2005). Homo socio-economicus: Foundational to social economics and the social economy. *Review of Social Economy, 63*(3), 483–507. http://dx.doi.org/10.1080/00346760500255635

Opula, L. (2007). *L'appui à l'entrepreneuriat et l'intermédiation locale dans le développement territorial: Le cas de la zone du Canal de Lachine*. Doctoral thesis in urban studies, Université du Québec à Montréal.

Pecqueur, B. (2006). Quel "tournant territorial" de l'économie mondiale globalisée. In J.-L. Klein & C. Tardif (Eds.), *Entre réseaux et systèmes: les nouveaux espaces régionaux*. Rimouski: Cahiers du GRIDEQ.

Prévost, P., & Sévigny, B. (2006). Les collectivités apprenantes. In J.-L. Klein & D. Harrisson (Eds.), *L'innovation sociale*. Sainte-Foy: Presses de l'Université du Québec.

Rich, M., Giles, M., & Stern, E. (2001). Collaborating to reduce poverty: Views from city halls and community-based organizations. *Urban Affairs Review, 37*(2), 184–204. http://dx.doi.org/10.1177/10780870122185253

Sellers, J. (2002). *Governing from below: Urban regions and the global economy.* New York: Cambridge University Press. http://dx.doi.org/10.1017/CBO9780511613395

Seyfang, G. (2004). Time banks: Rewarding community self-help in the inner city? *Community Development Journal, 39*(1), 62–71. http://dx.doi.org/10.1093/cdj/39.1.62

Stöhr, W. (2003). Development from below: Vingt ans plus tard. In J.-M. Fontan, J.-L. Klein, & B. Lévesque (Eds.), *Reconversion économique et développement territorial: Le rôle de la société civile* (pp. 119–43). Québec: Presses de l'Université du Québec.

Stone, C.N., Henig, J.R., Jones, B.D., & Pierannunzi, C. (2001). *Building civic capacity: The politics of reforming urban schools.* Lawrence: University Press of Kansas.

Stone, C. (2005). Looking back to look forward: Reflections on urban regime analysis. *Urban Affairs Review, 40*(3), 309–41. http://dx.doi.org/10.1177/1078087404270646

Swyngedouw, E. (1997). Neither global nor local: "Glocalization" and the politics of scale. In K.R. Cox (Ed.), *Spaces of Globalization: Reasserting the Power of the Local* (pp. 137–66). New York: Guilford.

Tardif, C. (2007). *Les corporations de développement communautaire au Québec: Processus d'institutionnalisation et trajectoires socio-territoriales spécifiques.* Doctoral thesis in urban studies, Université du Québec à Montréal.

Tremblay, D., Perron, J., & Germain, G. (2002). Sacré-Cœur: Un exemple de dynamisme économique. *Organisations et territoires, 11*(1), 93–100.

Tremblay, P.A., Dubé, G., & Émond, M. (2006). Agir contre la pauvreté dans une ville de taille moyenne: Les représentations des intervenants locaux. *Canadian Journal of Urban Research, 15*(2), 225–44.

Tremblay, M., Tremblay, P.-A., & Tremblay, S. (Eds.). (2002). *Développement local, économie sociale et démocratie.* Sainte-Foy: Presses de l'Université du Québec.

Tremblay, M., Tremblay, P.-A., & Tremblay, S. (Eds.). (2006). *Le développement social: Un enjeu pour l'économie sociale.* Sainte-Foy: Presses de l'Université du Québec.

Urry, J. (2001). *Sociology beyond societies.* London: Routledge.

Vaillancourt, Y., & Favreau, L. (2000). *Le modèle québécois d'économie sociale et solidaire.* Montréal: Université du Québec à Montréal, Laboratoire de recherche sur les pratiques sociales, Collection Cahiers du LAREPPS, No. 00-04.

Van Kemenade, S. (2000). *Économie sociale et développement local.* Doctoral thesis, Montréal, Université du Québec à Montréal.

Veltz, P. (1996). *Mondialisation, villes et territoires.* Paris: Presses universitaires de France.

Viard, J. (1994). *La société d'archipel ou les territoires du village global.* Paris: Éditions De L'Aube.

9 Factors Influencing Wage Relations in the Social Economy

YVAN COMEAU

Introduction

Since the late 1990s, with the deployment of the social economy in emerging-activity sectors (home care, child-care, the environment, and local development, among others), the question of working conditions in the social economy has been the subject of debate. In the public realm, there are two sides to this debate. One side argues that the social economy integrates into its statutes and practices a democratic decision-making process that involves users and workers, and defends the primacy of persons and work over capital in the distribution of surplus and income (Groupe de travail sur l'économie sociale, 1996, p. 7). The other side is particularly critical of working conditions within the social economy. They object that these organizations offer low wages that trap workers in poverty and eliminate public service jobs that, in passing, were traditionally the preserve of women, encourages workfare and regards salaried work as sacred (Boivin & Fortier, 1998).

Our objective is to contribute to the debate from a research standpoint. Several researchers in Québec have examined the question of working conditions in the social economy and have conducted empirical studies on the subject (Paquet, Deslauriers, & Sarrazin, 1999; Bourdon, Deschenaux, & Coallier, 2000; Paquet & Favreau, 2000; Comeau, 2003a; Aubry, Didier, & Gervais, 2005). To determine whether jobs within social economy organizations have positive or negative characteristics for workers, we have chosen to determine, on the one hand, the factors that influence all types of organizations – private, public, or within the social economy – and, on the other hand, those that have a specific impact on the social economy. With this objective in mind, we first examine the structural and strategic factors statistically related to certain aspects of working conditions in the social economy. We then present some of the studies conducted on these factors in public and private enterprises. In concluding, we look at some possible strategies for enabling workers to improve their working conditions in the social economy.

From a theoretical standpoint, the analytical framework we have chosen is broader than a strict analysis of working conditions and adopts the perspective of the wage relation. The analysis of working conditions focuses on direct salary (remuneration) and indirect salary (social benefits and various programs), the concrete process of production (work, machinery, and tools), and employee qualification and mobility (individual, geographic, and between organizations). The wage relation perspective examines not only working conditions as defined above, but also the degree of inclusion of employees within the organization's power structure: that is, the relations of exchange and production (Aglietta, 1997, p. 65). This perspective introduces the political aspect of salary conditions found in an organization's legislative and internal regulations, and within relational dynamics among stakeholders.

Structural Factors Related to Employee Status in the Social Economy

We have used several empirical studies to help us examine employee status in the social economy (Comeau et al., 2001, 2002a; Comeau, 2003b, 2009). These studies share a similar methodology: establishing the parent population, sending a detailed questionnaire to social economy organizations, verifying sample representativity (composed of 126 to 335 organizations), and carrying out a statistical analysis using correlation tests. For the purposes of this chapter, we must first consider the structural factors that people, groups, and organizations must grapple with and over which they exercise very little influence, at least in the short term. These structural factors promote the pursuit and continuity of daily life in fairly set routines, which constitute the basis for anticipating interpersonal behaviour. At least four structural factors are related to various aspects of the wage relation in the social economy: territory, area of activity, size of organization, and external and internal regulations.

Territory

A territory's urban or rural features as well as its economy are related to many aspects of employment in the social economy, and there are several explanations for these correlations. In rural areas, social economy jobs emerge in particular sectors such as agriculture and forestry (Comeau, 2009). Urban areas have their own characteristics. With 27 per cent of Québec's cooperatives, Montréal is home to a large proportion of housing cooperatives (Lepage, 2005); however, these organizations employ few workers (Comeau, 2009; Bouchard, 2008). It would seem that the territory determines its sectors. The influence of territory is even more apparent in atypical zones, such as the Far North, where most organizations offer a wide range of services and employees are required to perform a variety of tasks. This is the case of the 13 cooperatives in Nunavut (6,000 members, 390 jobs, and $90 million in assets), each of which offers banking, postal, telecommunication, and tourism services, and provides various goods such as petroleum products and construction materials (Arteau, Brassard, & Malo, 2005, p. 7).

Each territory also has a particular labour pool. Statistical analyses that compare social economy organizations based on proximity to an urban centre and on poverty level reveal significant differences in terms of employment. In underprivileged and peripheral zones, the study data indicate that social economy organizations generally hire employees who do not have a university degree. Moreover, these organizations recruit coordinating staff with comparatively less management experience and less schooling than anywhere else (Comeau et al., 2002a; Comeau, 2003b).

A territory's economic situation influences social economy jobs in many other ways. In less privileged areas, social economy organizations offer more jobs created through integration programs. This can be explained by a greater need for occupational integration in underprivileged areas, and the fact that these programs provide new resources for organizations that have relatively few employees and limited budgets (Comeau, 2003b).

Each territory also seems to have its own social economy employment culture. Comparisons have been drawn between social economy organizations in Gaspésie and Montréal, both of which received support from the fund to combat poverty (Fonds de lutte contre la pauvreté). We observed that cities, like Montréal, more often adopt written policies on working conditions,[1] hire women for coordinating positions, and hire on a full-time basis (Comeau et al., 2002a). There are several explanations for this. It is likely that there are more social economy organizations in Montréal that specialize in the provision of particular types of services to individuals (for example, child-care services) and that recruit a majority of women. We can also assume that organizations are larger in Montréal than outside of the city; as noted in a later section, large organizations have a greater tendency to set out working conditions in a policy. Social economy organizations are also likely to have a territorial or even sectoral culture that influences their choices with regard to work relations.

Area of Activity

The area of activity dictates many aspects of the wage relation in the social economy, starting with employees' gender. Studies show that, overall, the labour force in the social economy is dominated by women.[2] The situation varies somewhat according to area of activity, however: In some areas, the labour force is dominated by women, while in others it is dominated by men.[3] Moreover, more women are employed by relatively small non-profit organizations that provide services to individuals (Comité sectoriel de la main-d'œuvre, 2000; Comeau, 2003b).

Other data show that there is a greater proportion of people aged 35 and under in the social economy, compared to their numbers in the general population (Comeau, 2003b). It may be that areas invested in by the social economy – such as the environment, recreation, and culture – attract more young people, or that, early in their careers, young people turn to the social economy to gain experience.

The area of activity also has an impact on remuneration, as shown by statistical correlations (Comeau, 2009). This can be explained by first considering the labour force profile in two areas of activity dominated by women: home care and child-care services. The wages and social benefits of home care workers are substantially lower than those of day-care workers. In all likelihood, there are intervening variables that account for these differences, namely the stronger presence of unions in child-care services. Regardless, in home care, the labour force is largely dominated by women (90 per cent) who have little schooling and are older than those in the community movement in general (Comeau & Aubry, 2003).

The profit level of each area of activity is also a determining factor for working conditions. To better understand this dynamic, let us examine the financial services sector. In Québec, the social economy enjoys an enviable position in this area. Indeed, with assets totalling $152 billion as of 30 June 2008, the Mouvement Desjardins is among the 100 largest financial institutions in the world, ranking sixth among Canadian financial institutions and first in Québec (Développement International

Desjardins, 2008). We can hypothesize that, in this situation, the social economy can offer wages and social benefits that are equivalent to those of its capitalist competitors. In fact, Desjardins is one of the rare social economy networks that offers its employees a comprehensive insurance and retirement package (Comeau, 2009), whereas its biggest competitor, the National Bank of Canada, ranks 14th among the 30 best retirement plans in Canada, according to the magazine *Benefits Canada* (June 2008). Retirement and group insurance benefits are only offered by a handful of social economy organizations, excluding financial and agricultural enterprises (Aubry, Didier, & Gervais, 2005).

Size of the Organization

The size of an organization implies a certain number of employees and a certain financial capacity. In the social economy (Comeau, 2003b, 2009), particular employee benefits increase with the size of the organization. We can assume that a large number of contributors and large sales figures boost an organization's financial ability to offer social benefits. Therefore, just as with large social economy organizations in the financial and agricultural sectors, almost all child-care centres (CPEs) offer particular benefits to their employees (group insurance paid for in part by the employer and unpaid holidays), while a small minority of other organizations offer these advantages. On average, child-care centres have some of the highest numbers of employees and revenue, with the exception of financial and agricultural social economy organizations.

The complexity of large organizations is one of the reasons why larger social economy organizations allow employees to play a role, based on various guidelines, in decision-making processes. This need is less prevalent in small organizations, where it is easier for employees to express their opinions in a more spontaneous manner.

The size of an organization also plays a role in the adoption of a written policy on working conditions. The smallest organizations are less likely to have a written policy on working conditions (although a majority of them do), while the tendency towards having written policies increases with the size of the organization. It is reasonable to assume that the complexity of wage relations and the risk of work conflicts, which increase in larger organizations, prompt management to set out explicit regulations with regard to working conditions. We must also take into account the increased financial capacity of a large organization. In fact, it has been statistically shown that the greater the proportion of recurring revenue in an organization's budget (guaranteed revenue for the next three years), the more likely it is that a written policy on working conditions exists. Not surprisingly, the predictability of revenue allows an organization to make its working conditions official.

With regard to job training in the social economy, organizations with 10 or more employees spend more money on training, and training is offered to a larger number of employees. When these observations were made (Comeau et al., 2001, 2003b), organizations with a payroll exceeding $250,000 were obliged by law to devote one per cent of this sum to labour force training.

Legislative Provisions and Internal Regulations

As we know, social economy organizations are governed by external and internal regulations. The main external regulations can be found in the act that legally constitutes the organization. The term "non-profit organization" (NPO) corresponds to a legal status recognized and made possible by Part 3 of the Québec Companies Act. As is the case in cooperatives, the rule of "one person, one vote" prevails; however, it is quite possible that, in an NPO, a category of stakeholders, such as employees, does not have the right to vote, or that their right is limited.

As a set of external regulations, the Québec Cooperatives Act includes various provisions, depending on the type of cooperative. In worker cooperatives, members are generally paid employees. Each member has a vote in the general assembly and is free to express opinions and vote on various issues such as wages and membership shares, as well as the hiring and admission of new members. Members elect their colleagues to the board of directors and can also be nominated to sit on the board.

All credit unions share the same associative structure and the same democratic governing structure (one member, one vote) by a group of people – in this case, a group of users. There is therefore a consumer logic that is expressed through these regulations, as opposed to a work logic as in the case of a worker cooperative. This explains, to some extent, why, in certain years, credit unions saw a considerable number of strike days (Lévesque, 1991).

Legally instituted in June 1997, solidarity cooperatives are the most recent type of cooperative. A total of 255 solidarity cooperatives had been constituted in 2004, primarily in the tertiary sector (223 cooperatives;

that is, 87.4 per cent of constituted solidarity cooperatives) and outside the large urban centres of Montréal and Québec (Chagnon, 2004). Solidarity cooperatives strive to meet the specific needs of communities by allowing the creation of a broad membership that brings together people and organizations with a common interest and varied needs. These cooperatives bring together at least two categories of members: user members who use the services offered by the cooperative, worker members, and support members who have a vested economic, social, or cultural interest in attaining the cooperative's objectives. This legal status therefore promotes the political inclusion of employees, as do shareholding workers' cooperatives. Legally recognized in 1983, shareholding workers' cooperatives bring together workers who collectively own a certain number of shares in the enterprise where they work, in proportions that usually vary from 10 to 40 per cent. By forming a cooperative association, workers can express themselves as a group and appoint representatives to the enterprise's board of directors (the number of representatives of the cooperative is determined by a shareholders' agreement between the cooperative and the private enterprise) (Lévesque, 1994).

In addition, there are external regulations that do not fall under the founding legislative framework of the organization, but that can limit management decisions and impose, to some extent, production methods or characteristics of the labour force. This phenomenon can be seen in a worker cooperative that benefits from an adapted work centre program, provided that they integrate people with disabilities who have varying degrees of work autonomy. This labour force requires particular work arrangements and, in some situations, limits the possibilities for autonomy at work (Comeau et al., 2002b).

The internal regulations of a social economy organization make it possible to move beyond legal directives and promote – or limit – employee inclusion. Studies on work cooperatives reveal that they generally adhere to the regulations set out in the legislation on worker cooperatives. However, some cooperatives are the exception and experience a long-term collapse of their democratic structure. These failures are usually due to the limited rights of some employees (for example, obstacles to becoming a member due to very onerous membership shares) (Comeau et al., 2002a). Moreover, a more or less prolonged weakness of the general assembly or board of directors can sometimes tip the scale of power in favour of management.

The Effect of Stakeholder Strategies

The available information enables us to identify three strategic factors that could have a significant impact on working conditions in the social economy: management philosophy, the occupational mobility of employees, and their capacity for collective action.

Management Philosophy

Few social economy organizations[4] offer a space for expression and decision-making with an institutional reach for employees, with the exception of the general assembly and the board of directors. Studies show (Comité sectoriel de la main-d'œuvre, 2000; Comeau, 2003b) that social economy organizations confer the right to vote more to users and volunteers than to employees.[5] Even rarer are instances in which management or coordinating staff has the right to vote at the general assembly. It seems that the logic of service consumption often takes precedence in social economy organizations.

An entirely different logic obviously applies to worker cooperatives. Compared to capitalist enterprises in the same sectors, workers enjoy greater satisfaction (Greenberg, 1980; Rhodes & Steers, 1981). The control they exercise over their work and their power within the enterprise represent their main sources of satisfaction, in addition to having a job in their chosen field and a friendly work environment (Comeau, 1993).

Occupational Mobility of Employees

Employees can individually change their working conditions by assuming other functions and by obtaining training. In fact, remuneration varies significantly in social economy organizations depending on the position held. Coordinating staff is the best paid (Comeau, 2003b, 2009). Remuneration also varies according to the level of schooling: Employees with university degrees receive the highest wages, while those who do not have a high school diploma receive the lowest wages (Comeau, 2003b). This reflects the prevailing trend in the job market, in which people with rarer skills are generally better paid. In some sectors where professionalization and a certain level of schooling are required, working conditions can prove to be the most attractive. For example, by law, child-care centres are obliged to hire workers who have college diplomas.

The ability to speak out in a social economy organization can lead to another job. However, in home care social economy organizations, providers may have difficulty asserting themselves and taking advantage of opportunities to speak out, even when opportunities arise (Comeau & Aubry, 2003, pp. 210–13).

Capacity for Collective Action

In sociology, it is a well-established fact that the power struggle between social stakeholders (unions and employers, not to mention the state) is a powerful social mechanism that determines wage levels (De Coster & Pichault, 1994). Let us take another look at the situation of child-care centres, sometimes referred to as day cares. We know that the rate of unionization is about 30 per cent in day cares, much higher than the 3 per cent rate in NPOs overall (Aubry, Didier, & Gervais, 2005, p. 23). The average hourly wage of day-care workers ($12.48 in 2001) was at least 10 per cent higher than that of production workers in other sectors of the social economy, such as home care and adapted enterprises (Comeau et al., 2001b). The impact of the collective capacity of employees to take action does not stop there. More often than in any other sector (one out of two day cares), an employee representative is allowed to sit on the board of directors. Moreover, the tendency to adopt a written policy on working conditions is greater in child-care centres and in less-commercial social economy organizations – that is, those associated to community groups; this tendency can be explained by the political culture of this network.

The role of social movements in the social economy can have other effects on working conditions. The demand for a minimum wage of $8.30, put forward by the 1995 Women's March, was promoted in the development plan of the social economy on home care released at the 1996 Sommet sur l'économie et l'emploi (Fournier, 2000); on 1 October 1996, the minimum wage in Québec was $6.70 an hour ($9.90 as of 1 May 2012).[6] We can also hypothesize that activism on the part of women and unionists helps to maintain fair remuneration in the social economy. Statistical analyses conducted in three different studies did not confirm the hypothesis of an unequal wage structure between women and men in social economy organizations (Comeau et al., 2001, 2002a, 2003). However, despite the presence of social movements, the social economy is not impermeable to the trends observed in society in terms of gender division in the workplace.[7] In fact, we see that, proportionally, men occupy more coordinating and management positions than women and that, proportionally, men occupy fewer positions in production than women. Furthermore, relatively speaking, women perform more office duties than do men (Comeau, 2003b).

The Social Economy's Unique Wage Relations

Now that we have presented the structural and strategic factors that influence working conditions in the social economy, we will examine certain specific aspects. Our main argument is that the social economy does not create a particular context for the exploitation of workers, nor does it guarantee better working conditions. We believe that determining factors, similar to those encountered in public and private enterprises with regard to establishing working conditions, exist in the social economy, although prevailing regulations and stakeholder strategies manifest themselves in a particular way. We must stress the fact that remuneration in enterprises in general depends on gender, race, level of schooling, qualification, unionization, the size of the enterprise, and the region (De Coster & Pichault, 1994, p. 303). Let us take a closer look at how these variables correspond to the factors identified in the previous statement.

With regard to territory, we looked at various processes that affect the wage relation in the social economy. For the purpose of generalization, we can refer to a recent study by Beach and Costigliola (2004) on day care workers in Canada, based on data from the 2001 Census which clearly show that working conditions (wages and work patterns) vary significantly from one province to the next. The variables analysed in this study are provincial training requirements and levels of public funding. Québec offers the most public funding, more spaces for children, and some of the best wages for day care workers in the country.

Territory represents a complex global framework that has an impact on the wage relation in any organization. It includes the economic, political, social, and cultural dimensions of a society, brings together several communities, and shapes various aspects of daily life. In a territory smaller than the nation-state, we find a regional mode of regulation that Krätke (1997) recognized and that distinguishes coordination among enterprises, the type of work relations, the sociocultural profile of regional stakeholders, and political mechanisms.

The data presented above show that sector is a determining factor for various aspects of wage relations in the social economy. This process also applies to other forms of organizations, as shown in Finnie's study (1998) on the remuneration of employees with a bachelor's degree in Canada. The author's econometric study establishes that the remuneration of employees with the same level of schooling varies according to the field in which they are employed.

The area of activity has a major impact on an organization's wage relation because it is framed by a technological and scientific reality that forces an organization to produce based on the processes available in a given place, at a given time. Various monographs on social economy enterprises[8] show that production processes are not unique and not particularly innovative in terms of work organization (Comeau & Lévesque, 1994). Working conditions are more precarious when the social economy is deployed in non-lucrative areas that have been abandoned by capitalist enterprises (Vienney, 1994), particularly when dealing with services that are useful but for which the demand is not solvent, or for services provided to the general public that are more or less recognized by the state.

In terms of the impact of the size of an organization on the wage relation, the social economy is no exception. It has long been established that the size of an enterprise is a significant differentiation factor (Blau, 1970). The data on Canadian enterprises show that size represents a basic characteristic that has considerable and varied effects on work hours, retirement plans, social benefits, and remuneration (Drolet & Morisset, 1998). In this respect, compared to private and public enterprises, McMullen and Schellenberg (2003) found that social economy organizations are generally small. This study is worth examining in greater depth, since it provides a comparison of para-public, for-profit, and non-profit organizations.

The study by McMullen and Schellenberg (2003) uses the information on 6,320 establishments and 23,500 employees that was published in 1999 by Statistics Canada in its *Workplace and Employee Survey*. The non-profit sector includes 463 organizations with at least one employee working in culture, recreation, health, education, and social services. The interest of this study lies less in the correspondence between the non-profit sector and the social economy and more on the possibility of identifying the processes that determine working conditions.[9] The best wages are found in the para-public sector, followed by the for-profit sector and, lastly, the non-profit sector. The following reasons for these discrepancies confirm the observations made thus far on the effects of the size of organizations, training, and area of activity.

First, the vast majority of work settings in the non-profit sector are small, generally employing less than 10 people. Second, in the para-public sector, there is a higher percentage of employees who have post-secondary education. The differences between these sectors are more prominent among managers and professionals than among office workers, technicians, and representatives; in fact, the hourly wage of office workers in the non-profit sector and the for-profit sector is virtually the same. Third, remuneration varies considerably when only taking into account the activity sectors.[10]

In terms of regulations, we saw that in Québec, social economy organizations are subject to two main legislative frameworks: Part Three of the Companies Act, and the Cooperatives Act. These acts do not contain the same stipulations for the political inclusion of employees, but several types of cooperatives (worker cooperatives, shareholding workers' cooperatives, and solidarity cooperatives) confer more rights, in this respect, than those granted by most private companies (for-profit or non-profit sectors) and public establishments. In our opinion, this is a particular feature of the social economy, which explains why, in the same activity sectors, worker cooperatives offer an economic performance that is comparable to private enterprises while paying higher wages (Defourny, 1990).

Despite these advances, there are no guarantees in the social economy when it comes to employee inclusion. We must consider three scenarios. First, the political inclusion of employees is based on the regulations set out by law and in agreements contracted outside an organization, through participation in a particular government program, for example. Second, in practice, the rights of employees, or a portion of employees, are limited; there may also be restrictions or inequities in the regulations and various situations may reflect weaknesses in employee organizations or representatives. Third, there is an expansion of democracy within the organization. In this case, regulations stipulate the presence of a variety of stakeholders in decision-making bodies, the creation of specific opportunities for expression and decision-making by employees, and the independent association of employees in a union.

Across the board, structural factors exist that have a considerable impact on the working conditions of social economy organizations, as is the case in other types of organizations. Moreover, among the factors examined in this chapter that affect working conditions in the social economy, regulations and stakeholder strategies are by far the most specific factors with respect to the wage relation in these organizations. Like any social phenomenon, the wage relation in the social economy is subject to the impact of the duality of structural factors and reflexive behaviour (Giddens, 1997). Indeed, structural factors are both the context and the result of the impact of reflexive and interactive phenomena (Giddens, 1997). In this sense, the collective action of employees can contribute to changing employee status, provided that they are prepared to accept the uncertain outcome of their actions. The conclusion includes some reflections on this notion.

Conclusion

This chapter attempts to show that the wage relation in the social economy involves elements of specificity. We saw that some elements are shared by other types of organizations in terms of the determination of working conditions such as territory, area of activity, and size of the organization. When social economy organizations operate in peripheral and underprivileged zones, invest their efforts in non-lucrative areas of activity and are small in size, there is a strong chance that their working conditions will not be advantageous. While working conditions are also influenced by institutional provisions (the "rules of the game") and group strategies that constitute the wage relation, the fact remains that working conditions are unique in the social economy. In some cases, legislative provisions, internal operating regulations underpinned by the principle of "one person, one vote," and the characteristics of the stakeholders working in social economy organizations create a unique wage relation.

If this interpretation were valid, we would have to accept that the strategies of employees and managers in the social economy are different from those in organizations where the wage relation is created by resolutely different groups. A first strategy consists of enhancing the reflexive capacities of stakeholders in the social economy. This strategy involves the various stakeholders in the social economy, depending on their familiarity with the social economy: It focuses on a better understanding of inclusive management processes (Davister, 2006), the nature of the social economy, and its internal functioning. A second strategy consists of reframing various aspects of the social economy. Wage earning in the social economy certainly deserves greater recognition and deeper reflection among employees themselves. For instance, shouldn't government contributions to the social economy be considered on the same footing as those made to private and public enterprises for the production of services (enterprises for the construction of roads, public buildings, hospitals, etc.)? Since the state compensates organizations with a public-interest mission, should it not purchase these services at market prices (Fortin, 2007) and take this into account when paying the labour force in the social economy?

A third strategy is based on the fact that social economy organizations draw on the principle of mutuality in terms of providing their employees with access to group insurance and retirement plans. The fourth and last strategy pertains to unionization, which should be practised in a particular way. In social economy organizations, there is no private appropriation of profit based on capital invested: The employer is an association, where the same democratic structures that define unions prevail (Mayné, 1999); class affiliation among management is often the same as that among employees; and a substantial portion of funding comes from the public coffers. Under these rather unusual circumstances, central unions could draw on the success of unionism in social economy organizations, adapt practices to these organizations, and establish new protocols for negotiating with the state.

NOTES

1   Setting out working conditions in a written document means that an organization tends to make public contractual agreements and avoids the risks of more arbitrary individual contracts.

2   In the Québec City and Chaudière-Appalaches regions, taking into account all financial and non-financial cooperatives as well as non-profit organizations, 76.6 per cent of the labour force is female (Comeau, 2009).

3   Women represent 98.5 per cent of employees in child-care centres (centres de la petite enfance); just 15.8 per cent of employees in funeral services, and 29.3 per cent in the agricultural sector (Comeau, 2009).

4   Specifically, this represents 3.2 per cent of the social economy organizations in the Chaudière-Appalaches region, excluding financial and agricultural cooperatives (Comeau, 2003b, p. 68).

5   On average, these organizations reserve 12 per cent of positions on the board of directors for staff, far behind individual members (68 per cent of seats) and users or people reached (28 per cent) (Comité sectoriel de la main-d'œuvre économie sociale et action communautaire, 2000). If we consider the question from another angle, 12 per cent of organizations confer the right to vote on the board of directors to at least one employee

representative, and 15 per cent confer the right to vote at the general assembly (Comeau, 2003b).

6 Remember that in Canada, women represented close to two-thirds of minimum-wage workers in 2003, while they constituted just less than half of all employees; according to Statistics Canada, one out of 20 women were working for minimum wage, compared to one out of 85 men (Canadian Press, 2004).

7 In 1998, 37 per cent of administrative positions in Canada were held by women (Hughes, 2000).

8 It is possible to consult numerous online monographs on social economy organizations, edited since the 1990s by the Centre de recherche sur les innovations sociales (CRISES) (http://www.crises.uqam.ca) and by the Laboratoire de recherche sur les pratiques et les politiques sociales (LAREPPS) (http://www.larepps.uqam.ca/).

9 In this study, the term "non-profit sector" is used in its fullest meaning to include museums, unions, philanthropic foundations, and community clinics. All of these are legally constituted organizations, separate from government and thus referred to as non-government, independent, non-profit, and voluntary. The study also focuses on 358 non-profit para-public organizations (elementary schools, high schools, colleges, universities, hospitals, and public infrastructure) and 5,501 for-profit entreprises.

10 In fact, hourly wages in the non-profit sector are sometimes higher than in the for-profit sector, such as in the retail sector (McMullen & Schellenberg, 2003, pp. 32–3).

REFERENCES

Aglietta, M. (1997). *Régulation et crises du capitalisme*. Paris: Éditions Odile Jacob.

Arteau, M., Brassard, M.-J., & Malo, M.-C. (2005). *Les secteurs et le mouvement coopératif québécois: Portrait et défis*. Gatineau: Cahiers de la Chaire de recherche du Canada en développement des collectivités, Série Pratiques économiques sociales. No. 26.

Aubry, F., Didier, S., & Gervais, L. (2005). *Pour que travailler dans le communautaire ne rime plus avec misère: Enquête sur les avantages sociaux dans les organismes communautaires*. Montréal: Centre de formation populaire et Relais-femmes.

Beach, J. & Costigliola, B. (2004). *Salaires versés dans le secteur des services de garde et la qualité du système*. Ottawa: Conseil sectoriel des ressources humaines des services de garde à l'enfance.

Blau, P.M. (1970). A formal theory of differentiation in organizations. *American Sociological Review, 35*(2), 201–18. http://dx.doi.org/10.2307/2093199

Boivin, L., & Fortier, M. (Eds.). (1998). *L'économie sociale: L'avenir d'une illusion.* Montréal: Éditions Fides.

Bouchard, M.J. (Ed.). (2008). *Portrait statistique de l'économie sociale de la région de Montréal.* Montréal: Conférence régionale des élus de Montréal et UQAM, Chaire de recherche du Canada en économie sociale.

Bourdon, S., Deschenaux, F., & Coallier, J.-C. (2000). *Le travail et les conditions de travail dans les organismes communautaires: Faits saillants de l'enquête 2000.* Sherbrooke: Université de Sherbrooke, Collectif de recherche sur les occupations.

Chagnon, J. (2004). *Les coopératives de solidarité au Québec.* Québec: Gouvernement du Québec, Direction des coopératives.

Chantier de l'économie sociale. (2006). *Le Québec affiche ses couleurs. Sommet de l'économie sociale et solidaire: Rapport synthèse des travaux préparatoires.* Montréal: Chantier de l'économie sociale.

Comeau, Y. (1993). Les éléments de satisfaction et d'insatisfaction dans les coopératives de travail. *Coopératives et Développement, 25*(1), 31–46.

Comeau, Y. (2003a). *La diversité du rapport salarial dans le troisième secteur au Québec.* Montréal: CRISES, Cahier No. 03-05.

Comeau, Y. (2003b). *Le communautaire, la nouvelle économie sociale et leurs retombées en région: Chaudière-Appalaches.* L'Islet: Éditions Terres fauves.

Comeau, Y. (2009). *Réalités et dynamiques régionales de l'économie sociale et solidaire: La Capitale-Nationale et Chaudière-Appalaches.* Montréal: Éditions Vie économique, Collection Recherche.

Comeau, Y., et al. (2001). *L'économie sociale et le Plan d'action du Sommet sur l'économie et l'emploi.* Québec: Centre de recherche sur les services communautaires, Université Laval et ÉNAP.

Comeau, Y., et al. (2002a). *Les effets du financement étatique sur les organismes communautaires: Le cas du Fonds de lutte contre la pauvreté.* Québec: Éditions Sylvain Harvey.

Comeau, Y., & Aubry, F. (2003). Les rapports de travail et la participation des employés. In Y. Vaillancourt, C. Jetté, & F. Aubry (Eds.), *L'économie sociale dans les services à domicile* (pp. 201–33). Québec: Presses de l'Université du Québec.

Comeau, Y., Boucher, J., Malo, M.-C., & Vaillancourt Y. (2002b). Las configuraciones de las iniciativas de la economía social y solidaria. *Cayapa, 2*(3), 14–36.

Comeau, Y., & Lévesque, B. (1994). *La participation des travailleurs dans les coopératives de travail et dans les entreprises capitalistes au Québec.* Montréal:

Chaire de coopération Guy-Bernier, Université du Québec à Montréal, Cahier No. 0994-064.

Comité sectoriel de la main-d'œuvre économie sociale et action communautaire. (2000). Les premiers résultats de la plus vaste étude statistique jamais réalisée sur l'action communautaire et l'économie sociale. *Recto Verso* (286), 13–6.

Davister, C. (2006). *La gestion des ressources humaines en économie sociale.* Liège: Les cahiers de la Chaire Cera, No. 1.

Defourny, J. (1992). *Démocratie coopérative et efficacité économique: La performance comparée des scop françaises.* Paris: De Boeck.

De Coster, M., & Pichault, F. (1994). Les systèmes et politiques de rémunération. In M. De Coster and F. Pichault, *Traité de sociologie du travail* (pp. 301–35). Brussels: De Boeck Université.

Développement International Desjardins. (2008). Desjardins parmi les plus importantes institutions financières au monde. *Bulletin Finance et communautés, 9,* 3.

Drolet, M. & Morisset, R. (1998). *Données récentes canadiennes sur la qualité des emplois selon la taille des entreprises.* Ottawa: Statistique Canada, Document de recherche no. 128.

Finnie, R. (1998). *La rémunération des diplômés universitaires au Canada selon la discipline. L'importance du domaine d'études: Analyse économétrique des écarts de rémunération entre les bacheliers.* Ottawa: Développement des ressources humaines Canada.

Fortin, A. (2007). Organisation communautaire, développement local et financement. In D. Bourque, Y. Comeau, L. Favreau, & L. Fréchette (Eds.), *L'organisation communautaire. Fondements, approches et champs de pratique* (pp. 237–47). Québec: Presses de l'Université du Québec.

Fournier, J. (2000). Aide à domicile: Pour l'économie sociale demeure de l'économie sociale. *Nouvelles Pratiques Sociales, 13*(2), 193–206.

Giddens, A. (1987). *La constitution de la société: Éléments de la théorie de la structuration.* Paris: Presses universitaires de France.

Greenberg, E.S. (1980). Participation in industrial decision-making and work satisfaction: The case of the producer cooperatives. *Social Science Quarterly, 60,* 551–9.

Groupe de travail sur l'économie sociale. (1996). *Osons la solidarité!* Québec: Sommet sur l'économie et l'emploi.

Hughes, K.D. (2000). *Women and corporate directorships in Canada: Trends and issues.* Ottawa: Canadian Policy Research Networks.

Krätke, S. (1997). Une approche régulationniste des études régionales. *L'Année de la régulation, 1,* 263–96.

Lepage, D. (2005). *Coopératives du Québec. Données statistiques (édition 2005)*. Québec: Governement of Quebec, Ministère du Développement économique, de l'Innovation et de l'Exportation.

Lévesque, B. (1991). Coopération et syndicalisme: Le cas des relations du travail dans les caisses populaires Desjardins. *Relations Industrielles, 46*(1), 13–43.

Lévesque, B. (1994). Une forme originale d'association capital-travail: Les coopératives de travailleurs actionnaires au Québec. *Revue des études coopératives, mutualistes et associatives, 72*(251): 49–60.

Mayné, E. (1999). *Syndicalisme et économie sociale*. Brussels: Éditions Luc Pire.

McMullen, K., & Schellenberg, G. (2003). *Job quality in non-profit organizations*. Ottawa: Canadian Policy Research Networks (CPRN), CPRN Research Series on Human Resources in the Non-profit Sector, no. 2.

Paquet, R., Deslauriers, J.-P., & Sarrazin, M. (1999). La syndicalisation des salariés du communautaire. *Relations Industrielles, 54*(2), 337–64.

Paquet, R., & Favreau, L. (2000). *Qualité de l'emploi et micro-entreprises soutenues par la microfinance*. Gatineau: Université du Québec en Outaouais, Chaire de recherche du Canada en développement des collectivités, Série Recherche, no. 17.

Presse Canadienne. (2004). La majorité des travailleurs au salaire minimum sont des femmes. *Le Soleil*, 27 March, B13.

Rhodes, S.R., & Steers, R.M. (1981). Conventional vs. worker-owned organizations. *Human Relations, 34*(12), 1013–35. http://dx.doi.org/10.1177/001872678103401201

Scott-Clarke, A. (2008). The best made plans. *Benefits Canada*, 1 June 2008. Accessed 18 June 2011. http://www.benefitscanada.com/benefits/health-benefits/the-best-made-plans-813/2

Vienney, C. (1994). *L'économie sociale*. Paris: Éditions La Découverte.

Conclusion: Studying Social Innovation: Lessons From the Social Economy[1]

MARIE J. BOUCHARD

This book presents various facets of Québec's social economy, in order to highlight its innovative aspect within the current context. The concept of social innovation used in this work refers to social change. It takes into account the collective dynamics that underlie changes in organizations and institutions. Social innovation evokes the possibility that new ways of doing things may better meet the needs of persons and collectivities than do existing solutions. Aiming to attain systemic transformations, social innovation seeks support within an institution, an organization, or a community so as to entail sustainable collective social impacts (see the Déclaration québécoise pour l'innovation sociale du Réseau québécois en innovation sociale,[2] Québec Declaration for Social Innovation of the Québec Network for Social Innovation). Like a concept analogous to that of technological innovation in the analysis of economic dynamics (which explains increases in productivity but also "creative destruction" and, accordingly, crises), social innovation may be an operational concept in the analysis of social dynamics, their evolution, crises, and transformations (Bouchard, 2007).

The increase in interest in this concept of social innovation since 1960–70 precisely corresponds to the period when the social and cultural challenge of existing models began and during which the growth in productivity slowed. This productivity had sustained the period of growth following World War Two (the "Glorious Thirty"). Facing social, cultural, and economic challenges, developed economies entered a deep transformation cycle. New ambitions and new needs motivated the invention of new forms of labour organization, collective consuming, and territorial development. Among other things, this met the demands for participation by citizens, workers, and consumers in the democratization of the economy. Self-managed collectives, administrative decentralization, and cooperative and associative renewal are part of the features that characterize this wave of innovations. In the beginning of the 2000s, the crisis perpetuated itself and became multiform, affecting employment but also the relationship to labour, social exclusion, inequalities, environment, confidence in financial institutions, the solvency of states, etc. In the current context, in which capitalism seems to want to shake off any social or political constraints, the interest in social innovation and the social economy seems to increase exponentially.

The work performed by the Centre de recherche sur les innovations sociales (CRISES; the Social Innovation Research Centre) was a precursor; it developed a research program in the mid-1980s, the purpose of which was to determine how a society rebuilds itself during a crisis. As previously mentioned, and without ignoring the negative effects of the crisis, this is a period rich in social innovation vis-à-vis economic as well as social development, and in the reciprocal liaisons that the social economy tends to create. The Alliance de recherche universités-communautés and the Réseau québécois de recherche partenariale en économie sociale (ARUC-ÉS and RQRP-ÉS; the Community University Research Alliance and the Québec Partnership Research Network on the Social Economy) pursued this line of thinking by conducting joint research with actors in the social economy of Québec. Their publication highlights some of the research and thinking developed around what we might call the "Montréal School" of the social economy.[3]

Among other things, the research is characterized by an approach in which social innovation is analysed from three perspectives: social movements that are at the basis of social demands supported by the social economy; the institutional dimension that determines within relatively stable rules the compromises established by the social actors; and the organizational dimension in which the actors concretely apply their new production, consumption, and distribution relationships (see Bouchard & Lévesque, 2010). Research focuses not only on what occurs before (conditions for emergence) and after (conditions for dissemination), but also deals with the innovation process (creation) and the relationships in socio-territorial configurations. As an operating concept in the analysis of the social dynamics and its evolution, crises, and transformations, social innovation refers to the initiatives that accompany or offset the functioning of economic dynamics. From this point of view, the innovations borne by the social economy are testimony to more global contemporary phenomena, namely the quest for increased participation by civil society in the orientation of development.

The study of social innovations and social transformations is focused on the relationship to a paradigm of society or to a model of development. The emerging waves or clusters of the social economy correspond to reactions or propositions in dealing with capitalism's transformations. Unsatisfied demands and aspirations testify to the limits of a model of development and cause it to be challenged. Such an approach allows us to see the social economy as a critique of the capitalist economy and of its institutions and, at the same time, as an alternative that can reconcile economic, social, and political aspects. The social economy is perceived to be a witness to and an eye-opener of the tensions to which the development model is subject. From this point of view, the social economy is featured less as a general alternative to the capitalist economy or to a planned economy, and more as a field of experimentation, which, if such experiments become generalized, could have the effect of changing capitalism and public space enough that attaining greater democratization becomes possible.

Innovations are often undertaken by visionary leaders and even by those who deviate from the rules (Alter, 2002), but they cannot be disseminated without challenging established standards and the existing institutional system. One of the features of the social economy is to challenge the market's exclusivity in economic development and the central role played by the state in social development. The institutional environment may be either favourable to or wary of new experimentation, especially when it questions the fallout and the performance of the components of the institutional field (Hollingsworth, 2000). For the institutional system to be open to new proposals, shortcomings must first be identified, thereby underlining the role played by institutional actors in the social innovation process (Lawrence, Suddaby, & Lecca, 2009). In addition, new solutions may be thought up if the actors in place have relative autonomy, among other things, to establish constructive interactions between themselves. Social innovation supported by the social economy must therefore establish social and political coordination, spanning bridges between each of the levels represented by institutions, organizations, and communities. Social economy enterprises are especially innovative (Lévesque, 2004), not only because they integrate the social aspect into their values and practices but because they integrate the political aspect as well (Eme & Laville, 1994).

This book was written in light of the lengthy history of the social economy in Québec and the important role played by researchers in its development. By situating our writing in the context of the crisis, we have also explored the potential of the social economy to find innovative answers to problems caused by the crisis: social exclusion, territorial devitalization, "unsustainable" development, etc. The accent was placed on the relationships established between the social economy and its own employees, its networking with researchers, its relationship with public authority and with the market economy, its territorial links, and even with the Earth as an ecological environment, etc. The terms that describe these relationships underline their participatory features and the will to bring society closer to the economy and to political power: governance, partnerships, coproduction, co-construction, networking, etc. We note the capacity of actors in the social economy to participate in the definition and orientation of public policies, to create financing routes that are adapted to a mission based on the needs of persons and communities rather than the maximization of profits for shareholders, promote production and consumption relationships that are fairer and more sustainable, support the identification to territory, develop structuring relationships with public authorities and the other market actors, etc.

All of this may seem obvious, but the fact must be underlined that not all of the social economy innovates. When it does, innovation may be of short duration, becoming almost invisible under the effect of market pressures or standardization by the state. The practices of the social economy may also be disseminated to private enterprise, however, as can be seen with corporate social responsibility (CSR) exercises, or within the public service, as shown by the increasing importance of the social economy in social and health services (adapted transportation, ambulance services, medical services, perinatality and early childhood services, etc.). Such dissemination does not, however, necessarily cause a sustainable transformation of practices and institutions. Innovation may temporarily absorb system tensions without eliminating its contradictions. In this book, we have looked at some of the limits of the social economy, because it cannot, in itself, resolve all difficulties, such as poor working conditions in traditional environments, the inequality of social relations, and development without sustainable effects on the quality of the environment. There are also inherent limits to the very form of the social economy, whose legal structures embed unequally, for which traditional financial tools are often inadequate, the democratic results of which may be deficient, etc.

The social economy cannot change deep-rooted tendencies on its own. Nevertheless, it is a laboratory in which to explore alternative practices for production, consumption, distribution, and territorial occupation. It is also a crucible where new rules can be developed that are more democratic and respectful of the needs of persons and communities on a short-term and also on a long-term basis in a perspective of sustainable development. The growth of the social economy over the last few years – in Québec but also elsewhere in the world – shows that it does not occupy a residual space between the market and state, but tends to become an integral portion of a plural economy. More than the size of the social economy sector, it is especially its influence on the institutional aspect that counts. The social economy must not be seen strictly as a producer of goods and services but as a powerful agent of social and political coordination (Laville & Evers, 2004). It can provide for sustainable social innovations to the extent that its experimentation goes beyond the organizational stage, participates in the institutional field, and proposes another model of social organization of the economy.

The social economy is, however, confronted with the challenge of its representation, as it is extremely diversified by type of activities, modes of organization, and financing obtained. Lacking strong mutual and institutional acknowledgement, the social economy runs the risk of remaining fragmented and isolated from the locations where the important decisions for the economy and society are made. Confined to itself, without any connection to public and private actors, it could have only local effects that are limited in time. Without the vision of its contribution to the general interest, it may be perceived as simply reinforcing polarization and social and economic exclusion. Finally, the social economy must express a clear vision of the projected society to which it can and wants to contribute.

Because of its distinctive features and its capacity to innovate, it is important to get to know the social economy better. Due to these features, however, the practices of the social economy question established usage, which makes it difficult to interpret. The development of interpretation grids is, accordingly, an operation that must be based on a formal and thorough analysis of what characterizes the social economy, but it must also be based on the point of view of the actors concerned. From the standpoint of research, it must also be kept in mind that innovation is not an inherent feature of the social economy. Although considerable work[4] has shown its innovative feature, often thereby reinforcing the speeches and strategies of its actors, it is important not to assume what we want to establish and not to take as a given what is to be built (Eme & Gardin, 2003). An examination of concrete practices of the social economy shows that they sometime barely are distinguishable from those of other types of organizations (Frémaux, 2011).

Research on social innovations in the social economy must be centred on at least three challenges. The first concerns the uniqueness of the observed experiences and the uncertainty of their effects due to their experimental feature. Even without limiting the validity of the tools and the results of research to a case-by-case basis, it must be acknowledged that they cannot be extrapolated or applied only to contexts, the similarity of which could be empirically shown.

A second difficulty concerns the political feature of social innovation borne by the social economy, which conflicts with existing values, standards, and rules, but whose conditions for stabilization and generalization depend on its institutionalization, which in itself may take various forms and may even be desired by its social actors (see Lévesque, 2011). The researcher's vision about the role attributed to the social economy in economic and social dynamics must therefore be clarified (research is never neutral).

This leads to a third difficulty: the scientific construction of the field of social economy. Partnered research allows the researcher to become a close witness to the construction of the representations of the economic and social world on which action is based from the point of view of its actors. The risk, however, is that the researcher participates too closely in this construction, giving an anticipated answer to the questions raised by the research. Science is always socially constructed, and in tension between a tradition of research that targets theorization, and one that integrates the subjectivity of the actors it studies. This is true for all current social science research, but perhaps especially relevant to the study of the social economy from the point of view of social innovation.

NOTES

1   I wish to thank Allan Parvue for the translation of this conclusion.
2   See www.uQuébec.ca/ptc/rqis.
3   One of the founders of CRISES and ARUC-ÉS, Benoît Lévesque, stated that it would be necessary to "set the tone" ("faire école"). Since then, the two research centres developed well beyond Montréal by attracting researchers from almost all Québec universities: HEC Montréal, Concordia University,

Université de Montréal, UQAM, UQAR, UQO, UQTR, and Université de Sherbrooke.

4   In addition to the work performed by CRISES, ARUC-ÉS, and RQRP-ÉS, see also the work of the Centre de recherche et d'information sur la démocratie et l'autonomie (CRIDA, affiliated with the Laboratoire interdisciplinaire pour la sociologie économique LISE, CNRS; Democracy and Autonomy Information and Research Centre, affiliated with the CNRS Interdisciplinary Laboratory for Economic Sociology) and the Centre for Social Innovation (Stanford Graduate School of Business).

REFERENCES

Alter, N. (2002). L'innovation: Un processus collectif ambigu. In N. Alter (Ed.), *Les logiques de l'innovation: Approche pluridisciplinaire* (pp. 15–40). Paris: La Découverte.

Bouchard, M.J. (2007). Les défis de l'innovation sociale en économie sociale. In J.-L. Klein & D. Harrisson (Eds.), *Innovations sociales et transformations sociales* (pp. 121–38). Québec: Presses de l'Université du Québec.

Bouchard, M.J., & Lévesque, B. (2010). *Économie sociale et innovation: L'approche de la régulation, au cœur de la construction québécoise de l'économie sociale*. Montréal: CRISES and Chaire de recherche du Canada en économie sociale, nos. ET1103 and R-2010-04.

Eme, B., & Gardin, L. (2003). Introduction, retour sur la construction de l'économie solidaire. In *Organisations et dispositifs d'économie solidaire en région Centre* (pp. 5–33). Paris: Centre de recherche et d'information sur la démocratie et l'autonomie.

Eme, B., & Laville, J.-L. (Eds.). (1994). *Cohésion sociale et emploi*. Paris: Desclée de Brouwer.

Frémeaux, P. (2011). *La nouvelle alternative? Enquête sur l'économie sociale et solidaire*. Paris: Les Petits Matins.

Hollingsworth, R.J. (2000). Doing institutional analysis: Implications for the study of innovations. *Review of International Political Economy, 7*(4), 595–644. http://dx.doi.org/10.1080/096922900750034563

Laville, J.-L., & Evers, A. (Eds.). (2004). *The third sector in Europe*. Cheltenham, UK/ Northampton, MA, USA: Edward Elgar.

Lawrence, T.B., Suddaby, R., & Lecca, B. (Eds.). (2009). *Institutional work: Actors and agency in institutional studies of organizations*. Cambridge: Cambridge University Press. http://dx.doi.org/10.1017/CBO9780511596605

Lévesque, B. (2004). Les entreprises d'économie sociale, plus porteuses d'innovations sociales que les autres? In *Le développement social au rythme de l'innovation* (pp. 51–72). Québec: Presses de l'Université du Québec et Fonds de recherche sur la société et la culture.

Lévesque, B., 2011. *L'institutionnalisation des services québécois de garde à la petite enfance à partir de l'économie sociale: Un processus qui s'échelonne sur plusieurs décennies.* Montréal: UQAM, CRISES, no. ET1105.